THE POLITICS OF C

THE POLITICS OF COMMUNITY

A feminist critique of the liberal–communitarian debate

Elizabeth Frazer
Nicola Lacey

New York London Toronto Sydney Tokyo Singapore

First published 1993 by
Harvester Wheatsheaf
Campus 400, Maylands Avenue
Hemel Hempstead
Hertfordshire, HP2 7EZ
A division of
Simon & Schuster International Group

Typeset in 10/12 pt Erhardt
by Pentacor PLC, High Wycombe

Printed and bound in Great Britain by
Biddles Ltd, Guildford and King's Lynn

British Library Cataloguing in Publication Data

A catalogue record for this book is available from the British Library

ISBN 0 7450 0861 5 (hbk)
ISBN 0 7450 0862 3 (pbk)

1 2 3 4 5   97 96 95 94 93

Contents

Preface

The seeds out of which this book has grown were planted in an informal social and political theory reading group which we began in 1988. The reading group was a response to the lack of institutional space in which to share thoughts about feminist social theory in Oxford University. It was also a product of our frustration at the way in which liberalism continued to dominate the shape and content of most of the political theory debates going on within the University. By chance, we read Alasdair MacIntyre's *After Virtue* and Catharine MacKinnon's *Feminism Unmodified* one after the other. This juxtaposition set us thinking about the resonance between some aspects of feminist thought and the communitarian ideas which were beginning to form a distinctive critique of liberal individualism. We drafted a paper in which we set out what we saw as the common methodological assumptions and political concerns of feminism and communitarianism, and in which we sketched an analysis of what we saw as the political dangers of communitarian thought from a feminist point of view. Encouraged by the interest which this paper attracted when we circulated it to some colleagues and presented it at a couple of seminars, we decided to develop the ideas in the form of a book on feminism and political theory.

During the period of writing, a number of philosophers and political theorists (including both feminists and writers associated with communitarian views) have begun to explore some of the pitfalls of the communitarian critique of liberalism. But, so far as we are aware, no one has yet provided a systematic feminist critique of the liberal–communitarian debate which integrates the feminist issues with the broader concerns of critical social theory. Nor has any of the critical literature presented a general assessment of the implications of the debate for the relationship between political theory and social theory – a relationship which we see as crucial to the development of a political theory which would be adequate from a feminist point of view. These, then, are the projects on which *The Politics of Community* embarks.

During the last five years, the indifference to interdisciplinary feminist research which characterises the intellectual climate at Oxford has come to seem relatively benign as compared with the increasingly difficult research conditions prevailing at many other institutions. We recognise how fortunate we have been in the research time, library and other resources which have been available to us. None the less, our work would have been both more difficult and far less rewarding had it not been for the interest and encouragement of colleagues and students who shared our sense of the importance of feminist research. In particular, Beverley Blakeney, Michael Freeden and Sabina Lovibond read the whole of the manuscript and made many suggestions which were of great importance to us in preparing the final version. They will all find things to disagree with in our final position, but their criticisms enabled us to avoid a number of mistakes and helped us to formulate our views much more sharply than would otherwise have been the case. Hugh Collins, John Gardner, Sabina Lovibond and Megan Vaughan read and gave very useful comments on the original paper out of which the book developed. Papers based on parts of the book were given at a joint seminar in Law and Women's Studies at Warwick University; the Human Sciences Seminar at Manchester Polytechnic; the Criminology Centre at Sheffield University; the Politics Reading Group at Southampton University; the Department of Politics at the University of York; the Political Science Department at Stanford University; the UK Political Thought Conference; and the Oxford University Women's Studies Committee Seminar. We learnt a great deal from our discussion with the audience on each of these occasions. Elizabeth Frazer enjoyed the hospitality of both the Law School and the Politics Department at UCLA in the Spring of 1990, and benefited from discussions there with Frances Olsen and Carol Pateman. Stanford Law School provided an exceptionally warm and intellectually stimulating environment for Nicola Lacey during the early summer of 1992, and she benefited in particular from the interest and support of Barbara Babcock, Tom Grey, Janet Halley, Mark Kelman,

Susan Moller Okin, Peggy Radin, Deborah Rhode, Carol Sanger, Bill Simon and Kathleen Sullivan, all of whom took the time to read the drafts she was working on, to make suggestions for reading, and to give her their acute, but always encouraging, comments. Susan Christopherson, Janet Zollinger Giele, Brian Loynd and David Soskice gave useful comments on a number of draft chapters. To all these people we express our very warm thanks.

Last, but certainly not least, the encouragement and enthusiasm of our editor at Harvester Wheatsheaf, Clare Grist, has been of great importance to us. The understanding with which she met several requests for extensions of the delivery deadline were a far more effective stimulus to the book's completion than a less sympathetic response would have been, and her personal interest in and commitment to the book kept us going at moments when our own confidence wavered or when other obligations seemed overwhelming. We hope that she and all the other people we have mentioned will feel that the finished project in some measure justifies their encouragement.

Elizabeth Frazer
Nicola Lacey

New College, Oxford
December 1992

Introduction

This project began when we asked ourselves whether recent themes in political theory, which have been characterised as 'communitarian', really constitute an advance, in feminist terms, on the liberal, Marxist and other theories and practices they seek to refine and replace. Political theory is a contested terrain. There are disagreements about issues of method and issues of substance, and many parties to each disagreement. The dominant position, though, is occupied by liberalism; and in this book the so-called 'liberalism–communitarianism debate' has a prominent place, although we also touch on some communitarian arguments with aspects of other political theories such as conservatism, Marxism, and anarchism.[1] Similarly, a debate with liberalism has been central in the development of feminist political theory.[2] Notwithstanding the historical fact of contemporary western feminism's roots in liberal thought and politics, communitarian themes have been present in feminism since its inception. The striking similarities between some feminist and some communitarian arguments, as well as the differences between them, are the subjects of this book.

Communitarianism can briefly be characterised as the thesis that the community, rather than the individual, the state, the nation or any other entity is and should be at the centre of our analysis and our value system. This thesis has had its place as a significant strand in political thought and philosophy from Plato to the present day. However, it has not been systematised in contemporary work, as Rawls, for example has systematised a particular version of liberalism, or as utilitarianism is a system, or as Marxism offers a 'grand theory'. And although many individual writers are quite prepared to accept or claim the title 'liberal' or 'Marxist' or 'feminist', this tends not to be the case for the communitarians; they have usually had the label ascribed to them by others, and tend to think of themselves variously as conservatives or socialists or liberals. Neither does communitarianism map at all neatly onto contemporary western party politics. Whereas philosophical liberals will tend towards liberal and social democratic parties, and Marxism has its place in socialist politics, the communitarian theorists we discuss in this book range across the party political spectrum. So characterisation, analysis and criticism of 'communitarianism' is even more hazardous and complex than is the case with other 'isms'.

In recent debates communitarianism has undoubtedly been a largely critical or negative position, defined by what it is not – not liberalism or anarchism, nor state socialism, nor social democracy; not atomistic individualism, nor structural determinism. But core positive themes recur in the work of writers who are identified as communitarians. Primarily, there is the social nature of life, identity, relationships and institutions. Communitarians emphasise the embedded and embodied status of the individual person, by contrast with central themes emphasised in particular in contemporary liberal thought which construct an abstract and disembodied individual. They tend to emphasise the value of specifically communal and public goods, and conceive of values as rooted in communal practices, again by contrast with liberalism which emphasises individual rights, and conceives of the individual subject as the ultimate originator and bearer of value. The centrality of the real, historical individual person in communitarian theory, though, distances it equally from certain varieties of Marxism, specifically strong varieties of historical determinism. The centrality of the value of 'community', too, distances the communitarians from those varieties of state socialism where power is highly centralised.

In the course of their critique, the communitarian theorists identify weaknesses in liberalism's social theory. There are several levels of analysis. To begin with, the communitarians can be understood to be conducting a straightforwardly prescriptive argument: human life will go better if communitarian, collective and public values guide and construct our lives. Second, though, there is a descriptive thesis: that the communitarian conception of the embodied individual is a more true and accurate model, a better conception of reality, than, say, liberal individualism or atomism, or structuralist Marxism. The descriptive and prescriptive levels of analysis can be fused – communitarians argue that given the state of the world, certain social, political and normative arrangements and values are unviable. For example, a society which understands itself to be constituted by atomistic and autonomous discrete individuals, and which makes that kind of autonomy its highest value, will not work. Similarly, a top-down imposition of values (as in Stalinism) or the attempt to completely subordinate the individual to the state (as in modern fascism) will fail (as well as being morally repellent and indefensible). Here, arguments in the field of political theory are fused with arguments at the level of a wider, or underlying, social theory (the exact relationship between the two remains, of course, to be specified). In the vocabulary of social theory, the communitarians will reject methodological individualism and empiricism (which they identify as bound up with liberalism); and also reject structuralism (which has been connected with certain variants of Marxism).

We analyse the themes of communitarian theory under the headings of *social constructionism* (by which we mean the claim that social reality is contingent rather than given) and *value communitarianism* (the commitment to collective values, public culture and a concern with the collective aspects of human life). They coincide with much in the thought and theory of contemporary western feminist movements. Women's political campaigns have focused on sexual violence, childcare, health, the domestic division of labour – all issues where the body is central, practically speaking, and cannot be ignored or abstracted away from in theory. Feminist campaigns have always been, at least in part, for public goods. Safe transport, non-sexist health care, street lighting, childcare, cannot be provided purely privately and individually. In practical politics and theory feminists have emphasised group processes and group identities, and have been critical of existing political practices (whether in socialist, liberal democratic, Marxist, or conservative parties). Feminists have insisted that the facts of sexual inequality and oppression are not natural facts, although they may appear to be so. Social facts, social reality and social beings are socially constructed. This suspicion about the status of 'facts' and 'reality' has its counterpart in feminist social theory, specifically in the idea that a purely political science or theory is untenable, and more broadly in the feminist challenge to conventional understandings of 'the political'.

The relationship between political and social theory is central to our concerns. The debates are complex and we hope to clarify them. First there are substantive arguments about social theory to deal with – the disputes between empiricists and structuralists about explanation in the social sciences, for example, and the way these are connected with or have implications for disputes between liberals, Marxists, social democrats and others in political theory. Second, there is a more subtle argument about whether social theory is relevant to political theory at all. Liberal political theorists have been especially likely to answer 'no' to this question. They argue for the autonomy of the political realm, political categories and political discourse, understanding these as free from, or indifferent between, ontological commitments (that is, commitments about the nature of existence and things that exist). This position is bound up with liberalism's broad acceptance of the fact/value distinction – which is to say, with liberals' broad acceptance of empiricism. We shall argue that this acceptance itself implies some ontological assumptions, so that the liberal aspiration to freedom from ontology is unconvincing.

In the twentieth century structuralist theorists of one sort or another have sustained a powerful attack on liberalism and its individualistic metaphysical underpinnings.[3] But this debate has resulted in a dilemma which is widely understood now to be sterile, if not vicious – the 'agency–structure' opposition, which is mirrored at the level of political and moral theory by the 'free-will–determinism' opposition. The communitarian political theorists develop a social theory which we consider in most cases tends too nearly to the structure, and determinism, side of this pair of oppositions. The questions feminists and members of other progressive social movements must ask are, whether this is an inevitable outcome of this debate in any event, and if so, whether the terms of the debate must be questioned.

In Chapter 1 we address a number of important definitional and methodological problems that have been raised by our characterisation of the project. Our enterprise is one that tends to call forth a great deal of scepticism. Some of this comes from feminists, who are frequently sceptical of the validity or worth of work in the field of a specifically political theory at all, and some of whom are hostile to theoretical enterprises as such. Many political theorists, for their part, are sceptical about the political relevance or admissibility of the category of gender. We tackle these sceptical positions and in the process attempt to make clear our own position as feminists and as political theorists. This involves us in an explication of some of what are for us key theoretical terms like power, discourse, practice and critique.

In Chapters 2 to 5 we explore what novel substantive issues emerge when this methodological framework is employed in political theory – what, in other words, this methodology suggests is problematic about conventional political theory. Specifically, in Chapters 2 and 3 we characterise liberalism and outline the critique which has been developed by feminists and others. We give this critique concrete content by discussing the shortcomings of the liberal framework for progressive social change, as demonstrated in European and North American equal opportunities legislation. At this point, we see that specifically communitarian themes are emerging from the analysis. In Chapter 4 we examine and discuss in more detail the communitarian critique of liberalism as it has been rehearsed in recent debates; and communitarianism's less well-rehearsed critique of rival political theories and traditions of practice. In that chapter we discuss in some detail the affinities between certain themes in feminist theory and politics and communitarianism. In Chapter 5 we move on to develop a feminist critique of communitarianism. In Chapter 6 we attempt to move beyond the liberalism–communitarianism debate, and elaborate and develop the methodological framework with which we began so as to outline a political theory which is adequate to encompass feminist political concerns.

In the course of our discussion we make three claims, First, that 'the liberalism–communitarianism debate' can only be properly understood as a multiplicity of debates, which need to be located in a broader context of arguments in political *and social* theory. Second, that there can be no *political* theory without *social* theory constitutes a serious problem for communitarians, who find themselves committed to dubious theories of the individual and social reality. This means, third, that in so far as there are real affinities between feminism and communitarianism, difficult questions about feminist social theory, values and politics are raised, and must be faced.

To begin with we turn to the two major discourses with which our project is concerned – feminism and political theory – and discuss the troubled relationship between them.

1

□

Feminism and political theory

Introduction

In this chapter we aim to characterise contemporary feminism and argue for political theory's relevance to feminist projects. There is, of course, a substantial body of feminist political theory, criticism and scholarship, and our analysis draws on this. Nevertheless, neither feminism nor political theory are simple objects and the relation between them cannot be taken for granted. First, there have always been competing feminist analyses – Marxists, socialists and radical feminists, among others, have disagreed in their understanding of women's oppression.[1] But further in recent years, consciousness of differences between women have led in the first place to the fragmentation of contemporary western women's movements, and second, to the argument from some theorists that in light of this 'feminism' has no coherent meaning and that the category 'woman' on which it has been built has no referent.[2] We have already alluded to the contested nature of political theory. Not only do liberals, Marxists, conservatives and others disagree in their understanding of political institutions and events, but there is broader disagreement within the discipline about the conception of 'the political', and about the relation between political theory and other disciplines.

At this point we begin to elucidate feminist criticisms of political theory, in order to clear the ground for our assessment of the communitarianism debate. Here we offer an initial outline of key elements of our version of feminist theory and method – discourse theory, the concept of practice, the method of critique, and a particular conceptualisation of power. Our characterisation of feminism in the next section is broadly theoretical; in later chapters we shall be discussing more concrete aspects of feminist political activity and organisation.

Feminism

Clearly it would be absurd to attempt to unite the diversity of women's movements and feminist thought past and present in any very particular definition. Marxist, liberal, radical, revolutionary and other species of feminism offer rival analyses of the nature and explanation of gender relations in general and women's disadvantage in particular. Moreover, these analyses vary from one political and historical context to another – British and French radical feminisms, for example, have significant differences.[3] However, common core concerns can certainly be identified. We consider it sensible to say that all feminists are concerned with the oppression, subordination and exploitation of women as women; they are committed to understanding the nature, form and history of women's oppression, and to making an effort to dismantle it. This characterisation is question begging, so we shall immediately address some of the questions.

First there is the question of the implications of the term 'women as women'. There are two aspects to this. The first is to do with explanation; does the very idea of feminist politics commit us to any particular theory of gender? For example, is feminist politics compatible with the Marxist position that women's and men's class identity is more fundamental, theoretically speaking, than their gender identity, *and* with the liberal position that our status as persons is more fundamental than our status as gendered beings? Is feminism compatible both with the theory that gender identity is explained biologically (by genetic structures, for example) and with the theory that men have an erotic interest (which is not reducible to biology) in the oppression of women?[4] Our formulation of the common core of feminism defines it in part as the project of researching and discovering explanations for women's oppression. However, within feminist politics there have sometimes been assertions to the effect that this project is already complete, and that feminists can be *defined* by their acceptance of particular analyses of women's oppression.

These assertions have led to political disputes and sometimes to splits within groups and campaigns.[5] We do not have space in this book to systematically set out and discuss all these rival theories of gender, although we shall assess some such theories in detail where it is relevant to our argument. We can, though, note some broad distinctions.

Marxist theories tend to explain gender relations by reference to the interests of the capitalist system or state. Within Marxist feminism there is controversy about the extent to which the capitalist state has a direct interest in the oppression of women (for example, because women's subordinate role is necessary in keeping subsistence costs, and thereby men's wages, down) or a merely contingent interest (it would not matter to capitalists if gender distinctions disappeared and both men and women were directly exploited in production relations). This controversy is at the heart of 'the domestic labour debate', and of the debate about whether 'capitalism' and 'patriarchy' are two separate systems, and whether and how they are connected.[6] Radical feminist theories emphasise the special interests men as a group have in oppressing and exploiting women. Different writers have discussed men's interest in exploiting women's domestic labour, their interest in dominating women sexually, and their fear of women stemming from women's unique ability to bear children and/or cultural definitions of feminine sexuality as dangerous or evil.[7] Liberal theories see gender oppression as a profound injustice which must be righted by appeal to and the reassertion of individual rights and the equality between human beings.[8] In addition, psychoanalysis and its variants offer specific theories of gender.[9]

As well as these disagreements about the explanation of gender inequality, theorists disagree about the appropriate strategy for change. One major controversy is about the liberal strategy of national and local legislation in favour of sexual equality. This has generally taken the form of equal opportunities legislation. Critics of this strategy argue that equal opportunities legislation overlooks the issue of the reasons for women's subordination. If men dominate women because there are pressures on them to do so from the wider mode of production, or in their own interests, something more than legislation is needed. In this connection critics of liberalism argue that the strategy of rational and logical argument about individual rights or human equality is unlikely, on its own, to alter gender relations.[10] Feminist theorists have differed greatly on what, in addition to rational and logical argument, must be done to bring about change. Should we focus on culture and representations (changing how the world is understood and represented in literature, film, advertising and so on); on direct action against bastions of male power; on encouraging women to live separate lives from men, to engage in birth strikes, to refuse to participate in heterosexual relations; should we concentrate on getting women into positions of power in the job market and the education and political systems; or any of the above?[11]

When we look closely at the various theories of gender and the various strategies for change encompassed within feminism we find an underlying tension which surfaces again and again in feminist politics and thought. This is the tension between asserting the basic equality between men and women and looking forward to a time when gender differences and inequalities are overcome, and asserting that there is a genuine difference between men and women, both now and in the future, and looking forward to a time when women's subordination is overcome. This tension has been present in feminism since its inception in the West in the seventeenth century.[12]

This tension also shows itself when we discuss the second aspect to the question of the implications of the term 'women as women'. The problem here is: does the very idea of feminist politics, with its reference to a particular interpretation of femininity, presuppose that all women have something crucial in common? The sceptical and critical response to this possibility is that this something – femininity, womanhood, a shared position in a structure of power relations – is a fiction or a theoretical construct, and assertions that it is otherwise do violence to the reality of differences between women. This problem, too, has been a recurrent one in feminist politics. At some times the idea that feminism is for and about only some women (usually white and middle class) has been taken for granted or specifically argued for, and the thought that working-class women or black women may be encompassed in feminism's projects explicitly dismissed.[13] At other times more universal conceptions of the common interests or common identities of all women have been developed, and there have been impassioned protests against the idea that any women can be excluded from 'womanhood' or feminism.[14] Equally often, women who do not conform to dominant feminist identity have protested that feminism has been hijacked by a certain group, with the result that unwarranted assumptions about the interests, needs and situation of all women actually oppress many. The feminist categories of sisterhood and solidarity define women without their consent, and thereby only perpetuate the kind of oppression women have always suffered from men (who are masters of the art of defining others).

Much feminist scholarship, conversely, has constructed links and commonalities between the situation of women in different ages and cultures. For example, parallels have been found between the coercive nature of contemporary western fashion and the old Chinese practice of footbinding, between the sexism and misogyny of much modern medicine, and witchburnings (many 'witches' were practising midwives and healers). Contemporary lesbianism has been put in a continuum with female friendships in earlier historical periods. But critics argue that this project, and the political categories of sisterhood and solidarity which it generates, conceal crucial differences in women's situation in different times and places which belie the existence of a constant historical force – misogyny, or the oppression of women – which we can identify and oppose as such.[15]

These debates have been pursued at a somewhat more abstract level in social theory, where the issue is the correct conceptualisation of social identity and social structure. In particular theorists have criticised the tendency to think of social identity in an aggregative fashion – that a person is white, and female, and working class, and heterosexual. This tendency has had undesirable political outcomes: when much feminist discourse is examined it becomes clear that in effect it is postulated that underneath a black skin is a white woman.[16] Instead we must develop a theory of identity which acknowledges that within any single society the definitions and expectations of what it means to be a woman will vary greatly, by race, by class, by status, by generation.[17] Similarly what it means to be working class will vary by gender, by race and so on. This kind of analysis has profound implications for social theorists' conceptions of structure. We discuss this concept in more detail later in this chapter. For now we must note that theorists have usually employed spatial metaphors, conceiving of a power structure in which individuals have specific positions. Even when it is acknowledged in a theory that an individual may be relatively powerful on one dimension (say class) and relatively powerless on another (say race, or gender) the tendency has been to postulate a series of parallel structures, and to conceive of social identity as fragmented. But many theorists have made theoretical departures, attempting to conceptualise 'structure' as fluid and processual, as itself constantly shifting, as not having a determinate shape.[18]

Some theorists have argued vigorously that any idea of 'women as women' is empty, or incoherent, for the sorts of reasons outlined above.[19] We disagree. Some of the time women do find themselves being treated as and acting as women (no matter how fervently they wish to be treated as 'persons' or professionals or intellectuals).[20] It may be that the category 'woman' has no simple or unitary content, but then neither do the majority of categories, especially in the field of social theory. This experience, of being treated or acting as a woman, is only a part of one's total experience but it is an element of experience which has particular social and political consequences, and which is only possible given a particular kind of social and political context (one in which gender is a structure). The undoubted reality of this structure, processual and fluid as it may be, is the basis for feminism.

The second major question begged by our core characterisation of feminism is the question of the place of 'understanding'. The commitment to 'understanding' does not imply that to be a feminist one must be a philosopher or a theorist, although many disputes within feminist politics have revolved around the place and role of theorists and intellectuals, and especially the tendency for women who do not want to or cannot engage in writing, theory, intellectual discussion and so on to be excluded or oppressed within feminist movements. However, it is central to the greater part of feminist politics and particularly to our analysis that theory and understanding are implicit (and sometimes explicit) in practice. Further, feminism does depend on a degree of consciousness. A woman may be locked in mortal combat with her son or husband over an issue like domestic work. This fact alone is not sufficient to make the combat a feminist combat however. That depends on her actions and practices being bound up with an understanding (implicit or explicit) that the situation they are all in has to do with sex or gender. That is, we cannot understand this woman's struggle as feminist if she attributes the men's behaviour to some fact such as that they were dropped on their heads as babies. Even if she is inclined to say 'typical men', a lifetime of discontent but resistance to change really cannot count as a feminist life as such. (However, feminists do identify 'proto-feminism', the foundation on which feminist movements and struggles have been built, in such circumstances.)[21]

Third, the question of the unity of feminist politics and tradition is raised. Women have fought with and against men and in solidarity with one another (as women) for power and freedom throughout history and in all corners of the world, although accounts of these conflicts have frequently been lost to history, and their significance has been denied. These can all be understood as feminist conflicts, and they are based on women's identification of themselves as sharing a position, sharing interests, in some aspect of their lives. However, it is important not to make the fallacious move from the assertion that women have frequently engaged in feminist conflicts, to the assertion that *the* feminist conflict has continued or recurred throughout history. There is not one feminist movement, but many. In many contexts women find that they have interests which are opposed to men's. But we cannot say in advance exactly what those interests are, how they are related to other (conflicting or coincident) interests, how they will be understood and enacted by the participants in the situation, or what categories are appropriate for characterising the process.

This is crucially important in the context of this book. We are concerned with the inter-relations between feminism and political theory. Political theory is a particular discourse, historically and culturally specific to the 'West', and the historical transitions from ancient and traditional societies to modern, and even post-modern, ones. The categories, concepts, understandings and practices enshrined here, with which some feminists, such as ourselves, negotiate, and which are partially constitutive of particular forms of feminism, are by no means universal, by no means applicable to or illuminating of all feminism.

Nevertheless, all feminism aspires to be transformative, and aims at applying understanding of the possibilities for human life, moral commitments, and understanding of how social institutions can and should work, to the project of overturning male dominance and oppression. Feminist politics consists of criticism of and protest against sexism, heterosexism and misogyny wherever and whenever they appear. Critique reveals how these are enshrined in social and political institutions; protected by the design and execution of social policy; perpetuated by social practices which construct and socialise persons, their goals, their skills and their understandings; and celebrated and taken for granted at the level of the discourses which are bound up with these social practices. Understanding the histories of these institutions, policies and discourses brings knowledge of the conditions of their transformation. The project of transformation, of course, involves envisioning the possible shape of future social and sexual practices and institutions.

Our analysis of gender relations will be explicated with reference to a variety of recent discussions. Drawing illustrations from the UK, we identify three sites of social practice which are crucial to an understanding of women's oppression. In the first place, labour is a sphere in which segregation, discrimination and devaluation of women's contribution is endemic in ways that are deeply harmful to women's material well-being. In the UK women's wages are still considerably lower than men's; women are disproportionately employed in low-status and low-paid occupations; women in high-status professions are disproportionately located in low ranks; and work traditionally done by women is either poorly paid in the public labour market or confined to the 'private' sphere where it is either unpaid or part of a low-paid and legally marginal 'hidden economy'.[22] Second, sexuality is an important area of practice in which women are subordinated, both by coercion and physical violence, and by the ideological assertion and practice of masculinity. The social facts of male violence against women, the construction of female sexuality as passive, the sexual objectification of women in sexual practice, pornography and popular culture, and the cultural sexualisation of violence, all constitute strong reasons for any feminist analysis to focus on sexuality.[23] Finally, access to political power remains a central concern for feminism. The UK is not alone among 'developed' nations in experiencing radical under-representation of women in positions of political power, both elected and non-elected (such as the high-level civil service and judiciary).[24] However, the problem of powerlessness extends beyond the public political sphere into every area of social life, with the result that even when we are physically present women's voices are seldom heard in the way men's are in the whole range of decision-making and executive contexts. These three sites of oppression are, of course, interconnected. The sexual harassment experienced by women in the workplace contributes to powerlessness and oppression at work; the sexualisation of women's bodies helps silence and marginalise women's political speech; women's lack of political power is a barrier to the reconstruction of working practices; women's low pay and lack of economic power feeds into our political marginalisation, and so on.

We want to emphasise three things about our analysis at this stage (all suggested by our earlier discussion). First, the influence of each of these axes of oppression and the relation between them will vary both across time and cultures, and in the lives of particular women: no generalisation about their relative importance or interrelation can or should be made. This means we resist any feminist analysis or practice which privileges in a general way any one of these aspects of women's oppression. Second, we believe that any adequate feminist analysis must give equal weight to social and material, and symbolic and discursive aspects of subordination (this distinction is discussed below). Finally, our approach, although primarily oriented to an understanding of women's oppression as compared with other sites of social oppression, does not privilege gender as a significant social relation. Indeed, we are committed to a non-reductionist and pluralist approach in social theory. This recognises the coexistence of multiple forms of social oppression, and analogies and connections between them, while also acknowledging their distinctiveness. In the UK we would currently take gender, race, class, ethnicity, generation and sexual preference to constitute the most important among such axes. Only by pursuing this kind of pluralist approach can the diversity of women's experience begin to be properly theorised and acknowledged in political practice.

This makes the gap between ourselves and some other feminist theorists clear. Some radical feminists, for example, analyse all forms of the oppression of women as a manifestation of an underlying trans-historical misogynistic force.[25] Marxism defines much of the work that women do as insignificant, and understands sexual oppression to be derivative of class oppression, and many Marxist feminists accept this analysis.[26] Some liberal feminists accept that many of the processes which prevent women exercising all their citizenship rights are indeed beyond the bounds of political theory.[27] It will be obvious that our commitment to the kind of pluralism we have outlined means that we reject all these positions. There are further reasons why we reject certain versions of liberal and conservative feminism. As we have said, feminism is committed to changing gender relations. This commit-ment entails that all feminists must believe that gender relations are the kind of things that can be changed. In our analysis, it entails social constructionism – the theory that social facts, however much they seem to be natural or objective, are actually based in social practices. They therefore would change if the relevant practices changed. In later chapters we discuss in more detail how social constructionism rules out certain liberal feminist strategies and reveals inconsistencies in conservative versions of feminism.

Discourse

In our analysis we call feminism, and political theory, and liberalism, Marxism, social democracy and conservatism, *discourses*. By this we intend to convey something quite precise. 'Discourse' is more than just another word for 'theory', 'set of ideas', or 'ideology'. Feminism and political theory are indeed sets of ideas, or inter-related sentences, which have a certain kind of institutionalised coherence. But more, they are bound up with the construction of social reality. The use of the term 'discourse', then, distances us from the position that there is a given social or political reality which is just named or described by language users and theorists. By alluding to institutional coherence, too, we are not saying that the ideas or sentences are necessarily logically consistent in any rigorous sense. Certainly critics may take them to task if they fail tests of internal consistency – indeed, we shall be doing just that in this book. But even internally contradictory discourses can still be socially viable, which is to say they can endure over time and play a constructive role in the maintenance and reproduction of a society.

Sociolinguists and other social theorists use the term 'discourse' in a variety of ways which can be confusing. Sometimes it denotes nothing more than its neutral, minimal, linguistic sense of 'language above the level of the sentence', or, more often, 'a set of related utterances (written sentences, and so on)'.[28] In this minimal sense, in so far as political theory and so on consist at least partly of language it is (trivially) valid to call them discourses. This definition does not illuminate very much, because the nature of the relation between utterances or sentences is not specified. According to this all writing and language use by liberals constitutes a discourse; so does all journalism, all remarks ever made about women, all remarks ever made by Margaret Thatcher and so on. And all utterances can be said to be related to all others in some way.

In the influential work of Michel Foucault, the relations between utterances and sentences are more closely specified so that 'discourse' has a more specific and technical reference. The modern scientific disciplines are the paradigmatic discourses for him – he was particularly interested in the human sciences of psychiatry, medicine, criminology and so on.[29] Here the relation between the sentences and utterances of a discourse is an institutional one. To analyse criminology as a discourse is to emphasise the primary part language itself plays in science; it is to *problematise* (in a way that needs further specification) the natural existence of 'criminals'. Foucault was particularly interested in the social sciences' place in modern life, the way these sciences define abnormality, and make the 'abnormal' an object of study; science and modernity are characterised by the 'objectifying gaze'.[30]

Some theorists employ the concept of discourse in place of that of 'ideology' in certain contexts. Critical theories of ideology ask how it is that people can have beliefs and ideas about the world that are false, and which are in opposition to their interests. (Thus, both nineteenth-century *laissez-faire* liberalism and Marxism have been understood, by opposed analysts, to be paradigmatic ideologies.)[31] Contemporary social theorists inevitably focus on language when exploring the theory of ideology, as it is now widely taken that beliefs and ideas are not separable from their linguistic articulation. So ideology is a certain kind of discourse – one which serves certain purposes, and affects people in certain ways.[32] Further, for some theorists the notion of ideology has come into disrepute because it makes a sharp distinction between appearance and reality, and between truth and falsehood, in the social world. In much contemporary philosophy and theory these distinctions disappear, and the postulation of a genuine or authentic reality behind the appearances is dismissed. Thus, at one point the idea that *all* is discourse, and discourse is all there is to analyse, was influential.[33] This analysis is now pretty much discredited; critical theorists accept the fusion of material relations, practices (a concept we discuss in the next section), and discourse, without rejecting the distinctiveness of these categories.

Undoubtedly, there are many problems with discourse theory. First, there is the wide variability in theorists' and researchers' specification of the relations between sentences, which has already been mentioned. Second, even given a clear specification of this relation, the boundaries of a discourse are problematic – is 'alternative medicine', for example, part of medical discourse proper, or outside it? In taking political theory (the academic discipline) and liberalism, Marxism, conservatism, communitarianism, and so on (which have frequently been called 'ideologies' in a neutral sense) as discourses, we inevitably have to face these methodological issues. What warrants our identification of any particular text as part of the discourse of communitarianism, for example? How do we analyse socialist feminism, or Marxist feminism – as *part* of the discourse of feminism, or as hybrid discourses in their own right? In what follows we frequently face these methodological problems but this does not vitiate the usefulness of the term. Social reality is not monolithic or static. What counts as 'medicine', or 'physics', or 'liberalism' varies over time and, more to the point, is the subject of negotiation, dispute and conflict. We should not, therefore, expect the boundaries of discourses to be stable or determinate.

Clearly it is in the term's favour that 'discourse' emphasises the non-neutrality of language, and the responsiveness of 'social reality' to discursive categories. What citizenship *is*, for example, depends (to a degree which must be explored) on what citizenship is *conceptualised as* in a political order (bearing in mind that there may be political orders which do not have citizens at all). Second, discourse theory emphasises the fusion of mental phenomena such as beliefs, logical items such as concepts and categories, linguistic entities like descriptions and explanations, and social phenomena like institutions and (most important to our analysis) practices. We earlier argued that we must not privilege either the purely material aspects of women's oppression (as some varieties of Marxist feminism have), or the purely symbolic (as some varieties of cultural theory have). The theoretical use of 'discourse' emphasises the fusion of these two levels.

Practice

The other key theoretical term in our analytic apparatus is 'practice'. In contemporary social theory 'practice' refers to human action which is socially based and organised, underpinned by formal or informal institutions, usually a combination of these.[34] In the case of crafts, professions and other occupations, for example, there are governing bodies and lines of authority, with written rules, procedures, standards and regulations. In other cases (motherhood, sexuality, social interactions and events like dinner parties or demonstrations) rules, procedures and standards are still articulable (usually with most clarity in the face of a breach, as the rules of etiquette become clearest when we encounter a drunk at a party). Indeed, 'authorities' might enforce these. Practices are bound up with discourse which is both produced by and produces the practice – like law, scholarship, fashion journalism, or barrack room, bar room or changing room talk. Practices and discourses pre-exist particular social subjects – chess grandmasters, seven-year-old chess learners, psychiatrists, mental patients, students and academics, can only exist as such by virtue of the prior existence of practices, discourses and their institutions, yet they are also constituted by constellations of human action and behaviour.

For our purposes a number of connected issues are raised here. The first is methodological. The invocation of the concept of practice in empirical and normative analysis challenges a number of tendencies in social science, including the very idea that empirical and normative analyses are easily separable. In social science empiricism concentrates on the measurement of observable variables – attitudes, opinions, revealed preferences, age, educational attainment, social class, etc. Social states of affairs are conceptualised as the summation of individual behaviours, and individuals are effectively clusters of variables. Structuralism, on the other hand, sees individual behaviour and action as determined by structures and forces which are not easily observable (although they are deducible by scientific method). In contrast to both of these, use of the concept of practice emphasises the materiality of the social reality we inhabit, and the centrality of human action in that reality.[35] But the individual human actor is not, in this analysis, conceptualised as the irreducible and unified ego of Cartesian philosophy or liberal politics. Second, normatively speaking, the analysis is non-atomistic – actors are connected with each other, and are not atoms, either of the autonomous and self-driven, nor of the billiard ball variety (at the mercy of external forces).[36]

We take it that these arguments about the methods and presuppositions of social science are connected with arguments about the moral commitments of liberal and other varieties of political philosophy. Ontological commitments in social theory (whether one understands society as the sum of discrete rational individuals, or as a totality of relations, for example) constitute a framework which rules certain normative principles in or out. The historical link between empiricist science and liberal culture is incontrovertible, although that is not to say that its exact nature is simple or obvious, nor that logically it is impossible to be an ontological holist and a moral individualist.[37] Structuralist theorists have certainly taken it that their analysis has political implications, and the hostility to structuralist methods in the humanities and social sciences has had a clear moral dimension.[38] Indeed, the important question arises here whether description and prescription can be clearly separated (as both empiricism and liberalism have supposed) anyway. Feminists' use of the concept of practice illustrates this issue.

Liberal feminism of the current wave introduced a new concept into language. 'Sexism' was defined as a particular set of attitudes, and a particular and discriminatory way of treating women and men. The liberal feminist project was one of changing attitudes: feminists and their critics were pessimistic or optimistic about this project as they tended to believe in genes (the pessimists) or reason (the liberals and the optimists). The optimists of course lived constantly with the shadow of pessimism, as there was vagueness about precisely how the force of reason was to prevail, and how change was to come about. It was not long, however, before the feminist critics of liberalism were pointing out that the whole analysis tended to individualism (individuals have attitudes, and individuals 'treat' other people one way or another) and was by this fact flawed.[39] By contrast, in anti-individualist or 'post-liberal' feminism the concept of practice is brought to bear, both theoretically and practically, both critically and positively. Feminist theory understands male power as exercised and maintained in and through practices. And feminism adds a reflexive twist to the analysis of practice, as it is itself, in its contemporary forms, rooted in the practice of consciousness-raising. The concept of practice is an irreducibly political concept – practices involve the exercise of power which calls for justification or critical scrutiny.

To begin with, the way things are done in groups, meetings and campaigns, is problematised (that is, cannot be taken for granted) and their constructive and normative functions explicitly discussed. Campaigns and committees have been organised non-hierarchically. Consciousness-raising (the practice in which women's and men's understandings of women's social position and how it works has often been developed) involves sharing and comparing experience, and finding much in common, in groups, and thereby changing the meaning of the experiences in question, and so changing the experiences themselves. The group process is governed by rules which are more or less tacit or articulated: 'honesty' is valued, as is acceptance of other people's experience; equality of participation, of access to the floor is a rule; listening has to be supportive. There has been argument (among sociolinguists and other social theorists) whether this form of communication is a naturally feminine, women's way of doing things.[40] Whatever the answer to this question – and we don't think that anything biological or essentialist can be going on here – it is notable that participants often find the norms strange at first. Many articulate women find it hard not to interrupt, or jump in to fill silence. Feminist identity, then, is rooted in practice, and the practice is constitutive of the identity.

The development of this practice transforms the liberal conceptualisation of 'sexism' too. Women's own practical experience of the power of rules, structures, and processes brings a new understanding of rape, sexual harassment, parenting and childrearing, the sexual division of labour. These are no longer seen as matters of individual attitudes, or one person's treatment of another. There is much more to it than that: sexual harassment, for example, is understood as norm and rule governed (although these norms and rules are, of course, contested). It is underpinned by social institutions of masculinity and normal sexuality: whether one is doing masculinity right is not up merely to one to decide – there are public, objective facts of the matter about standards. The practice itself is an item in a matrix of sexual practices that are constitutive of a particular and concrete masculine sexuality. The practice and the institutions have their counterpart in discourse: pornography, men's talk, women's talk, and other discourses of gender from women's magazines and romantic fiction to psychoanalyis and sociobiology.

Critique and deconstruction

Our other methodological technique is *critique*, and this is connected to discourse theory. By critique we mean two things: first the analysis of existing reality to discover the power relations and institutions, meanings and assumptions, and values, that sustain it. This involves discovering what must be changed to change social reality itself. Some of these conditions are quite overt and clearly articulated, others are repressed. Second, the analysis of texts (in this case the texts of political theory) to discover the meanings, assumptions and values which make the argument make sense. Critique also reveals contradictions in argument, shows up incoherences and the ways in which and perspectives from which an argument does not make sense.[41] Critique, whether or not it is referred to in these terms, has been an essential tool of women's movements in all their phases. What looks like 'common sense' or the way things just are, has been revealed by feminist criticism to be the outcome of elaborate processes of socialisation, mystification, definitions of 'normal' and 'abnormal', and right and wrong, of exclusion, coercion and persuasion. Critique has been the basis of women's movements' wide variety of practical and theoretical projects of challenge and reconstruction.

A good example of feminist critique is found in arguments about sexual harassment. We define sexual harassment as 'sexual attentions (usually, but not only, to women) in situations in which these are inappropriate and/or unwelcome, especially but not only when they are persistent'. Feminist analyses of sexual harassment aim to reveal what moral and political values and presuppositions about social life and social actors underlie it, and what real effects on people's lives it has; and then, of course, to expose and oppose these values and effects. Feminists have analysed sexual harassment on the basis of the accounts and experiences of those who harass, those who are harassed, and others who have to deal with harassment (those to whom complaints are made, legislators, judges and lawyers, the colleagues and friends of the parties involved, journalists and other commentators, and so on). Feminist analysis reveals that the practice of sexual harassment presupposes that women do not have the right to define when sexual attentions are or are not appropriate. Second, that women are presumed to sexualise hitherto non-sexual environments, so that it is always appropriate to treat a woman sexually, even in nominally 'a-sexual' places like the office or factory or on public transport. And the appropriateness of this treatment is understood as being due to something about women themselves. The further presupposition is that the only way that men and women can and do relate to each other is sexually. Third, there is the implication that male sexuality is imperative, uncontrollable, insatiable, and so on – men are always potentially sexual and if women cross their path male sexuality is triggered. Fourth, it implies that women and anti-sexist men do not have the right or power to enforce and institutionalise alternative motifs of sexuality, for example, equality, respect and agreement, love, affection, friendship. That is, it entails that the sexual order is a hierarchy of power relations.[42]

Here we have a mixture of empirical generalisations and normative judgements about sexual behaviour which are politically institutionalised in culture, social convention and law. This is not to say that they are straightforwardly set out or written down in these terms anywhere. But our culture represents and reproduces this version of male and female sexuality; the sexual harasser can always say in his own defence that 'he couldn't resist her', and people will understand this. Law itself defines male sexuality as active and female as passive.[43] Seeing sexual harassment as transgressive, harmful, anti-social, and above all challengeable presupposes a standpoint from another culture, another set of conventions, and the vision of an alternative set of institutions and norms. It also presupposes an alternative vision of persons and social-sexual behaviour, a vision which many feminists and anti-sexist men are already trying, with more or less success, to make real, in the face of opposition.

Another term that is often used to characterise this kind of analysis is that it is deconstructive. Deconstruction is a response to structuralist social theory. Structuralism comes in two broad versions. First, many theorists, notably social anthropologists in the tradition of Claud Lévi-Strauss, understood social reality as structured by binary relations.[44] These theorists reasoned from the study of social institutions, societies and historical processes that stability and change were explained by something like a balance of opposing forces. In some cases they reasoned that this reflects something fundamental about human mind or thought. Structuralist anthropologists, for example, have identified ideas and definitions of the sacred and the profane, or the raw and the cooked, or male and female, as fundamental in the social structure of human societies. Lévi-Strauss considers that such oppositions mirror something essential about the human mind, that is, that the human mind is such that thought and knowledge rely on the discernment of such pairs of opposites.[45] In the case of structuralist Marxism the crucial opposition is between the exploiting and the exploited class (landowners and serfs in feudalism, capitalists and proletariat in capitalism). Marx himself did not, though, consider this kind of opposition to be inescapable, or 'hard-wired' into the mind. Indeed, Marxism as a revolutionary and transformative theory looks forward to our escaping these patterns, into the freedom of communism and autonomy.[46] But, structuralist Marxism (like other varieties of structuralism) emphasises how what we do, which we may think we do freely and out of choice, is actually determined by these structures, which are not present to our consciousness, and can only be discovered by science. Structuralists understand these binary structures to be inescapable; and they attribute to them an existence quite independent of and not susceptible to alteration by social beings (the structure determines the social beings, not the other way round).[47]

The second version of structuralism does not emphasise binary relations in this way, but employs the metaphor of a 'skeleton', or the 'structure of a building' or other piece of engineering. This metaphor is applied both in descriptions of human thought or knowledge, and in descriptions of aspects of social reality. Again there is the idea that the structure will always shape and generate the actual fabric of reality, whether this is the detail of fairy stories, or of social roles and relations (just as the design of a bridge will constitute a constraint on what material it can be made from). In the work of the psychologist Jean Piaget, the structure of human thought, reasoning and knowledge is transformed developmentally – it goes through stages, toward completion.[48] The linguist Ferdinand de Saussure emphasised that natural languages partake of a common structure, which it is the business of scientific linguistics to discover and study (as it is the business of engineers to study the structure of bridges in general, so that they can throw light on why this bridge in particular stands or falls).[49]

Saussure's picture of language has subsequently been employed metaphorically in social theory. The idea that societies are structured, that structures are made up of elements which are related quasi-grammatically, and that the structure thereby has a determining role in the detail of our lives (as the grammar of a language determines the order of words in a sentence) has been highly influential in sociology.[50] The structuralist functionalism of Talcott Parsons, and more recent developments of the concept of autopoiesis (the mechanism of maintaining and policing one's own boundaries) emphasise the autonomous existence of a structure, and the existence of its own mechanisms for maintaining itself.[51] Parsons' structural functionalism has passed out of fashion, and obviously the idea of the radically autonomous nature of structures is by no means commonsensical. But a random selection of sociology books from any shelf will reveal the (admittedly rather imprecise) use of the term 'structure'. In all these cases, even where theorists obviously think of structures as patterns which result from individuals' free choices, the term has connotations of givenness, immutability, and independence.

A plausible structuralist understanding of sexual harassment (in either of these versions) can obviously be constructed. Male and female is a fundamental divide in our society. The public sphere is the world of men, and the private sphere is the world of women. It follows that women in the public sphere are violating this pattern. The presence of women therefore pollutes the purity of the masculine public world. Unsurprisingly, then, masculinity is threatened, and men's response is to put women in their place, to reassert the proper relations between men and women by emphasising that women are primarily sexual and domestic beings. Now strong structuralism would hold that this binary relation will always assert and reassert itself. Alternatively, we can understand the social order as a structure in the second sense, in which certain roles, functions, forces and patterns are maintained, and see sexual harassment as a mechanism or means of keeping the structure stable.

But deconstructionists and other post-structuralists argue two main things.[52] First, that structuralism as a full blown social theory is wrong. Second, that nevertheless the dualistic element of structuralist modes of thought and metaphors have a grip on the western imagination and western discourses, and ordinary mundane language tends to reproduce these structuralist ideas in an uncritical way. They especially point to the undoubted dominance of dualistic schemes in western thought, ideas and language – for example, the centrality of the oppositions male and female, black and white, good and evil. Hence, the critical thought that 'structures' are *constructs* (constructed by 'us', furthermore), and can and must be deconstructed. ('Must' here is intended in both its positive and normative senses – structures will, as a matter of fact, fail, and they should.) The independence and immutability of the structure is very dubious given the amount of trouble people have to go to to maintain it. Structures seem to be much more fragile than the theory suggests. Furthermore, the fragility seems to come from within them – they are to a great extent self-destructive and internally contradictory. Deconstructionists deny that what structuralists and dualistic modes of thought imply are opposites really are such. In language one pole cannot be said or thought without invoking the other pole as the two poles of an opposition are not independent of one another. On the contrary they are precisely dependent.[53] The profane constantly invades the realm of the sacred and it must do, because it is profane human beings who engage in sacred behaviour. The masculine and feminine spheres cannot be maintained intact. If a woman behaved as a 'total woman' she would not be able to live. And so on. Some deconstructionist theory has suggested that structures are 'merely imaginary' but we don't have to fall into the trap of ricocheting from the immutability of structure to its nullity. Masculinity and femininity are social realities which we live, practices in which we engage and which we oppose, discourses which we speak, and speak against. They are real; and we can change them. That is the essence of feminist politics, and one of the main motivations of the critical argument of this book. In their criticism of and campaigns against many aspects of culturally, economically and legally enshrined male–female relations feminists have precisely used deconstructive arguments. However, feminist criticism is not entirely negative. It does not stop at the destruction of 'structures'. Like political theory, feminism goes on to engage in prescriptive and visionary thought, thinking of ways of making novel and better social arrangements. This utopian thought must be, though, and in feminist politics is, accompanied by thought about what would be viable. Utopian thought in this context does not entail the design of blueprints for society, with the implication that a feminist political programme must involve the imposition of such a design. The emphasis must be on the visionary.[54] Deconstructive criticism must be followed by reconstructive thought and action.

Political theory

The academic discipline of political theory is extremely diverse, encompassing the whole spectrum of substantive political approaches. There is argument about how it is to be distinguished from political science, political practice and political policy. It is also (inconsistently) distinguished from political philosophy, political economy, ethics, social theory and critical theory. We shall adopt a broad definition of political theory, according to which it is the enterprise of systematically characterising, and explaining, the salient features of particular forms of political organisation, and of providing arguments and justifications for and against particular forms of political organisation. This definition begs the question of the reference of the term 'political'. Unsurprisingly, we find that this varies from one version or theory to another. In liberal thought, the political realm has been demarcated from the personal, and from the realm of private economic transactions; people are studied in their roles of citizen, voter, tax payer or benefit claimant. Challenges to this tradition have questioned the autonomy of political relations – orthodox Marxism, notably, takes political relations to be reducible to economic relations. Feminism, equally notably, has challenged the distinction between personal and political, asserting the political nature of allegedly private and personal relations such as that of marriage and parenthood.

In feminism, practice and theory, campaigning, discussion, thinking and writing have always been closely linked. More particularly, it has been central to the women's movement that the theory which is implicit in any campaign or organisation be made explicit, and, concomitantly, that theory be genuinely illuminating of practice and experience. This is not so clearly the case in all political practices – certainly academic political theory can seem to be quite unconnected with any political institutions. Nevertheless, political thought and political theory *have* been very important in shaping the social world. What were radical or shocking notions are absorbed over time into common sense. In some instances (notably the framing of constitutions) theoretical writing and discussion about concepts and institutions like equality, liberty, law and political obligation, representation and citizenship are applied in the construction of political institutions.[55]

Feminist political theorists have engaged with the debates about the conceptualisation and institutionalisation of equality, citizenship and the rest, and we shall be alluding to these arguments throughout the book. In this section we want to clarify two particular topics in political theory which are crucial in what follows. First, we want to elucidate the way political theorists and others have conceptualised 'modernity', and why some theorists have been *against* modernity, while yet others think of themselves as *post*-modern. Second, we want to discuss the concept of power.

Modernity, anti-modernity and post-modernity

The inception of the 'modern era' can be located in the Italian and later Northern Renaissances of the fifteenth and sixteenth centuries, although historians trace its roots back much earlier.[56] The explicit consciousness of 'modernity' and discussion of the fact that a new modern era has been entered appears in the writings of the French and Scottish Enlightenment in the eighteenth century. Renaissance and Enlightenment thinkers explicitly rejected certain aspects of medieval thought and feudal relations, and 'rediscovered' certain ideas and values from the ancient worlds of Greece and Rome. Of course, different theorists and thinkers emphasise different issues and are preoccupied with a variety of problems. Mike Featherstone distinguishes four distinct concepts under the heading of modernity. These are: 'modernity' proper, which is an epochal or historical category; 'modernité' which is an experiential category capturing a particular state of mind and being, a particular quality of human experience which is typical of the modern era; 'modernisation' which refers to material developments such as industrialisation, the development of a certain level of technology, and to particular kinds of economic relationships; and 'modernism' which refers to particular cultural and aesthetic values and practices.[57]

Here we are first and foremost concerned with the epochal conception of modernity (and specifically its political aspects) and with 'modernité', or the experience of being an individual in modern society. Under these headings we can refer to a particular and new conception of the relation between the individual and state or society, and the perception of and normative commitment to individual freedom and formal equality between all men. This raises in a new and specific form the issue of the legitimacy of political authority. In a society of individuals each must in some sense choose to participate. A legitimate political order must be organised around the rule of law, and a just constitution. These ideas are bound up with the idea of the, in principle, potential rationality of the individual and thus the possibility of the rational organisation of society. On the other hand, freedom can be felt as isolation, and choice means that the individual feels a weight of responsibility which is novel. The 'rule of law' has two connotations. First the normative one that we can design good laws to order society and guide social behaviour. Second, the positive conviction that social life is governed by discoverable laws, as the physical world seems to be. This second, and later, connotation is connected, obviously, with the rise of modern social science.[58]

The ideas of 'Renaissance', 'Enlightenment', and 'modernity' itself have clear positive and progressive connotations. It may be difficult to see exactly how the miners and labourers of nineteenth-century Britain were much better off materially than their peasant forebears. But, as Marx insists, the form of exploitation was radically and irreversibly altered: the nineteenth-century labourer *sold* his labour power in an individual relation of exchange of goods with his employer which presupposes a formal equality between the two parties.[59] The institution of formal equality did not immediately bring an end to the institution of slavery – it was maintained in the United States of

America until 1865. But slavery was now rendered problematic by the new premises of political life. Thus, the 'individual' (a specifically modern conception) emerges as the ultimate bearer of value in a relationship with state authority (rather than embedded in a hierarchy of relations with other men).[60] Not only slavery, but state and society itself needs a new legitimation. Thus the world of the family, where the individual head remains in a to some extent archaic set of hierarchical relations with others (children, wife, servants) is distinguished from civil society (voluntary market and other social relations) and from the state (where the individual has given up much of his own sovereignty and accepted subjection to law and government).

The agenda for political theorists in the modern era then is rather different from that which exercised earlier political thinkers. Aristotle and Plato, in their critique of democracy, were concerned with the discovery of the authentic good, and the attainment of wisdom by rulers. Later on, thinkers were preoccupied with the place of virtue (specifically, the Christian virtues) in just and successful government.[61] By contrast the first modern thinkers (Hobbes, Locke and Rousseau) are preoccupied with the relation between the state and the citizen, and the problem of political obligation. Rather than wondering how rulers are to attain wisdom or virtue, they wonder how states and governments are to attain legitimacy. Whereas classical democracy and later European republican politics presupposed pre-modern social relations and a small polity or citizen body, the rise of the modern state as the unit within which modern political relations are organised means there has been a significant alteration in scale which affects the agenda of political theory.[62] For later modern thinkers another category has entered into analysis – that of society, social relations more generally, the possibility of our scientific knowledge of these, and their impact on politics and the citizen–state relationship.[63] For contemporary political theorists it is generally accepted that liberal democratic society *is* legitimate, but the limits of state and others' interference with the individual are still to be questioned, as is the pattern of social relations generally.[64]

In liberalism the values of liberty, equality, and the rule of law are developed in a sophisticated way but liberal thought immediately attracted criticism from two directions. Conservative thought was reactionary, and opposed both individual liberty and the connected idea of individual right, and equality. Conservatives like Burke also had a rather different analysis of law, harking back much more to ideas of 'the word' or the wisdom of fathers and monarchs than the rational or scientific wisdom which is central in the work of the modern theorists like Montesquieu and Bentham.[65] Conservative thinkers agreed with everyone else about the enormity of the facts of material and moral social change – the fact of formal freedom and individualism, the decline of traditional patriarchy, the inception of equality and so on. They differed from more or less everyone else in their evaluation of these changes.

Right from the start, too, other major contemporary political theories (Marxism, social democracy, anarchism, feminism) developed critiques of the liberal interpretation of the values and concepts of the modern era. All these theories are rooted in an acceptance of the modern condition, and premissed on individual freedom in this sense so they share a great deal with liberalism, and differ from conservatism in the same way. But for Marx, for example, the 'freedom' of industrial society was, while undeniably a progressive move away from feudal bondage, nevertheless a grotesque sham: to him, capitalist society is incapable of delivering the freedom it heralds and trumpets. Marxists' attention is focused on the alienation and atomism of modernity, and Marx himself thought that the modern state was quite incompatible with community.[66] Feminists also emphasise how liberalism has fallen short in its own aims, and in some versions aim radically to reinterpret the concepts of freedom and equality. They criticise continuing patriarchy, either seeing this as a true continuation of elements of pre-modern relations, or understanding patriarchy as having a distinctively modern form.[67] Socialists criticise the continuing failure and inefficient and unjust outcomes of market relations.[68] But these differences are based in a common set of premises and categories – Marxism, socialism, anarchism and feminism are undoubtedly modern theories.

We can now see the sense in which the enterprise of political theory is bound up deeply with liberalism, for liberalism positively embraced and developed the values on which modern social relations are based. Liberalism accepts and fosters the distinctions between political relations, and economic and other social relations, while its critics tend to challenge these distinctions. Meanwhile, of course, there are problems for liberalism's critics in maintaining their specific criticisms of liberal values *and* their distance from each other. Perhaps it is evidence of the power of dualistic thought we discussed in the last section, but in this as in any other debate it is easy to construct an understanding of the 'fors' and the 'againsts' and make of the 'againsts' one party. In their understanding and analysis of historical changes, too, sociologists and political theorists, conservatives, socialists and liberals, use a series of dualisms: pre-modern and modern societies, mechanical versus organic solidarity, traditional versus rational relations, community versus society.[69] This last is central to the subject matter of this book. There is no dispute that in modernity 'community' is problematic but there is and must be a great deal of dispute about exactly what the problem is and what is meant by community. It is a pervasive motif of conservative thought that in the modern era we have suffered loss – loss of authority, of stability, of community. Socialists, feminists, anarchists and other critics of liberalism also identify its inability to sustain or deliver community as a problem. But there has been confusion over acceptance of the conservative tendency to respond to that loss by asserting the need and desire for *restoration* – in the case in point, restoration of the kind of community that featured in pre-modern societies.

There have been two strands of anti-modernist theory, then. First, a commitment to the modern values of equality, liberty, the rule of law, together with a criticism of how the modern era, and liberal politics, has actually failed consistently to protect these values. Second, a rejection of those values themselves, and the desire to return to or reconstruct quite different, older, social relations, values and practices. The subject of community, notably in the context of the communitarianism–liberalism debate, has crystallised this division.

More recently, of course, we are encountering 'post-modernism' as a general critique of modernity in its manifestations in politics, ethics, aesthetics, and social and psychic relations.[70] This is a third anti-modernist position. Post-modernism is complex and many-stranded. Some post-modern thinkers think that contemporary reality *is* post-modern, that a new (and perhaps the last) historical era has begun. Central to this position is an emphasis on the peculiar significance of such material developments as new information technologies and, in the sphere of politics, the decline of traditional political authority and institutions and the rise of new social movements.[71] Others emphasise post-modernism as a new critical and normative perspective on contemporary reality (although both *criticism* and *normativity* are, of course, quintessentially modern practices!). This perspective is characterised by an enhanced awareness of the failure of the liberal project of rationality, and the rule of law both in its prescriptive sense of a rational and fair system of justice, and in the descriptive sense of laws of social life which can be understood by social science and perhaps harnessed in the interests of progress. The modern liberal project of rationalisation, and the accompanying values of liberal individuality, freedom and equality are understood to have been authoritarian, and biased in the interests of powerful groups. 'Grand theories', like Marxism and utilitarianism, with their claims to truth, have similarly been treated at least sceptically, or even as repressive instruments of power.[72]

When we use the word 'modern' or 'modernity', then, we refer to the entire modern era (notwithstanding uncertainty about the exact date of the commencement of that era!) We distinguish this from 'contemporary' thought or politics, some of which is undoubtedly modern, but some of which is or has pretensions to be part of the post-modern era and movements. We refer to ancient, feudal and absolutist political relations in contrast, while wishing to maintain clear consciousness of the transformation of the conception of 'politics' between these eras.

Power

'Power' is arguably the key concept in practical politics and political science, and many political and social theorists have produced empirical and theoretical analyses of power relations.[73] However, it is strikingly neglected in the liberalism–communitarianism debate. The indices to Rawls' *Theory of Justice*, Dworkin's *Taking Rights Seriously* and *A Matter of Principle*, and Nozick's *Anarchy State and Utopia* do not feature 'power'. Neither do those of Walzer's *Spheres of Justice*, McIntyre's *After Virtue*, Sandel's *Liberalism and the Limits of Justice*, or Kymlicka's *Liberalism, Community and Culture*. Consideration of why these writers do not see power as problematic, or even bother to address the issue raises a larger question about the relation of political theory and philosophy to other social theory and science.

The accusation that liberal philosophers and empiricist social scientists neglect questions of power is familiar. It has been made by Marxists, feminists, and structuralists (although these critics will themselves have differing theories of power). It is more striking that the communitarian critics of liberalism also neglect it. There are two possible explanations. First, it may be that power is taken for granted as the context of individual actions – much as space and time, and the fact that we have to breathe, are. That is, questions of obligation, freedom, equality, and so on, can be said to presuppose a theory of power, but nobody bothers to state it. The second possibility is that these political theorists deny that power relations are significant. Neither of these is satisfactory. We argue that power relations certainly are significant, that they are indeed presupposed by conventional political discourse, and that they must be explicitly theorised. The absence of this theorising is a genuine weakness in the literature we have cited.

Modern political philosophers are responding to the questions 'how is social order possible?' and 'what legitimates particular sets of political arrangements?' These questions require an interpretation of the relations of dominance, submission and oppression in a society.[74] There are two major approaches to this question, either of which is explicitly adverted to or implicitly taken for granted in most contemporary political philosophy.

First, the model of society as an aggregation of individuals bound together by common commitment to a social contract, or by rational choice and expectations of others' choices and actions has, as we shall see, been taken by some political philosophers to be an adequate generator of a substantive answer to the questions 'is social order justifiable?' and 'what kind of social order is justifiable?'.[75] Rational choice and expectations theory is an influential model for *explanation* of individual and group social action and, derivatively, of (some) social relations and social institutions.[76] Although contemporary contract theorists explicitly deny that the contract is intended to be an adequate sociological account of the possibility and actuality of social order, rational choice and expectations theory does assume for itself descriptive and explanatory power in empirical sociology. The problem with this approach is that a theory of social institutions is needed, yet is not offered by the theory. People can only become and act as rational calculators in a particular social context, one which fosters those forms of individuality. The second, now less influential, approach to modelling the process and procedure by which social order is maintained makes reference to processes of socialisation and the internalisation of norms.[77] The problem with this approach is that it cannot adequately account for deviance and conflict, which can only be understood as failures of social forces.

Despite the fact that political philosophers often completely neglect the question of power as such, normative political philosophy inevitably implies some view about the basis and organisation of power. The contract or choice approach to social order, for example, goes hand in hand with a voluntarist conception of power – where power is exerted, legitimately or illegitimately, by one individual or group over another. In the other approach, power is conceived of as being exerted on individuals through norms, social forces, structures, or similar phenomena. Political scientists study, in part, the distributions and workings of political power. They are therefore more likely to attend to power as such, even if they do not develop wholly satisfactory conceptualisations of it. For them, the question arises as to the impact of different kinds or domains of power on politics. Can political science just study political power and develop theories and hypotheses about this independently of theories about economic, cultural, domestic and sexual power? The claim that political power is affected by, even shaped by, economic power is widely accepted. This would also, of course, have to be the case for theorists like Rawls and Walzer for whom economic inequalities are of the first importance in thinking about justice in a social order. Political scientists have been less impressed though by the claims of feminists and other radical theorists that domestic, cultural and sexual power is also socially and politically significant, and must be analysed in tandem with economics and politics in the conventional sense.

The feminist argument is that the social order is importantly, in all known societies past and present, a gender order, maintained by power relations. The argument that gender is socially constructed and maintained is an obvious challenge to the liberal conviction that the 'private' or 'personal' is or can be an area of freedom, for it is in our personal relations that our gender identities are forged and maintained. The feminist and radical emphasis on our very personal selves as the outcome of power struggles has also issued in other insights. Foucault for example emphasises how all social identities – man or woman, citizen, proletarian, and so on – are the outcome of processes of power that act directly on the body, embodying us in a series of disciplinary processes.[78] The individual is an embodied site of material forces. The liberal response to the disciplined body has always been to empower it by giving it rights. However, from the Foucaultian perspective this move only introduces another process of discipline on the body, a fact that liberalism tries to suppress by conceptualising the individual as an *abstract* site of moral and ethical status and rights.

So there are broadly two approaches to the study of and conceptualisation of power. First, and rather crudely, is the idea of power as a property of individuals who exercise it (and, of course, have it taken away from them and have power exercised over them by others, or acquire more of it, or band together to pool their resources of power, and so on). Political science has studied this distribution of power, examining how people exercise it, how conflicts are resolved, how and when the exercise of power is deemed legitimate.[79] The second approach is structural. The 'exercise' concept is criticised for being inadequately subtle and overlooking the real and efficacious workings of power without deliberate consciousness and intentionality on the part of the powerful.[80] Foucault, further, has challenged the whole idea of power from a source – whether the picture painted by liberal political science which sees a plurality of power holders in a society and an economy of power so to speak, or that of Marxist science which sees the dominant economic class as a monopoliser of power, or of a radical feminism which sees all power as residing in the dominant sex. For Foucault power is widely dispersed between individuals, and holds them, rather than in any way being held by them. For him, in the modern era, power resides in discourse and in knowledges (that is, in regimes of truth associated with particular discourses) which construct social persons. (In previous times it has resided in symbols, specifically the symbolic person of the sovereign, or the deity.)[81]

But crucially, now as then, power engenders resistance.[82] However, Foucault's conception of resistance is woefully underdeveloped, and the concept in general raises many problems for political theorists. First of all, our conception of power must be able to encompass the phenomenon of resistance. There are many problems with voluntarist conceptions of power, but clearly they are more easily able to fulfil this task than structuralist conceptions can. Second, it is easy to fall into the trap, if our analysis runs along Foucaultian lines, of seeing all resistance as progressive and to be applauded. But individuals resisting power may be themselves acting or attempting to act oppressively. Valerie Walkerdine, for example, has analysed how little boys in a classroom who resist the power of the female teacher and the school disciplinary regime sometimes do so by using conventional sexist masculinity.[83] James Scott, among others, has described how strategies of resistance can fail to actively challenge power relations in any really significant sense (although of course power relations which are challenged are significantly different from those which are not challenged at all).[84] Despite such difficulties the phenomenon of resistance is theoretically and empirically central to the phenomenon of power.

We argue that it is important that the two approaches to conceptualising power – voluntarist and structuralist – are not seen as mutually exclusive. It is important that recognising that power cannot be seen purely as a possession or attribute of individuals does not result in our locating it in 'structures' where these are completely beyond our understanding or control. All exercises of power presuppose a network of social relations which make the exercise possible and significant.[85] When a parent exercises power over a child (and gets the child to do something she would not otherwise have done) the social relation of parent, or adult, and child is presupposed. When middle-aged men dominate in a group discussion and effectively silence the young and the women, that is an exercise of power which can only occur given the social structures of gender and age. These structures are constituted by discourses (what it means to be young, what value is attached to middle age and masculinity) and practices (how group discussions are done) which are bound up with the distribution of material goods like income and wealth (and even guns). This means that the analysis of the exercise of power cannot be confined to an analysis of the relation between the parties directly involved – those actually present in the discussion, for example. But this does not mean that the participants in the situation are all the effects of power, in the sense of 'mere' effects, for the men in this situation are *doing* something. They are participating in practices in a particular way, working with or against structures of power. And their interlocutors may or may not resist. According to this analysis power is both an exercise (or more properly an action, or practice) concept, *and* a structural one.

We must also make clear that power is complex and fragmented. Individuals who are on the receiving end of power in one context by virtue of one structure can be beneficiaries of power or practitioners of domination in another context. This complexity can be significant not only in explaining an individual's different power position from one context to another, but also the complicated nature of an individual's power position in any given context. The power of a female teacher in a class of boys or a researcher with subjects is not susceptible of simple analysis. There are many examples in the empirical literature which vividly illustrate this point.[86] This might seem so obvious as not to be worth saying; but both the pure voluntarist conception and the pure structuralist conception of power tend to obscure it. We think that our conceptions of power, structure, discourse and practice offer a potentially illuminating framework for the development of political theory.

Feminism and political theory

Clearly, feminism and political theory have concerns and projects in common. However, the forging of an intellectual link between the two has proved controversial and problematic. This is due both to feminist scepticism about the worth and motivation of political theory as such (as evidenced by feminists' challenge to the very idea of the political) and to a mixture of scepticism, ignorance and closed-mindedness on the part of political theorists about feminism, and about the significance of gender itself.

The attitude of modern political theory towards issues of gender has, naturally enough, varied over time. Like the classical and medieval political theorists, some Enlightenment writers had a good deal to say about women's position in society and about femininity generally.[87] Feminist critique of political thought reveals how important it has been for women's subordinate position to be maintained institutionally and justified ideologically. Gender inequality, the social fact, has then functioned as a metaphor which illuminates the meaning and nature of categories of political thought like 'citizen', or 'autonomy'. So even those theorists who imply (although they rarely insist) that women are at least formally equal to men, nevertheless clearly indicate that women cannot be political subjects in the same way men are, and implicitly use the same masculine-feminine contrast to define politics.[88]

From an early stage, though, feminist and pro-feminist writers like Mary Astell, Mary Wollstonecraft, Harriet Taylor and John Stuart Mill launched an attack on the subordination of women and its so-called justifications.[89] It is now widely agreed that their powerful arguments have won the day. Misogynist passages in the earlier writers are now usually dismissed as reactionary and wrong. They are said to be understandable, given the widespread commonsense misogyny of their time. This is despite the obvious fact that all of these writers are notable mainly for their refusal to be spellbound by common sense, and for their courage in going against the contemporary grain. It clearly will not do as an account of and response to past misogyny in political theory. Modern political theory now assumes formal gender equality, and the full citizenship of women. But this assumption is never cashed out in the elaboration of a theory of politics which would genuinely give men and women equal access to political processes and goods, power and authority. We might cynically suppose that these theorists, as much as Rousseau and Aristotle, actually cherish a social order of gender inequality.

Instead of the old elaboration of a misogynist ideology of femininity, though, it is now the absence of any reference to or analysis of gender which functions to justify this inequality. Most political theory – liberal, Marxist, social democratic, or anarchist – simply fails to advert to gender as a significant social category at all. This gender 'neutrality' then functions ideologically to mask the gendered reality behind the concepts of political theory. One, but not the only, reason why this is the case must be that the vast majority of political theorists are men. This is not to claim that all male political theorists are sexist (although undoubtedly some are), but rather to see that in our culture and in the tradition of political theory, men's viewpoint and their experience of masculinity is widely understood to be 'objective'. Men escape experiencing themselves as gendered beings in the way women must, given the social facts of and problems of femininity. They are hence unaccustomed to reflecting on issues of gender.

One of our central arguments follows from this observation. We argue that in its analytic, explanatory, and normative project, political theory must proceed from an empirical social basis. Any political theory, implicitly or explicitly, invokes a social theory, and a theory of subjectivity, and the adequacy of these theories has an impact on the adequacy of the political theory. In all societies and throughout the period we are concerned with, gender relations and a gender order have strikingly and significantly determined the distribution of power and resources, and have been central in social identity. Any explanatory political theory which simply fails to advert to gender will be deeply flawed, for it will fail to account for an important aspect of the very social relations it seeks to analyse. A political theory which represents as genuinely democratic a country in which women have practically no political voice and suffer serious social disadvantage, is making, in its own terms, a serious intellectual mistake. And social facts are crucial to the validity of any normative or utopian project. No utopian political theory which proposes a programme which fails to address substantive issues of gender is likely to realise its own goals.

Similarly, the provision of formal equality in various areas of social and political life has often failed to generate the substantive fairness which was sought.

Feminist engagement with political theory

The case for political theory to engage with gender issues seems clear enough but does the argument work the other way? We shall argue that there is a great deal to be gained from feminist engagement with political theory, albeit that political theory will be transformed in the process.

The core project for feminism is the understanding of how gender relations and a gender order are socially constituted and maintained. The other important task is critique. This involves three enterprises. First is the reappropriation of normative concepts generally used by political theory in ways that are insensitive or antipathetic to feminist concerns: equality, autonomy, welfare, justice, need, exploitation. Furthermore, feminism has also constructed new concepts, like sexual harassment, which both radically re-describe the social world and embody a distinctively feminist normative analysis. Second, feminists work practically against discriminatory, exclusionary, and oppressive institutions. Action by action, practice by practice, discourse by discourse, feminism attempts to understand the concrete processes by which women are oppressed in specific ways by specific institutions. (Of course, this second project is intimately bound up with the first: feminist opposition to the institution of sexual harassment relies on their having constructed the concept in the first place.) This second project, which is conceived and carried out at the level of mundane existence presupposes a third: like political theory, feminism goes on to engage in prescriptive and utopian thought. Once again, the close link between practical and theoretical projects is evident, as is the inseparability of psychological, cultural, social, economic and political processes.

However, both utopianism and theory have been sources of ambivalence within feminism. Feminist suspicion is based on the consideration that 'grand theory' can function as ideology, and totalitarianism attends any process which makes a blueprint of a perfect society and then tries to make reality conform to it.[90] Some feminists are also suspicious of abstraction, on the grounds that abstraction involves effective bias and the repression of difference and complexity within whatever is being abstracted from. Theorists have also been accused, quite justly in many cases, of exclusivity and elitism. These charges focus on issues such as the inaccessibility of much theory to people without higher education; the autonomy and priority of grassroots practice and the ways in which this can be undermined, ignored or marginalised in theory; and the male domination of the academy and the suspicion that feminist theorists are essentially playing a male-defined game.[91] (On the other hand, there has, of course, been a strong utopian strand in feminist thought itself, with the usual emphasis on the design of a society along rational lines.)[92]

We share many of these misgivings, but think these do not discredit theory and utopianism themselves. Theory does not entail the assertion of any single principle explaining social reality. Neither does the attempt imaginatively to conceive a totality of actual or alternative social institutions and relations imply totalitarianism. Our 'utopia' might consist in a great deal of indeterminacy and uncertainty; we might acknowledge the impact of coincidence and serendipity on social change. Nevertheless, however we understand society as it is, and whatever kind of social order we look forward to, we must seek to understand how the separate institutions and practices that make it up actually relate to each other. All language, all attempts to grasp and articulate reality, involve abstraction, so hostility to abstraction as such is misplaced. This does not preclude criticism of certain instances of abstraction – for example, many critics think that the common modern model of 'rational economic man' wrongly abstracts away from essential aspects of human life, and wrongly privileges (in a biased manner) other particular aspects. Feminist theorisation of the world, inside and outside the academy, does and must emerge from consciousness-raising, everyday conversation, experience and reflection, as we have been at pains to stress. Even if written theory is more visible and receives more recognition, no dichotomy between it and practical theory can be maintained, for all theory has its roots in practical experience. Feminist scepticism about theory is best read as a justifiable hostility to a particular social practice, rather than as a generalised hostility to theory as such.

However, the suspicion about academic theory as a male-defined game has a second aspect which cannot so quickly be dealt with, and which relates to some fundamental distinctions within both feminist thought and political theory. Debates in political theory have often addressed, but also been structured by, the dichotomies of universalism and subjectivism, reason and passion, individualism and collectivism, mind and body. It has been argued that these dualistic patterns of thought and analysis themselves are peculiarly modernist (and we should now have moved on to post-modernism) and peculiarly male.[93] There are two possible strategies for feminism. First, to collapse the theory/practice dualism, that is, to deny that there is any absolute opposition here. Second, to devote itself to practice only, and eschew theory, on the grounds that in western dualistic thought theory, mind, reason and universalism have traditionally appeared in the same column as masculine and male, while practice, body, emotion and subjectivism are associated with femininity. In the project of embracing and revaluing femininity, we should reject masulinity and all its paraphernalia.

We certainly take this second idea seriously, and the age-old tension within feminism between revaluing what has been denigrated and rejected by men, and rejecting the male–female dualism altogether will recur and be discussed at several points in our argument.[94] Needless to say, we are more sympathetic to the first strategy, to the fusion of theory and practice (or we would not be writing this book). We do consider that the engagement of traditional political theory with feminist and other critical social theory and practice promises, in other words, real theoretical and political transformation.

2

□

Liberal individualism: the feminist critique

In this chapter and the next we want to draw out certain central themes and aspects of the liberal tradition, and pinpoint important issues in contemporary political theory which are problematic from a feminist perspective. First we set out our account of the central themes in contemporary liberal thought, and discuss the feminist criticism of liberal theories of the person, freedom, rationality, the state, public goods, social contract theory, public–private distinctions, and power. In the following chapter we look at feminist criticisms of the liberal value of the 'rule of law'. We do so through a detailed analysis of the liberal project and interpretations of equal-opportunity legislation. We also trace the implications of contemporary liberal theory for the analysis of sexuality and women's political participation.

Liberalism

In Chapter 1 we argued that the liberal tradition of political theory and practice has a peculiarly privileged position in the modern era. It would be false to say that the modern world has been shaped in liberalism's image. The development of modern material and legal relations have been understood in a number of competing ways, and in the terms of a variety of political perspectives. These various understandings and the competition between them have in turn shaped institutions and discourses. Nevertheless it is arguably the case that in the developed countries of the western world contemporary social and political institutions more nearly enshrine liberal values and principles than, say, socialist, anarchist, feminist, or even conservative ones. This is especially the case with political institutions and with law, not only in the sense that some liberal values have in some countries been explicitly legislated for (freedom of speech, sexual privacy and so on) but more fundamentally in the sense that laws construct persons as autonomous individuals, along the lines of liberal theory. In the modern era too the material and discursive distinction between state, society and individual is a social fact. Liberal theory applauds and seeks to maintain this distinction while, as we shall see, many of liberalism's critics are broadly critical of it. In this way, too, liberal values and institutions enjoy an ascendancy.

That is one reason for devoting what might seem to be a disproportionate amount of attention to liberalism. A second reason is that, in the context of political theory, liberal feminism is a dominant and significant discourse. Liberalism was at its inception and still at least partly is, a discourse and politics of liberation – from feudal relations, from oppressive social norms, from authoritarianism, from superstition and false belief. In theory, then, it promised individual liberty and equality for people of all races and social status, including women.[1] Feminists have long used liberal categories and arguments to argue for women's liberation, although liberal discourses and strategies have been fiercely contested within feminism. And third, there is no doubt that in the last two decades arguments between self-styled liberals, and about liberalism have dominated academic political theory, and set the agenda for debate. For example, although communitarian thought has a long and complicated history, recently it has been elaborated mainly in explicit opposition to liberalism.

We must here repeat however, that we do not want to imply that liberalism is a simple, unified, completely coherent set of doctrines, (indeed, neither is any other political ideology). On the contrary there is disagreement about whether particular texts and philosophers are within or outside of the 'liberal canon'. There are disagreements between liberals as to the proper analysis of liberty, equality, the relationship between the individual and society, and so on. Nor does liberalism enjoy a secure dominance, theoretically or practically. Critics offer competing analyses of these concepts, and sometimes challenge their validity altogether. Feminists, libertarians, some conservatives, lay claim to liberal principles and subject them to immanent critique, and this means that liberalism is potentially transformed. Institutions like law, which we argue enshrine liberal values, also enshrine conservative ones. Sometimes a tension or even contradiction between values in an institution can make it unviable, and therefore cause change – but not always.[2]

All this adds up to the relative instability of liberalism, and means that our analysis, like any other, relies on a method of ideal typification – the construction of a version of liberalism. This construction is the result of a particular reading of the history of ideas and an analysis of the pattern of concepts that constitutes liberalism. Our subsequent critique is both conceptual and logical, pointing out implications of the way the concepts fit together, and drawing inferences about what liberals would, logically, have to say about a range of issues (especially gender and the situation of women) were they to address them.

There has been a renewed vitality in Anglo-American liberal political theory in the last three decades, the centrepiece of which has been John Rawls' *Theory of Justice*.[3] A particular version of liberalism has been constructed in this revival and has enjoyed the upper hand in debates, at least until very recently when a number of critical attacks from within the liberal tradition have begun to appear. This version privileges notions of individual civil rights, the right to property and personal integrity, and a broadly negative or defensive conception of freedom.[4] These themes can be associated with the work of John Locke.[5] It also invokes a Kantian model of the person, which holds that the moral status of the individual is irreducible (the common technical word for this kind of theory of the person is 'deontological').[6] Thus certain strands of liberal thought are marginalised or rejected in this model. Notably, the emphasis on the values of public life, and on equal political liberties, which are associated with Rousseau, are downplayed, and Rousseauian suggestions that 'society' might have a moral or metaphysical status over and above that of individuals is dismissed.[7] The belief in the possibility of a rationally and scientifically organised society which has been an important motif of much welfare liberalism of the late nineteenth and the twentieth centuries tends to be marginalised as the value of individual liberty is given a central place, ruling out too much state intervention.[8] And Benthamite utilitarianism, which dismisses Kantian ideas as metaphysical, and takes the good to inhere in the maximisation of the aggregate utility across society as a whole (and therefore might find it permissible to deprive one individual of freedom or other goods in order to increase the total utility in a population) is also explicitly repudiated.[9] The deontological version of liberalism might be said to be a highly idiosyncratic version, or even a misreading of what the liberal tradition is really about.[10] On the other hand, its specificity might be said to be overstated, as the alleged distinctions between this version on one side, and the Rousseauian and Benthamite traditions on the second and third sides, are not completely clear cut. In particular the question of how far utilitarianism should be interpreted as an entirely consequentialist view is controversial. After all, it is a tenet of Bentham's that each person is to count for one and none to count for more than one. This may be seen as flowing from the original liberal concern for respect for the individual, therefore implying individual rights.[11] The conception of the equality of all (men) before God, the law and morality, is fundamental to the entire liberal political tradition in its reaction against feudalism, absolutism, and traditional patriarchy. Similarly, Rousseau's picture of the individual as ideally autonomous (albeit this autonomy is transformed and indeed threatened when man lives in society) shares a great deal with recent individualist liberalism.

Indeed, we consider the similarities between the various versions of liberalism to be more significant than the differences. Certain values seem to us to characterise and unify the liberal tradition. These are the values of individuality, individual rights and freedom, and a certain notion of equality; the conviction that all humans are (potentially) rational (and therefore that society and social life are potentially improvable); and an understanding of the individual as distinct from and in potential conflict with the state and society. Of course there is disagreement about priorities and rankings, about the proper analysis of these concepts, and about their logical implications.

None the less, the recent particular emphasis on a deontological individualism, which has attracted an enormous amount of criticism, from socialists, Marxists, feminists, communitarians, conservatives and from others within the liberal tradition, is reflected in the analysis that follows. We do attempt, though, to make clear how different emphases within liberalism might alter the picture we describe. Our analysis is divided into six headings: the individual (where we cover the concepts of rights and freedom), the state, rationality, equality, the rule of law, and science and progress.

The individual

The vision of the individual which has informed liberal political theory is an a-historical one; individuals come into the world with essential characteristics which proceed from their very humanity. All liberals agree that individuals are at least potentially rational, and have the capacity, which is not dependent on any particular social circumstances, to make choices and even to enter into contracts and agreements. Some (notably the Kantians, but also those in the Lockean and other social contract traditions) endow human beings as such with natural rights. The individual is therefore essentially and morally what has been called a 'disembodied self'; what makes her or him a person, a moral subject, are pre-social or transcendent features of human beings.

It is central in the liberal tradition that a person's moral status is not dependent upon the form of their embodiment. A physically deformed person, no matter how extreme their deformity, is no less a human and a moral being. (This may seem so commonsensical as to be not worth stating but it is important to remember how often human beings' physical characteristics have been taken as a sign of moral status.) Obviously most non-liberal political philosophers will be at one with liberals on this substantive point. In the liberal tradition this principle has often been derived from a conception of the individual as *pre-social*, that is to say, essential characteristics of the individual person are in place before he enters society as an embodied person. Thus in the social contract tradition rational individuals enter into an agreement to institutionalise social and political arrangements. Individuals' moral nature, on this view, is not dependent upon any particular social or political arrangement. It flows from this that the appropriate stance from which we may judge whether a society or a set of political arrangements are just is one which is external to society, that is, the original pre-social nature of men translates into men's ability to *transcend*, to rise above and out of, their actual social and bodily situation.[12]

In Rawls' theory, for example, the hypothetical people in the original position, who reflect on and choose the principles of justice from behind a veil of ignorance about their own conception of the good and the details of their own society, are conceived as being able to engage in a quasi-contractual process, and one which generates ethically privileged conclusions. They are conceived as 'selves' or as 'choosing subjects', but they are clearly not persons (even hypothetical persons) in the more mundane sense of that term. Further, each subject has exactly the same motivations and knowledge – they are in fact identical. The original position does not contain the recognisable political phenomenon of a group of persons engaged in discussion and the search for consensus, then. Instead it contains, effectively, only one disembodied, pre-social or transcendent self reasoning to reflective equilibrium.[13]

Such rights, needs and intererests as the individual already has when he enters society, then, must be respected by subsequent political arrangements. That is, the ontological conception of the person as pre-social and transcendent feeds into an ethical conception of the paramount importance of individual rights and negative liberties, and the value of individuality.[14] Indeed, on the most uncompromising versions of liberal (or libertarian) individualism, political society brings into being no new or additional rights or obligations beyond those which are validated by individual assent or arrangements. This vision presupposes an idea of social change as generated by individual agency channelled through the political process. Political agreement and decision, the organs of the state, shape the social world in accordance with the coordinated agency of individual citizens. The concept of *society* is essentially a derivative one on this model.

We should note that the derivative nature of society also holds for Benthamite utilitarians, who are criticised by Rawls, Nozick and Dworkin for failing properly to take account of the separateness of persons, and for allowing the 'common good' to override individual rights. But society, for Bentham, is nothing more than an aggregate of individuals, and the social scientist need look no further than individual actions and preferences to discover the nature of society.[15] Rousseau is frequently criticised for privileging the imperatives of society over those of the individual (and is often cited as a founder of socialism, and of Stalinism and fascism, on this ground).[16] But it is noteworthy that for Rousseau, man's natural (that is to say, pre-social) state of freedom and rationality retains a normative force, and he also understands society as the outcome of a social contract between free individuals.[17]

This robust individualism is not unchallenged in the liberal tradition. Just as utilitarianism can be understood as beginning with a conception of the 'social interest', so some liberals have derived theories of individual rights, freedom, the value of individuality and so on from such a starting point. This, arguably, logically commits these theorists to a conception of the individual which is very different from the one outlined above.[18] As we shall go on to argue, if liberals are logically committed to a socially based conception of personhood, this sets up strains within the liberal conceptual scheme.

The state

There is a dual, ambiguous analysis of the state in the liberal tradition. First, flowing from the focus on the moral individual we find a deep-seated aversion to state power, and an acute awareness of its dangers. This is accompanied by a similar aversion to *societal* pressures on the individual. But equally central is a belief in the power of state policy as the promoter of social change and, especially, social progress. In some senses there have been straightforward divergences between some theorists and politicians who emphasise the state's positive role for good (in the theory and practice of welfare liberalism) and others who have stayed with the emphasis on individual freedom and suspicion of state power.[19] But one cannot make a straight choice between these two paths – liberals must negotiate with the undoubted importance of both sides of the tension, and in the liberal texts we find a more or less unresolved tension still present.

One way in which the tension is realised, and an attempt made to resolve it, is in the separation between public and private realms. The state's activities are to be limited to a clearly demarcated public sphere, whilst human individuality and diversity is to be respected in the private sphere. This doctrine is expressed most famously in Mill's argument that the only reason for which the state should use force to coerce a citizen's conduct is the prevention of harm to others. This harm principle is not, however, as determinate as it might appear at first sight.[20] It is susceptible of various interpretations, depending on the conception of 'harm' adopted or, more fundamentally, on the relative weight attached to individual freedom and other deontological considerations on the one hand, and to utilitarian considerations on the other. So although many interpretations of Mill's principle generate an explicit public–private distinction (a good example being the British Wolfenden Committee's assertion of a 'private sphere' which is 'not the law's business' in their recommendations for reform of criminal law on homosexuality and prostitution) this is far from being the only way of conceiving the proper limits of state action.[21]

The tension between individual freedom and state power is also often resolved by asserting the state's neutrality as between the various conceptions of the good espoused by its citizens.[22] The job of the state is seen as being to ensure that justice is done. There is a clear separation, then, on this liberal view, between the 'right' and the 'good', and in political terms, the right has a clear priority. The priority of doing justice also ties in with the strong focus in liberal thought on the rule of law: the idea that all laws should meet certain procedural rquirements such as clarity, generality, publicity, and prospectivity. All citizens should be equal before the law, having the same laws applied to them in accordance with the dictates of procedural fairness. Hence all rational choosing subjects have the (formally) equal opportunity to organise their lives so as to avoid the coercive intervention of the state.

Rationality

A specifically modern conception of rationality characterises and serves as an ideal for the liberal individual. Classical ideas which tie rationality to the recognition of 'truth' or 'reality' are explicitly rejected. The idea that individuals' aims or conceptions of the good may be assessed in terms of political rationality is also rejected. This mirrors the priority of the right over the good. The individual envisaged in theories like Rawls' expresses an instrumental rationality which resonates strongly with the utilitarian conception of the self. On this view, rational action consists in the selection of appropriate means to chosen ends.

Added to this, though, the liberal tradition also operates with a normative conception of reason as impartiality. This means that an impartial judgement will be one that proceeds from an unbiased stance towards the possibilities that are being judged or chosen between. It also entails that the reasoner must stand apart from his own emotions, desires and interests. The paradigm rational choice, on this view, is made abstractly – abstracting, that is, away from the concrete situation.

Equality

Some idea of human equality (under a variety of terminology) is central in the liberal tradition. *All* individuals are presumed to be endowed with rationality (although some individuals' rationality may be impaired or undeveloped, for example, people with a mental illness or handicap). All are equal in at least this respect. This leads to some radical ideas; for example that each human life is worth the same as all others, all having the same rights at the outset. These principles, of course, have revolutionary and progressive consequences in societies where rights have been conceived as varying according to one's social standing, or where women's or black people's word is not admissible in courts of law, or where property ownership was taken for granted as a necessary condition of enfranchisement. The thinkers and philosophers who are now thought of as founders of the liberal tradition did not dream that the non-propertied should vote, or that women should be equal before the law with men, or even that slavery should be considered ethically and politically indefensible. However, it can be argued that all these and other developments can be derived from the logic of their original thought. And this, indeed, is what subsequent thinkers have argued: feminists, civil rights activists, those who attacked slavery in the United States of America, used liberal arguments and pointed out the logical problems with restrictions on rights.

However, there is still profound disagreement about the actual implications of liberal equality. First, although the feminist and anti-racist arguments have largely been won (certainly in terms of formal legal equalities, and in academic debates) the consideration that some differences between persons are as significant as the samenesses (and therefore that people are not, and in particular respects should not be, equal) keeps returning.[23] This question of the relationship between equality and sameness is still a live one, especially in the area of gender politics. Second, some in the liberal tradition have argued that substantive material equality is a precondition for the exercise of and securing of formal equality, of political participation and representation, before the law, and so on.[24] But others have stayed with the more conventional view that formal equality comes first, and does not imply any particular degree of substantive equality. Yet others have argued positively that any degree of material redistribution or other moves toward substantive equality are a violation of individual liberty and are therefore not permissible under liberal principles.[25]

The rule of law

The rule of law has a central place in all liberal thought.[26] Historically it is a value which meshes with liberalism's commitment to the sovereignty of the individual, which means that state authority is prima facie a threat to individual freedom. The state's legitimacy is therefore the first issue of liberal politics. The state can only claim legitimacy if it in some sense commands consent, and a particular, public, universal conception of law has been understood to be a condition of this consent.[27] There must be an end to arbitrariness. Monarchical absolutism (which was claimed in France prior to the revolution of 1789, and in England prior to 1688), feudal relations (which are premissed on radical inequality of status and the subjection of one person to another) and superstition, were all seen to enable the exercise of arbitrary power and authority. The liberal view is that we must put formal and institutional constraints on any power wielder. The public and universal conception of law has a commitment to rationality at its heart. If law is conceived as like the word of God, coming to men from an external agent, then it need not be rational. This conception of law had earlier undergone a transition when medieval philosophers argued that the natural law, or God's law, must partake of rationality if it is to be knowable, understandable, and executable by men.[28] With the inception of the modern era the idea that law comes from God was increasingly discredited. Natural law theory is by no means defunct but the dominant conception now is that law is made by man, for man, and is the product of human rationality and wisdom.[29] As well as this idea of rationality, the modern and liberal idea of law also has connotations of impartiality and universality. All individuals are equal before it; its content and implications do not chop and change from one case to another; it is public – in principle every individual can discover what the law is, and knows what is and what is not permitted. Similarly, we all know what will happen to us if we are accused of breaking a law, if we wish to bring a suit against others, and so on. Currently in liberal thought law is conceived of as a touchstone of legitimacy, as the institutionalisation and line of defence of individual freedom, and as an instrument of progress.

Science and progress

A commitment to the possibility and desirability of social progress is central to liberalism. As we have seen, the idea of the rule of law is important here; so also is the idea of law governedness in its scientific sense. The conviction that social reality is understandable and knowable, as predictable as physical reality has been proved to be by the rise of modern physical science, brings with it the conviction that social policy and technology might be used to ameliorate poverty, unhappiness and other ills.[30]

There are, however, tensions within the liberal tradition over the idea of the law governedness of social reality. We can see why this is when we consider that no sooner had the free liberal individual emerged onto the world stage, sovereign over himself and unencumbered by arbitrary authority, than he was threatened by the spectre of determinism. Certain free individuals began to observe how events in the physical and social worlds seemed to be regular and predictable, which set up the obvious conundrum that perhaps the modern individual was not free after all. He was no longer commanded by God, or his lord or monarch yet instead, his actions, beliefs, tastes and desires seemed to be determined by a chain of cause and effect which was susceptible of scientific study!

Some liberal thinkers have explicitly repudiated the idea that we can study social reality as physicists study physical reality, and have especially attacked the idea that history and society are law governed in this sense. Rather historical and social reality are the product of free human action, and are therefore not predictable.[31] Others have conceived of social reality as law governed, arguing that these laws are just like physical laws and cannot be flouted or altered. F. A. Hayek was doubtful whether economic laws can even be harnessed as successfully as men have harnessed, for example, the law of gravity in engineering.[32]

A more dominant current view is that rational action certainly is, in principle, predictable and understandable. That people are acting freely does not mean that they act arbitrarily or randomly (that is at the heart of liberal philosophy). How a human being will act is predictable, if we have sufficient information about his preferences and motivations, and about the context in which he is situated.[33] (This predictability though is not based on the kind of mechanical calculation that enables us to predict exactly where on the billiards table a billiards ball will come to rest if we have sufficient data about the force of the hit, the angles at which balls will collide with one another, with the sides of the table and so on.) Liberals have faith in the possibility of increasing the individual's opportunities for rational action, and thereby enhancing political value. By these means social relations and conditions might be improved. Belief in the potential rationality of all goes hand in hand with belief in the educability of all.[34]

The account we have given in this section suggests there is a connection between liberal ethics and political philosophy, metaphysics or ontology, epistemology, and methodology (the aims, methods and metaphysical commitments of science). The nature of these connections is a contentious issue. Here we have made the case for a close historical link between the rise of individualism and the promotion of the value of individuality to a central place in liberal thought. Later in this chapter we discuss in more detail whether this historical link is any more than accidental.[35]

Summary

Before we move on to the feminist critique of liberal individualism it is worth re-emphasising the degree of variance within the liberal tradition. We have pointed out tensions in the liberal tradition over concepts of equality, freedom, the status of rights, the problem of state power, the status of law (whether it is natural or man-made) and the susceptibility of human life to scientific investigation. Contractarian theories differ vastly from each other as to whether the contract or agreement is conceived as actual or hypothetical, as between real persons or transcendent subjects.[36] Modern liberal theories like that of Rawls are more receptive than are classical ones to the idea that social circumstances influence and shape human personhood, notwith-standing their reliance on a theoretical procedure in which choices which are, or would be, made by individuals abstracted away from their social situation, are taken to validate political arrangements. Liberalism has encompassed not only the radical consequentialism of Bentham and the strict deontology of Locke and Kant, but also the rights-respecting yet consequence–sensitive stances of Hart and Dworkin.[37] Some contemporary liberals have questioned the possibility of the state's neutrality as between conceptions of the good, and have affirmed the importance of public culture as a component of political value and a precondition for a just society.[38] Theorists like Rorty and Unger who are in some respects 'post-liberal' but nevertheless identify themselves with liberal values have asserted a strongly social construc-tionist stance on the question of political value and (to different degrees) human identity.[39] Some liberals have stuck strictly to *laissez-faire* economics and put property rights at the centre of philosophies which see all taxation and redistribution as tantamount to theft; others have been at the forefront of the development of welfare policy.[40]

In developing our argument with liberal individualism, we shall return to many though not all, these points of divergence. We shall try to give a reasonable number of examples, while avoiding the discussion's becoming too cumbersome. As well as dealing with this pluralism, any critic of liberalism also faces another difficulty. Sometimes finding concrete examples is difficult, because the target of critique is *absence* in a text or doctrine, rather than any positive claim. Feminists and other critical theorists frequently have to read a writer's work 'from the standpoint of an absence, extrapolate from things he says to things he does not, reconstruct how various matters of concern to feminists would appear from his perspective had they been thematised'.[41] The feminist challenge speaks to certain fundamental presuppositions of the liberal individualist world-view and the claims emerging from it, and it is with these basic assumptions and claims that we shall be primarily concerned.

The feminist critique of liberal individualism

The liberal tradition in political thought has generated an extensive feminist critique. Partly this develops criticisms of liberalism from other quarters, notably Marxism and critical theory. For the most part, though, the feminist critique develops directly from a consideration of gender as an aspect of social reality, as a political fact and as raising ethical questions.

The liberal conception of the person

As we have seen, the dominant strand of recent liberalism conceives of the moral subject as a non-embodied, unified individual who is the bearer of rights and interests. The relation between the liberal individual and his or her body is one of ownership rather than identity.[42] This means that certain aspects of embodied being, such as emotion, our physicality, and certain aspects of our sociability, are logically beyond the ambit of ethics and by extension politics, according to the liberal. The liberal individual is not gendered, not historically or socially grounded in any way. A common way of putting this is to say that the liberal individual is a transcendent subject, implying that the individual can rise above his bodily being (although he cannot, of course, shake it off altogether). Another way of characterising the situation is to say that the individual is pre-social, as if he pre-exists his bodily being.

Feminists have frequently argued that the desire to transcend bodily being is (in western culture) a peculiarly masculine desire. Further- more, in western culture, the ideal of transcendence of bodily being, the living of a lofty life concerned primarily with spirituality, or intellectual pursuits, or pure reasoning, is one that men have been systematically more able than women to live out. This is because of features of social and political life, such as women's disproportionate responsibility for daily care for children and others. We may be profoundly sceptical about the genuine possibility of men transcending their bodily life, let alone its desirability, yet nevertheless ideologically these are powerful notions.[43]

These conceptions of the individual, then, go a long way to explaining the absence of the important social category of gender from the analytic and critical focus of liberal political theory. For one thing, gender exploitation is particularly connected with the body.[44] Liberalism's normative focus on the disembodied individual leads liberal theory to practically overlook bodily processes (except in extreme cases of abuse such as torture) or take them for granted as below a threshold of significance. Equally, a theory which takes abstract individuals as its basic unit is ill-equipped to focus constructively and critically on social institutions and relations, such as gender, class or race. Individuals cannot be seen as members of groups whose destinies and fortunes are determined by their group membership, and this means that important kinds of social injustice are effectively invisible to liberal theory. It is equally unlikely to generate an account of society and culture which moves beyond traditional, concrete political institutions to accommodate diverse and less tangible factors such as discourses and traditions. Yet these, too, are crucially important determinants of human life, just as they are sources of stability, social change and the production of social meanings.

For example, although at various stages of his argument in *A Theory of Justice* Rawls acknowledges the power and relevance of social factors in determining political judgements, the legitimising basis of his theory – the 'original position' – consists in a hypothetical agreement between disembodied subjects who know nothing of their own preferences or conceptions of the good, or even of their social situation beyond some very general facts. As we saw earlier, Rawls' construction of the 'veil of ignorance', which constitutes fair conditions under which choice as to the basic principles of justice may be made, raises serious questions. First, we can question whether the original position constitutes an *agreement* at all, hypothetical or otherwise, for given the characterisation of the individuals involved, stripped as they are of everything that would make them distinctive (persons in the full sense of the term), it can be argued that there is really only one 'person' present.[45] Further, does the idea of meaningful choice make sense under such stringent conditions of uncertainty? In the real world 'choice' always implies a concrete context of options, our perceptions and understandings of these, norms and our understandings of these. The chooser must be a person with multiple responsibilities, affective commitments and so on. This is to say, choice only occurs in a social context. We might ask why the original position is in any sense a suitable starting point for reflection about the just society.[46]

If in fact the notion of a completely disembodied, degendered, yet choosing subject is incoherent or vacuous, then the choices represented as being made by such subjects must in fact reflect the judgements of some other kind of being – an embodied, gendered and otherwise socially-situated being. It is hard to escape the conclusion that the judgements are those of the philosopher himself, the construction of the original position having served only to obscure, to neutralise, substantive assumptions which should have been spelled out and defended. Far from being the product of an abstract, transcendent process of reasoning, the theory of justice is revealed as chosen from a very specific social position, that of a white, middle-class, liberal American male. Rawls has said that the original position only symbolises, is a 'device of representation' for, ideal conditions under which fair choices might be generated.[47] Yet these conditions themselves enshrine the very values which determine the principles which are meant to *emerge* from the original agreement. The original agreement is supposed to validate, not to presuppose, these values.

This is an example of an epistemological critique frequently advanced by feminists, which identifies a move within liberal theory to render objective, by means of what we might call neutralising strategies, views which are politically partial. This does not, of course, entail that the resulting theory is unattractive, but it opens it up to a particular form of scrutiny from which its pretensions to objectivity attempt to protect it. Feminist and other critique has related epistemological issues quite directly to what it sees as substantive ontological and moral problems with liberal individualism.[48] Specifically, it has been argued that liberal individualism is systematically connected with empiricist methods, the attention to 'observable' or 'experienced' facts and the connections between them. Empiricism is criticised as unsubtle, shallow and crude in its lack of critical attention to the processes by which experience and observation are structured, by which 'facts' come to be 'apparent'.[49] There is a connection with liberalism's tendency to take individuals' expressed preferences and intentions as the data for moral consideration, while neglecting the social structures and cultural factors which explain or generate these preferences and intentions.

Charles Taylor has recently argued though, that we cannot deduce from a theorist's ethical stance what his or her methodological or ontological stance will be.[50] One may consistently argue that all there is in the world are individuals (not collectives, or wholes, or relations); *and* that we ought to pursue collectivist policies, or work for the social good. Alternatively one may consider individualist ontology to be inadequate, and yet identify oneself as a liberal ethically and politically. Although we take seriously Taylor's logical point, we do not agree that the historical connection between individuality in ethics, individualism in metaphysics and epistemology, and empiricism in social science is wholly contingent. For example, Rawls' use of a rational choice framework as a descriptively adequate characterisation of modern societies and individuals, with rationality construed *individualistically* as described above, is undoubtedly connected with his use of it as a prescriptive device of legitimation for a liberal democratic polity. Ontological and methodological commitments can and do predispose a theory toward particular substantive commitments and absences. This means that epistemologies and ontologies themselves are open to both deconstruction and political critique.[51]

For instance, Drucilla Cornell argues that the very idea of the abstract individual divorced from its relations with others constitutes a profoundly anti-feminist denial of the mother.[52] Since as subjects we only become aware of ourselves in relation to others (and, primarily for most of us, in relation to our mothers) the pre-social or transcendental notion of subjectivity is incoherent in that it represents a denial of the necessarily relational aspect of subjectivity. We can, of course, engage in abstract reflection about subjectivity (including our own subjectivity), but we should not deny the relational character of that subjectivity. To do this would be both misleading and politically dangerous.

This idea of relational subjectivity leads us to a social constructionist account of the subject. This emphasises that we develop our complex identities in concrete social and historical situations and in relation to both social context and other persons.[53] We experience ourselves as embodied and socially-situated beings with multiple ties and commitments. Human life outside the context of human society, interaction and interdependence is evidently impossible. Therefore, the notion of the disembodied or pre-social individual is seen as an eminently unsuitable starting place for political theory, as is transcendence of our social being as a first political or ethical ideal.[54] This kind of approach turns the tables on liberalism, as it suggests that the liberal conception of the autonomous individual agent is itself a product of social construction, an ideal or model of human life which has emerged in this particular form with the liberal tradition. So if liberalism is true as a social theory, this is only because it is, in a wider sense, false.[55]

On this critical view, political theorists should not seek to transcend or stand outside of their own social location, any more than individuals should make transcendence of their social existence a prime political value. Instead, political theory should situate itself historically and take as its subject matter real people, whose identity is importantly constituted by their affiliation to certain communities, by their affective ties, and by important social practices and structures, one of the most important currently being that of gender. Persons are social beings, beings importantly constructed, furthermore, by influential social processes backed up by measures ranging from mere social norms and officially communicated standards of correctness, to common sense (and thereby more or less unchallenged) definitions of social categories, through informal but well-institutionalised sanctions like ostracism, social and individual violence, and coercion, to legal regulation and even state punishment. A person's critical, political consciousness can only be explained in terms of this socially situated conception of the self in which individual agency is not fully analysable in pre-social terms.

Of course, feminist theory is divergent, and some influential feminist theorists defend the transcendental conception of the person. For example, Susan Moller Okin defends Rawls' early conception of the original position.[56] Her argument depends on the possibility of our imagining a genuinely degendered (a really gender neutral) choosing subject, an imaginative possibility which we would question, given the structurally-gendered nature of the modern western world. In our view the appeal to gender neutrality in the original position cannot escape the implication of an actually masculine viewpoint.

It is noteworthy, though, that in response to social constructionist criticism of the liberal conception of the self, and to readings of *A Theory of Justice* which identify this conception with the original position, Rawls has developed his ideas in a number of articles in a direction which accommodates social constructivism to some degree.

These articles are instructive, for they illustrate the tensions within liberal individualism to which this move gives rise.[57] Rawls' progressive revisions make three related modifications. In the first place, he now acknowledges that justice as fairness indeed assumes a particular conception of the person (as distinct from a universal theory of human nature), while denying that this conception is of a transcendental subject, prior to its ends.[58] Rawls' distinctions between conceptions of subjectivity, personhood, and human nature are difficult to fix between his various formulations. What is clear, however, is that the conception of personhood he now offers is conceived as of limited application: it is a conception of public or political personhood which resonates with the liberal emphasis on the priority of justice and the limits of the political. Second, his clarification or reconstruction of his conception of the person is accompanied by a characterisation of the original position as political, rather than metaphysical, as concerned with the question of discovering and explicating the basis for an 'overlapping consensus' in real societies as the foundation on which just institutions may be based. Third, this brings with it an explicit recognition of the 'primacy of the social' and the need for the original position to generate both the 'social point of view' and the basis for the public institutions and culture which are recognised to be fundamental to human life.[59]

These modifications seem at first sight to have been bought at the cost of making assumptions about the possibility of political consensus and the homogeneity of political culture which would raise the eyebrows of any sociologist. Furthermore, many of Rawls' supporters have been dismayed at the extent of his concessions.[60] Rawls himself does not see all or even most of the views put forward in his later articles as modifications of his original stance, but rather presents them as clarifications. However, they certainly mean that he acknowledges the importance of criticisms from the social constructionist perspective (ontological, methodological, and prescriptive). Indeed, Rawls' eagerness to dissociate himself from any pretensions to transcendent or objective grounding is further reflected in his rejection of Dworkin's reading of 'justice as fairness' as grounded in a commitment to natural rights.[61]

But it is far from clear that Rawls can achieve the goal of his modifications while holding to the idea of the original position at all. In the first place, the model of hypothetical choice under radical conditions of uncertainty seems inherently incapable of *generating* the social point of view which Rawls now claims it aims for. Rather, the parties to the Rawlsian contract would have to have a particular social point of view (that of the pluralist society) at the outset. This is at odds with the veil of ignorance requirement that the choosing subject detach herself from both her embodied self and her social context. Furthermore, at many points Rawls appears, despite his constant denials of reliance on a conception of the person as prior to its ends and attachments, to continue to rely on just such an abstracted or transcendental notion of subjectivity:

> As free persons, citizens claim the right to view their persons as independent from and as not identified with any particular conception of the good, or scheme of final ends. Given their moral power to form, to revise, and rationally to pursue a conception of the good, their public identity as free persons is not affected by changes over time in their conception of the good.[62]

As Kymlicka insists, there is a distinction between regarding personhood as being distinct from attachment to any *particular* scheme of ends or attachments, and as being distinct from any such scheme at all.[63] Rawls is making the former, more modest, claim. None the less, even this claim assumes some morally relevant source of personhood which is prior to and independent of any particular social context or conception of the good, (that is according to the above quote, which is prior to these 'subjects' status as *citizens*). So it is, in this sense, pre-political and pre-social, or entails that persons can transcend their social being. 'Personhood' as the capacity for a sense of justice and for responsibility for one's ends and as a self-originating source of claims, constitutes the 'public identity' of citizens. This is distinct from persons' socially embedded 'private identity' and has independent moral significance.

Any anthropologist would instantly recognise this conception of personhood, and the public–private distinction it involves (which comes out even more strongly in Rawls's recent statements of his position) as historically and culturally specific. Yet if Rawls means to make his claim a thoroughly socially contingent one (his mode of expression is disarmingly ambiguous) he does so without offering a shred of evidence for social consensus that these capacities are indeed the ones taken as defining personhood in 'our' culture. If he is genuinely abandoning the claim to transcendence, what kind of grounding other than social consensus could there be? It is hard to escape the conclusion that Rawls' modifications to the conception of the person and the original position have served rather to highlight than to resolve the tensions in his theory between the impulse to ground the conception of justice in a transcendent or pre-social conception of personhood and the contrary impulse to conceive the idea of justice as fairness as a politically and socially grounded, culturally-specific conception of a just society.

The burden of the critique of liberal individualist conceptions of the self, then, is that political theory should start out instead from a full recognition of the embodied and socially situated nature of human life. However, it is not surprising that some commentators have been dismayed at Rawls's gestures and concessions in this direction. For this kind of approach raises its own problems about the relationship of human agency to social structure. How do we prevent the slide from the radically disembodied subject to the radically embodied subject who is merely a victim of, completely determined by, his or her social circumstances? This is an important question for feminism, many varieties of which are susceptible to a 'biology as destiny' interpretation.

The liberal conception of freedom

The notion that human beings have some fixed, pre-social or transcendent nature as individuals is closely related to ideas of freedom and rationality (of the conditions for human freedom and the nature of rational choice) which have also been the object of feminist and other critique.[64] The classical liberal conception of freedom has tended to be a negative one: freedom is the absence of constraint. The paradigm is humans' freedom to pursue their conception of the good, to satisfy their tastes and preferences, with as little intervention from other individuals and the state as is compatible with the similar freedom of others.[65]

Certainly, several influential modern liberals have emphasised the equal importance of a more positive conception of freedom as the capacity for self-realisation and fulfilment. J. S. Mill, who is often identified as a theorist of negative liberty, himself recognised the importance of positive conditions such as education for the effective realisation of individual liberty.[66] It is also possible to conceive negative freedom more broadly by recognising external factors such as lack of power and resources as effective limits on freedom.[67] But notably, modern liberals who acknowledge the need for positive social provision for the realisation of freedom, writers such as Rawls and Dworkin, are not always able to follow through the implications of this insight for the structure of their theories. For the priority of a narrow conception of negative freedom is deeply connected with the liberal notion of the limited state, and in particular with the state which is neutral as between competing conceptions of the good.

From a feminist perspective, a primary concentration on a narrow conception of negative freedom is deeply problematic for we know that, given actual social patterns of gender hierarchy, political analysis in terms of negative liberty means a failure to perceive gender exploitation. Similarly, the political practice of negative liberty means the perpetuation of the status quo – the consolidation of the positive freedom, to act, to be sovereign over self, of those with power, in the name of freedom for all. This is not simply the point that a normative commitment to negative freedom entails state non-intervention, for supporters of the idea of positive freedom also recognise limits on the scope of legitimate state action, as well as its limited efficacy. It is rather the broader point that the commitment to negative freedom as the politically valuable thing implies the *de-politicisation*, the construction as outside the proper ambit of politics, of many instances of powerlessness which give rise to genuine *unfreedom*.

A narrow conception of negative freedom, formal equality and the rule of law have long been targets of political critique from those political perspectives which espouse the cause of the powerless, for they recognise that these ideals have little cutting edge in addressing existing substantive disadvantage.[68] Absence both of regulation and, more fundamentally, of the recognition that these problems give rise to *political* injustice, means that those who cannot exercise their capacities, due to lack of self-esteem, lack of respect from others, lack of resources such as money and education, can hope for little from what holds itself out to be a progressive political doctrine.

Rationality

The notion of rationality employed in liberal individualism is, as we have seen, conceived in instrumental terms: rational choice fixes upon the most efficient means to chosen ends, the ends themselves being outwith the scope of assessment as politically rational or otherwise, except in terms of their instrumentality to further ends. This idea is in turn related to the conception of the self as prior to and separate from its ends and attachments. The notion of rational choice by persons in particular social contexts can certainly accommodate the idea that the choosing subject's identity and conception of herself, not only her goals but also her values and affective dispositions and attachments, are relevant to and indeed important determinants of what it is rational for her to do. But the construction of much rational choice theory fails to build such factors explicitly into the model. Indeed, we might be doubtful whether rational choice theory as such can offer a method for the research and discovery of such factors. Instead these are construed as *ends*, which are the *objects* of reflection, reckoning and choice. That is, these factors are outwith the sphere of rationality itself.[69] The idea that ends and goods are outside the sphere of rationality is one which has been widely challenged by theorists who emphasise the historical contingency of this distinctively modern view.[70]

The modern instrumental notion of rationality both offers an explanatory model of how humans think and behave, and has normative dimensions. In making rational choices the individual is expected (like political philosophers) to 'speak from nowhere': to achieve an impartial, detached stance from which she weighs up 'pros' and 'cons', and to apply relevant rules, coming to a considered balanced judgement.[71] Rational choices on the instrumentalist conception can be, and in a sense inevitably are, selfish or partial choices when they are directed to the fulfilment of personal preferences but a deontologically rational choice is not *contextualised*, not a choice in which the choosing subject's affective ties or personal history is engaged or relevant. Indeed, this conception of reason is defined in terms of an opposition between reason and affectivity, emotion or desire. As Iris Young has put it:

> the impartial moral reasoner thus stands outside of and above the situation about which he or she reasons, with no stake in it, or is supposed to adopt an attitude toward a situation as though he or she were outside and above it. For contemporary philosophy, calling into question the ideal of impartiality amounts to questioning the possibility of moral theory itself.[72]

Critique of this model of rationality as impartiality focuses on two issues. First, it is criticised for being reductive – it assumes that all objects of moral thought are susceptible of reduction to a common measure. Marx excoriated Bentham for taking it that all the richness of human life was reducible to economistic preference and reasoning, and this theme has been played again and again by critics of liberalism.[73] This desire for reduction, for finding a common measure, has been construed as oppressive by many critics, and interpreted as sharing the logic of the desire to make uniform, to rule out difference and heterogeneity.[74] Second, the dualism between reason and emotion, affectivity and passion, has been criticised. In the first place, the emotionless impartiality which is valorised is seen as actually impoverished and dangerous. In the second place this dichotomy is gendered, with women being identified in western culture and in practice with emotion, as opposed to reason, and thus being identified as non- or less ethical beings.[75] This identification at the level of ideas of course has its counterpart in what might be called social stereotypes and expectations, and therefore on material pressures and constraints in women's lives.

However, once we move on to a conception of the self as implicated in its ends, its roles and attachments, the dichotomised opposition between reason and emotion collapses. The emotional and affective is implicated in, and not separate from, the rational. On the one hand, there can be no pretence that the affective and emotional really is or can be suppressed in choice or decision; on the other, the affective and emotional are brought into the sphere of reason and justice.

Perhaps the best illustration of the practical import of this argument is the well known Kohlberg–Gilligan debate.[76] Carol Gilligan noted that on current psychological tests of moral development, young women scored less highly than their male peers. On analysis, this appeared to reflect distinctive modes of reasoning on the parts of the two sexes. Males tended to conceptualise moral problems in terms of rights, obligations and rules: they adopted precisely the standpoint of normative reason, categorising the moral situation in terms of abstract standards and thus finding it relatively easy to come to determinate judgements. Conversely, females tended to contextualise moral issues, analysing problems rather in terms of relationships and respon-sibilities, which characterised their own and others' positions, and generating more complex, less clear-cut decisions. On the criteria of moral development used by the test designed and developed by Lawrence Kohlberg, this resulted in females scoring less highly on average than their male peers.

Gilligan's research is itself problematic in that it takes gender division as given and monolithic. It is, for example, susceptible of a biologistic interpretation which few feminists or indeed liberals would find acceptable. Questions have also been raised about her method and interpretations. These, however, do not impinge on the important question for feminism and political theory. Is the culturally dominant notion of rationality as the abstracted reasoning process of a genralised, non-situated individual, really gender neutral? If not, is the connected idea of rationality as impartiality therefore oppressive to women? Further, can we make sense of the idea of gender-neutral moral concepts in a gendered culture?[77]

The dominant conception of rationality undoubtedly marginalises other forms of reasoning which may be argued to be equally or even more deserving of the attribution rational – forms which contextualise problems and speak explicitly from an articulated viewpoint and situation. These alternative forms, which eschew the notion of impartiality and of the opposition between reason and emotion, have been associated in our culture with women; and the judgement that women are deficient in rationality and moral sensibility has a long pedigree.[78] Why would an ethic based on judgements focusing on relationships and responsibilities be said to be any less rational, or any less ethically compelling, than one based on rights and duties? Here again, feminist argument is concerned not only with the substantive inadequacy of liberalism, but also with the way its epistemological stance ideologically underpins the hold it has on our imagination. For if, as we suggested in our discussion of the liberal subject, the very notion of transcedence is incoherent or is inconsistent with other important liberal commitments, then it merely acts as a cover for situated judgements. The notions of objectivity and impartiality can be exposed as nothing of the sort, but rather the characterisations of a politically and culturally particular conception of reason, and one which has oppressive implications.[79] The unified, transcendent, reasoning moral subject is not only an intellectual construct but a political one: the objectivity and impartiality attributed to his reasoning stance is in fact a mark of his political power, constituted and conferred in a concrete social situation.

State neutrality and the priority of the right over the good

The idea that the liberal state should aspire to complete neutrality as between its citizens' conceptions of what constitutes a good life flows from the priority of the right over the good, that is, the idea that the state is properly concerned only with doing justice, and not with doing good. As we have noted, this feature of liberal theory has been criticised by some who identify themselves as liberals but it remains an important aspect of the modern liberal tradition.[80] The issues raised here shade into the feminist critique of 'the public–private distinction' and of liberalism's failure to develop a conception of public goods.

The liberal theorist who emphasises state neutrality most strongly is Ronald Dworkin. He conceives of the state as providing a just framework of respect for rights, whilst leaving a wide sphere for citizens to develop and pursue their diverse conceptions of the good.[81] The liberal self-interested individual has instrumental reasons for entering society. He is willing to sacrifice some liberty of choice and action for the sake of the security and other benefits society can bring, but his moral and metaphysical status as, in essence, a pre-social rational being, means that there are clear limits to the demands that can be made on him by others or by society collectively. Specifically, his cherished right to his own autonomous rationality amounts to his right to choose his own good, his own goals, his own moral and aesthetic standards, according to his own tastes and preferences.

One flaw, by its own standards, in this anti-perfectionist vision is that it seems to be informed by at least a partial conception of the substantive good for human beings – the good of a life chosen and led freely. But even if the anti-perfectionist feels his or her position is undisturbed by recognition of this framework conception of the good, the critique can be pushed further. For several of the concrete policy proposals which Dworkin defends entail a departure from the ideal of neutrality. He argues, for example, in favour of affirmative action in certain contexts. Michael Sandel points out that the argument turns not only on the assertion that no rights are violated by affirmative action, but also, positively, on a vision of the kind of community which it might help us to realise – a community which is not characterised by systematic inequalities of distribution along racial, sexual or religious lines.[82] This community, in which goods would not be distributed on hierarchical racial or sexual lines, is implicitly valued, as part of a substantive conception of the good. Joseph Raz, too, has argued that the notion of neutrality is self-defeating: the state which purports to adopt a neutral stance is in fact one which affirms the desirability of citizens' lives involving wide autonomy and individual choice.[83] Indeed, the other central liberal value of progress, and the linking of this with individual freedom, is clearly in tension with the ideal of neutrality.[84] From a feminist perspective, these critiques are significant, for they reveal how neutralist liberalism obscures the substantive values which it in fact pursues behind a stance of objectivity and impartiality.

An adequate feminist political theory would reveal gender patterns and structures as politically meaningful, rather than as accidental, legitimated by the exercise of free choice, or natural. In the world as we know it, the liberal state which adopts 'neutral' policies on gender logically cannot, as we shall argue, include affirmative action. For it turns out to be a state which acquiesces in gender hierarchy. From a feminist perspective, the state's omission is not innocent: omission as well as intervention calls for justification, even if the structure of the justification is different. We should note here that the individual freedom-respecting preoccupations which underpin Dworkin's commitment to state neutrality implicitly paint a very strong picture of the potential power of the state. This is true not only in terms of its repressive potential but also in terms of its positive powers to initiate social change or sustain certain kinds of social practice.

Public goods and collective values
The priority of the right over the good, the doctrine of neutrality and the liberal focus on the individual as the basic moral unit, have meant that recent liberalism has not developed a thorough-going conception of the good.[85] But it is not simply conditions of the good life for individuals which liberalism has defined as outwith its ambit. Liberal theory, in its recent construction, has devoted rather little attention to the analysis of development of public goods, or collectively valued and distributed resources, nor has it been conspicuous in its recognition of other-oriented, solidaristic values. Even for recent welfare liberals, redistributive policies and state provision of some goods is a matter of the defence of the interests and autonomy of the individual.[86] For example, the design of the British welfare state recognised that some children had to be protected from or compensated for their parents and family circumstances, although in some strands of liberalism welfare rights proceed from a conception of the social interest.[87]

To say that justice is the first virtue of social institutions and that the state's primary role is to do justice between individuals, is very different from emphasising the maintenance of a shared public culture, the values of benevolence and solidarity, and concepts of public duty. Yet these all form a necessary backdrop for the living of worthwhile lives in society. Where liberals have attended to these issues, acknowledging the need for something more than justice among individuals, this has given rise to tensions between competing aspects of liberal theory.

For example, Rawls accords priority to the principle of liberty over his second equality principle, known as the 'difference principle' which enshrines, first, equality of opportunity and second, the need for distributive inequalities to be justified by their contribution to the position of the worst-off members of society. At first sight, this ranking expresses a rather clear individualism. Yet, as G. A. Cohen argues, the difference principle can be shown to rest on egalitarian commitments which are in conflict with his assumption that better-off citizens are *entitled* to demand the extra wealth which their skills or other advantages can command.[88] The difference principle assumes that *inequalities* may well be to the advantage of the worst off, because it assumes that wealth creators will not be willing to work as hard as they might without additional incentives in terms of extra earnings. This factual assumption is, in effect, given normative sanction in the difference principle. But if it is right to redistribute wealth to the badly off in the way Rawls assumes, what justification can the well off have for refusing to work other than for extra financial rewards? Either those who endorse justice as fairness are genuine egalitarians, or they are individualists who, like Robert Nozick, reject the legitimacy of redistribution. If, as Rawls implies, they are the former, Cohen argues they should not be able to voice their refusal to work to create wealth to be redistributed to the badly off without implicitly denying the very community or common citizenship which justice as fairness is meant to engender and express. In other words, Rawls' substantive principles seem to embody a half-baked ideal of community which sits uneasily with his motivational assumptions and the priority of liberty.

With the gradual move towards the recognition of the primacy of the social in both Rawls' recent work and that of Dworkin and Raz, liberalism has begun to explore and rediscover ideas of fraternity (sic!) and public culture.[89] In his recent work, Rawls emphasises that the notion of fraternity is an important value of justice as fairness.[90] But, as Cohen's argument reveals, the real extent of and basis for any genuinely solidaristic values in Rawls' principles are unclear. Moreover the existence of the public culture which Rawls acknowledges is needed to sustain justice as fairness is simply assumed to be implicit in modern western societies, waiting to be elicited via the attenuated model of the original position. If we look for any elaboration of the features of this public culture, let alone the social institutions which it might engender and depend upon, we find that the extent of discussion is minuscule as compared, for example, with the attention Rawls gives to basic individual liberties. And whilst we find some general discussion of the institutional aspects of public culture, any discussion of culture in the broader sense, encompassing traditions and discourses, is conspicuously absent.

In *Law's Empire* Dworkin too emphasises the notion of fraternity in the true 'community of principle', but the foundation for this community is the notion of the individual's right to equal concern and respect, and it is the individuated features of political argument and practice, that is, rights and their institutional realisation, which continue to dominate Dworkin's political and legal theory.[91] Will Kymlicka asserts the importance to liberalism of people's cultural membership, but the basic motivation of his argument remains a concern with the individual's rights and interests and the survival of cultures as necessary conditions for the living of autonomous lives.[92] Raz, whose position most thoroughly among liberals acknowledges the need to foster a public culture, sustains his argument only at a relatively abstract level, with little discussion of institutions.[93] Whilst his model certainly holds out the greatest promise of accommodating this importance of culture in a broad sense to political theory, this aspect of his argument is relatively underdeveloped in terms of the working out of implications for concrete practices. In any case it is implicit in Raz's position that while a particular kind of culture is necessary to foster individual autonomy, cultures themselves can be judged by whether they afford individual autonomy the highest value. Raz does not discuss the possible attractions of solidaristic political values, which might be suggested by this recognition of the importance of culture.[94]

In terms of detail and sophistication, then, although the last decade has seen a significant move in liberal political theory towards a recognition of the importance of the social, the most developed features of liberal theory tend still to be individual rights and individual freedom, and their place in a just civic or political order. The political importance of the social and cultural, and the importance of other-regarding values which the recognition of the primacy of the social might suggest, are just beginning to appear on the liberal agenda. But our argument would suggest that the very conceptual framework of liberal theory will hamper its development of these insights.

From a specifically social constructionist and feminist stance it is clearly nonsensical to claim that women are or have been constituted by their social ties and situation to a greater extent than men. All human beings are socially situated in this way. ·But there may have been historical differences in terms of how far women and men have experienced and identified themselves with (have acknowledged their identity as being bound up with) particular affective ties, cultural bonds and social responsibilities.[95] Critical feminist politics has been strongly concerned to emphasise the facts of human interconnectedness and, flowing from this practical insight, to argue for the reassessment of values and practices which flow from ideals of reciprocity, sisterhood and solidarity. And at an analytic level, a broad notion of culture as comprising practices, discourses, structures, institutions, cutting across public/private boundaries, has been central to feminist thought. The need to analyse the role of culture and the significance of solidaristic and reciprocal values to a wide range of social institutions, not only the traditional 'organs of government', but also the family, welfare institutions, pressure groups, trade unions, educational establishments, has been central to feminist theory.

Doubtless specific aspects of women's ethical reasoning and understanding have flowed in part from the consciousness produced by participation in activities such as child rearing, which have historically fallen to women in our culture, and which have been marginalised in terms of political significance and economic value. Feminist politics therefore must question a theoretical framework which focuses on issues of justice between individuals, and a politics which privileges economic entitlements, each to the virtual exclusion of public provision and collective and other oriented goods. The dichotomy between individual and other which this kind of liberal structure presupposes is highly artificial. The move from individualism to inter-subjectivity brings with it a move from individually oriented values to those which recognise and affirm human inter-connectedness and dependence on social life.

Feminists have also been critically literal-minded about 'he-man talk', revealing how allegedly gender-neutral uses of masculine pronouns and categories do as a matter of fact have gendered meanings for language users, and reinforce ideas of masculinity as the norm.[96] In light of this feminists would be well advised to cast a critical eye over recent rediscoveries of the value of 'fraternity' by these political philosophers. Of course, fraternity is one of the three elements of the slogan of the French Revolution. In modern political theory, elaborations of the concept, by contrast with the concepts of liberty and equality, have been few and far between. Carole Pateman has recently identified it as a discursively suppressed, but no less central, value of liberal politics, and insists that we must take its gendered nature seriously. It is not just a synonym for 'solidarity' or 'community', where these are understood as genuinely gender-neutral.[97] In this connection, we might say, the concept of 'fraternity' at least has the virtue of being explicitly masculine. Gender neutral language frequently hides or suppresses gender issues.[98]

Feminist scholarship and research in many disciplines has emphasised how male individuals actually rely on and are constructed by masculine solidarity and inter-connectedness and how this forms a basis for individual men's oppression of individual women.[99] Cultures of masculinity and femininity construct definitions of sexuality, fit work for women, notions of normality and deviance, and so on. 'Male bonding' and masculine cultures have been notoriously damaging to women's well-being. Pateman argues that this kind of male solidarity is central to the apparently individualist social contract tradition. We turn to this next.

The metaphor of contract

In our discussion of liberal conceptions of the self we have already touched on the regularity with which liberal theorists have relied on some version of contractual argument as the legitimising device for their principles of justice. The notion of agreement or assent, actual or hypothetical, has an important role in the work of writers as diverse as Hobbes, Locke, Rousseau, Kant, Rawls and Ronald Dworkin. Many of the difficulties which feminist theory identifies with this intellectual device flow from the features of abstract individualism which have already been discussed. The construction of the contract or auction inevitably participates, to a greater or lesser extent, in a decontextualising move. This is done by positing the participants as sufficiently equally situated to allow for the legitimacy of the outcome of the process – to allow for the application of the notion of pure procedural justice, in Rawls' terms. The most important assumption, of course, is that the conditions of the relevant agreement ensure equality of bargaining power among the participating parties. Thus even in Dworkin's auction, in which participants have a far greater degree of knowledge about themselves and their society than do the persons behind Rawls' veil of ignorance, the construction does not allow for reflection upon inequalities of access to effective participation in the auction in terms of articulacy, self-knowledge, self-confidence, assertiveness and power or authority distinctions between the parties.[100]

The failure of any liberal contract or quasi-contract theorist to reflect on this kind of substantive issue has important implications for gender politics. In a sexually unequal society, gender neutral procedures and gender neutral language do not lead to gender fair results. Instead the position of gender neutrality has served as a cover for what are implicitly male concerns and interests, which are thereby constructed as objectively valid. Questions of gender equality of bargaining power are relevant, and we must be doubtful about the suppression of ethically relevant questions of difference in the abstract individualist construction of the contract. Furthermore, we might well have hesitations about the very discourse of 'bargaining' as a legitimising device, for it expresses the idea of competitively self-assertive individuals, thereby presupposing a relatively equal power structure, and being at the outset less open to associational and collective values than a social constructionist would argue to be important. In other words, not only should we be doubtful about the substantive political vision expressed by contract methodology, but also about the methodology itself, which far from operating as a neutral grounding device, is itself founded on the values it is supposed to generate.

Recently, this feminist critique has been further developed by Carole Pateman through a critical reading of the classical contract theorists, Hobbes, Locke and Rousseau.[101] Pateman notes that the social contracts envisaged by the early theorists were, often quite explicitly, contracts between men. They were designed to found the conditions for fraternity (by implication a community of men of equal standing) as opposed to patriarchy. In this respect their liberal credentials are quite impeccable, and they represent a genuine repudiation of the older patriarchy. However, impeccable liberal credentials are not, in this analysis, impeccable feminist ones, for the very idea of the social contract in these texts presupposes a prior contract between the men, governing sexual access to and, in effect, ownership of, women. This prior sexual contract underpins the exclusion of women from political life and, most importantly, removes a dangerous source of conflict among men – access to women.

Pateman's argument does not establish that agreement as the basis for legitimising political arrangements *could not* include women. However, her work contributes a good deal to the understanding of the social contract tradition, and throws a great deal of light on the absence of any discussion of gender relations in political theory – these are essentially *pre*political. Her argument implies, at the very least, that contemporary exponents of contract-type arguments must be aware of this dimension of the contract tradition and make explicit efforts to counteract it. No such contemporary theorist has done so. Indeed, the subjects in Rawls' work are 'heads of households' with the clear reiteration of the principle that family and sexual relations are beyond the ambit of political theory.[102] Pateman's argument is also strengthened by her analysis of traces of 'sexual contract discourse' in modern institutions such as marriage and prostitution, and in the liberal critique of these.

Public–private distinctions

Perhaps the best-known, and most deeply contested feature of feminist critique of the liberal tradition is its attack on the dichotomy between public and private, in both its analytic and its prescriptive aspects. As we have seen, the liberal conception of the limited, neutral state carries with it an implicit conception of a private, non-political sphere in which state intervention is inappropriate and where individual autonomy is to be exercised.[103] Feminism is critical of this argument for several reasons, yet itself takes up a somewhat ambivalent position.[104]

In the first place, feminists have argued that the public–private distinction is analytically flawed. At a material level, it turns out to be extremely difficult to identify where the line between public and private is to be drawn. There have been many shifts over time: in the nineteenth century, *laissez-faire* liberalism constructed the economic market as private; in the late twentieth century, mixed economy liberalism has shifted this boundary, and the quintessentially private sphere is seen as being constituted by the family and sexual relations. In recent years the state/civil society distinction has been resurrected, in the context both of 'western' and of East European ex-communist systems. The revival of free-market ideology has begun to push economic relations back into the 'private' sphere. And in actuality in most modern states, family life itself is hedged around with regulation and intervention, with legal definitions of marriage and divorce, conditions under which the custody of children will be granted or maintained, conditions under which state support will be given, and so on. So in a sense there simply is no 'private sphere' in twentieth-century liberal states.[105]

Furthermore, even to the extent that there is a difference in the level of intervention and regulation between different spheres, feminism contests the assumption that the distinction between intervention and non-intervention is of absolute significance. Non-intervention is just as political as intervention, and calls for its own justification. Furthermore, what from one point of view is seen as non-intervention, from another appears to be intervention. Consider the issue of marital rape. From the point of view of some feminist campaigners the call has been for the state to step in and regulate relations within marriage. But that marital rape has not been and in many states still is not a crime is, of course, the upshot of state regulation of the marriage relation and legal definitions of a wife's status. Arguments like these tend to engender a straightforwardly sceptical analysis of public–private distinctions, which aims to reinterpret their significance for political theory.

However, liberals counter this kind of scepticism about the public–private distinction by reference to its normative credentials: the ideal of the limited state and the worth of individual human freedom. Feminists, as we have seen, reply with the argument that negative freedom is worth little if it is not accompanied by the positive conditions for self-determination. Indeed, it is women's lack of these with which the public–private distinction is associated. More than this, feminists focus on the discursive power of the distinction, a power which somehow survives its analytic incoherence.[106]

The idea of public and private spheres is often hived off from the freedom-based argument for the limited state, and is applied in an apparently descriptive, yet ultimately question-begging, way to particular activities and institutions. Once a sphere is labelled 'private', normative conclusions that no intervention is appropriate are drawn, usually without the full argument for non-intervention being spelled out. The attribution of privacy, which should be the conclusion of argument, is taken for the argument itself. And the discourse of privacy in areas such as sexuality and family life has, in political fact, become a mechanism whereby women's oppression is not only constituted and maintained, but also and most damagingly, rendered apolitical. Similarly, the ascription 'public' has been unproblematically associated with the state, leaving out of account the interpenetration of state and non-state institutions. In modern societies there are a number of non-state forums for public, political debate, such as social movements, trades unions, pressure groups, etc. Hence it is no longer possible (if ever it was) to elide the terms 'state' and 'public', any more than it is appropriate to see political theory as concerned only with state power. It is against this political marginalisation of women's subordination, and against the narrow conception of 'the political' that feminists have taken up the slogan 'the personal is political'.

Whilst we accept both the importance and the essential validity of the critique of the public–private distinction we would argue that there is a need to draw a sharper distinction than have many recent feminist analyses between the argument about state intervention on the one hand, and the depoliticisation of 'private' issues on the other. For although liberalism itself is disingenuous in its assertion of the illegitimacy of state intervention in the private sphere, given such massive intervention in all social domocratic liberal states (intervention which is unquestioned as such by social democratic liberal theory) the feminist critique of this tension within liberalism has often led to a simplistic conclusion in favour of the appropriateness and legitimacy of state intervention in the private sphere. The answer, it is suggested, is simply to extend state regulation of women's oppression into the private sphere.

Leaving aside evident difficulties about both the potential efficacy of state regulation in many areas of life, and the identification of 'state' institutions (especially in a time when such functions as policing and social work have been to some extent and might be further 'privatised') it is clear that this solution is not only too simple, but also too risky. For it appears to commit feminism to the view that there are no moral limits on proper state action. The proper goal for feminism should rather be the reinterpretation of some form of public–private distinction along less gender-exploitative lines.[107] For women even more than disadvantaged men in our culture have suffered from the lack of a real 'private' space in which to pursue our own concerns, given the double burden inherent in current gender arrangements which means that most women have, in effect, both more than one job and relatively few resources. A total critique of the public–private distinction in terms of a rejection of the idea of some limits on proper state intervention and control would be a grave mistake for feminist politics.

Furthermore, the inference from the critique to a solution in terms of legal change partakes of what we argue to be a naive and distinctively liberal attitude to how social change comes about. For it assumes that deliberate state intervention, via legal regulation of, for example, the family or the labour market, would be the best way to tackle the problems engendered by the traditional public–private divide. As we shall argue, however, an adequate theory would rather see potential for political change in terms of gradual changes in culture and practices brought about in important part by the operation of critical discourses such as feminism and, indeed, liberalism. On this view, the really important feminist claim here remains intact. This claim is not so much about state intervention or lack of it, as about the recognition of the political significance of aspects of life lived in what have been culturally constructed as private spheres. The recognition of the political relevance of women's family responsibilities for their effective access to political power, their position in civil society, the 'public' labour market and so on, are a fundamentally important aspect of feminist political theory. Indeed, this insight engenders a critique which has relevance beyond the way liberal political theory has continued to construct its notion of 'the political'. It also, by the same token, reveals the inadequacy of a construction of 'political institutions' as the traditional organs of government.[108] This conception is utterly inadequate for theorising the conditions of the modern social democratic state, in which a wide range of institutions ranging from the legislature through quangos, pressure groups, businesses, banks, unions, the family, the church and so on must all be acknowledged to wield what are properly seen as forms of political power. And political theory must attend not only to relatively concrete institutions, but also to institutions in the broader sense of cultural practices and discourses, if it is to give a satisfactory account of, let alone an attractive vision of the potential for, political society.

The historically contingent but politically significant fact, then, that women have lived their lives to a disproportionate extent in what has been known as 'the private sphere' marks out the ideological power of the public–private distinction as an important focus of feminist deconstruction and critique. But the crucial part of the argument is the reconstruction of 'private' matters as political, as of central importance to political theory, rather than any general prescription about remedies in terms of state regulation of the private sphere. The feminist argument is that the private sphere is not beyond political critique: this does not imply any general prescriptive position on the aptness of state intervention in response to the critique.

Power

Clearly issues of power are implicit throughout the feminist critique that we have been outlining. Liberals have certainly always been concerned to limit the power and authority exercised over the individual, both by the state, and by 'society' and other individuals. They have always been concerned to ensure that the power and authority that is exercised over the individual is justified. Yet we have seen that the adequacy of this liberal exercise is severely restricted by four factors.

First, and most important, for the liberal the ideal society is in important respects *power-free*. Some power is necessary, and some justified, but all power is undesirable.[109] Arguably what has happened in recent liberal political philosophy is that there has been a conflation of this ideal with actuality. This is surprising, given liberalism's common commitment to the fact/value distinction. Certainly, the ideal seems to have deprived liberal theorists of the conceptual and methodological tools for the study and analysis of power. They, paradoxically, mistake how things are for how things ought to be, by their lights. Further, when abuses of power do become visible, then the society in question is condemned as illiberal as though that is a sufficient analysis.

Second, the construction of the public–private distinction and the definition of certain social relations and institutions as beyond the realm of politics leads liberals to overlook the social (and deny the political) significance of relations of power in certain spheres, notably the family, sexual relations, and so on. Similar to this is the neglect of culture in a broad sense – institutions, practices, discourses and norms. These are also the site of power relations which in our analysis are politically significant. Third, liberal theory begins with the conviction that all persons are equal in essential respects, and ends with the normative conviction that they should be treated equally, irrespective of their race, sex, moral creed, and so on. Again, we have seen that this normative gender (and race) neutrality effectively means that liberal theories do not see and cannot take account of the realities of power exercised along these dimensions and the resulting disadvantage to certain individuals. Fourth, liberals tend to be oblivious to the power of their own discourse and practice, to the way in which liberalism itself has been constructed into a position of political ascendancy and hegemony, which means that those who protest at its gender or ethnicity 'blindness', or argue that housework or rape are political issues, need not be heard.

3

□

Liberalism and feminist politics

On a liberal individualist world-view, the freedom of the individual subject is the paramount value, and is best guaranteed in the context of a political society whose public institutions respect the rule of law. Each individual should be equal before the law, which should be applied to her or him in accordance with the dictates of procedural fairness. Clearly, this has been a progressive political doctrine in the history of our culture, and continues to be of paramount importance in resisting many forms of elitism, authoritarianism, prejudice, totalitarianism and brutality which threaten the conduct of political life in the western world. As far as issues of gender are concerned, the liberal commitments to formal equality and the rule of law have been crucial in many political struggles.

In developing a critique of this ideal, we and other feminists are of course not denying the historical and contemporary importance of liberal discourse to gender justice. Rather we argue that, and explicate the ways in which, the radical and critical potential of liberalism is limited by its conceptual structure, and the substantive assumptions and conclusions of liberal theory. These limits, it will be argued, can be demonstrated by the many ways in which liberal political practice has either failed to deliver the kind of gender justice it promised, or lacks the critical tools to identify remaining and significant forms and causes of women's oppression. Feminist critique suggests that in many areas of social life the progressive potential of liberalism has been exhausted, and that an alternative political analysis must be developed. If we are to construct political theory in terms which offer real insight into the nature of women's oppression and the possible means of social transformation, analysis must move beyond questions of formal equality to substantive questions of power, and must be informed by a more sophisticated social theory. We shall now turn our attention to political practice, in order to show how political action and change carried out in the name of liberalism and under the aegis of the rule of law have been of limited efficacy from a feminist perspective, and the extent to which they display limitations which correspond to the theoretical critique we have outlined.

The contribution of any political doctrine to progressive social change depends on the prevailing conditions of the time and the receptiveness of particular societies to the messages and values proclaimed by the doctrine. The contributions of liberalism then, must be assessed historically, and of course, liberalism has been associated with major progress not only for women but also for other oppressed and socially disadvantaged groups. In the context of societies such as the UK in the nineteenth and early twentieth centuries, when women were specifically excluded from a number of spheres integral to full political status, the liberal notion of formal equality was a powerful political argument which effected material advances. In a world of overt discrimination and exclusion, ideas of formal equality and the rule of law were powerful in arguing for women's access to education, to suffrage and citizenship, to the professions from which they had been excluded, and so on,[1] and liberalism has continued to take up causes of concern to feminists. Indeed, liberal feminism has become an important social and intellectual movement in its own right.

However, as women have slowly made political progress over the last century, the limitations of liberal feminism (the drawbacks of gender-invisibility and the ideal of gender neutrality) have been revealed. Paradoxically, the very successes of liberal feminism have deprived it of the critical foothold it used to have, for its successes have consisted primarily in the dismantling of gender as an explicit category of political decision and distribution. Reforms like the British Sex Discrimination Act 1975, the Equal Treatment Directive issued by the European Community, and the modern interpretation of the Equal Protection Clause of the US Constitution, operate to realise equality by *decategorising*. In other words, they proscribe the use of the category of sex or marital status as a basis for decision or action in particular spheres. Progress has therefore meant an increase in gender invisibility in social decision-making, and has lent itself in many areas to the marginalisation of gender issues. It has been possible to pretend that gender is no longer a problem; women have attained formal equality – what more do we want?

Evidently, much more is needed, not least because the instantiation of formal equality in the public sphere, given a history of inequality and given the effect of private subordination on a person's capacity to take up public resources, results only in further (yet less clearly illegitimate) gender hierarchy. In response to the evident inadequacies of this position, liberalism and liberal feminism have increasingly relied, over the last twenty years, on the notion of equality of opportunity.[2] This idea seeks to overcome the limitations of formal equality by focusing on a more programmatic and dynamic goal, and one which, it will be noticed, sits nicely on the fence between positive and negative conceptions of freedom.

Although programmes of equality of opportunity seem to promise positive empowerment, in practice they offer rather a guarantee of the removal of certain barriers. The liberal discourse of equality of opportunity constitutes an advance on that of formal equality, but its cutting edge remains limited. For gendered patterns and results which feminism takes as symptoms of social injustice (the manifestations of continued oppression and subordination) can be written off by equal opportunity theory precisely because of its liberal basis. Here the contours of actual political debate and strategy can be shown to connect directly with those conceptual features of liberal individualism which have been subject to feminist critique. For the primary focus on the individual choosing subject as the moral centre of liberal analysis, combined with its limited conception of the politically relevant 'public' sphere, depoliticises the nature of substantively unequal, gender-structured outcomes which persist in the face of equal opportunities policies.

In considering some specific examples drawn from the three areas of social life we identified in Chapter 1 – work, sexuality and political representation – we shall find three problems recurring again and again. These problems are to do with the conceptual framework of liberal political analysis. First, we shall see that given this conceptual structure, liberal politics is incapable of removing even some of the more obvious aspects of gender hierarchy. Second, and more fundamentally, it is incapable of identifying genuine instances of gender hierarchy in the first place. Third, when we examine the issues we find that we are faced with problems of *social* theory. Liberalism tends to over-emphasise the power and relative importance of 'traditional' political institutions. This excludes from consideration certain important aspects of social structure and hence sources of social change. Indeed, claims that liberalism is a political, not a social, theory are disingenuous: the pursuit of a 'purely political theory' in this way itself is an implicit (and unsatisfactory) social theory.

Waged work

The principles of non-discrimination and equal pay for women and men in the public labour market have been politically and legally established for nearly two decades in the United Kingdom, yet the labour market is still massively sexually segregated and characterised by significantly lower status and wages for women workers.[3] Although this at first sight seems to represent a failure on the part of liberal egalitarian politics, liberal individualist discourse contains the tools for quite simply explaining away substantive sex inequality as a political problem. For example, it can be said that women choose certain kinds of lives – that men and women exercise their freedom in different ways – and that this free choice legitimates whatever outcome emerges. The gender pattern of the outcome becomes politically irrelevant because women are assumed to be operating as equal and autonomous choosing subjects: the factors which structure their choices in certain ways (such as their disproportionate responsibilities in the 'private' sphere) are removed from the ambit of the political.

The removal of formal barriers to women in a variety of jobs was obviously an important first step, but we can see that it has done little to realise an even distribution of jobs across gender.[4] Furthermore, the retention of certain 'protective' limits on women's employment in jobs such as coal mining have proved highly problematic for liberal feminism, in that 'accommodation of difference' seems to threaten the basic premise of equality and to be susceptible of naturalistic interpretation.[5] This is well illustrated by problems encountered in the legal treatment of pregnancy. Statutory schemes for paid maternity leave appear, paradoxically, to have worked against women in the labour market, in that they act as a disincentive to employers who regard employing women as more costly than employing men.[6] The history of the application of anti-discrimination legislation to pregnant employees in the UK illustrates precisely the dilemmas encountered by liberal analysis. The premise of equality has led at one time to a denial that pregnancy discrimination is really discrimination, because it cannot constitute less favourable treatment than that accorded to *similarly situated men*; at others to affirmation that it may be discrimination on the basis of comparison with the treatment which would have been accorded to a sick or disabled man (thus assimilating pregnancy into the category of sickness).[7] The opposition of the ideal of formal equality to the seemingly inevitable need to recognise difference has been a constant problem to liberal feminism, and one which it shows no sign of being able to resolve.

In general, liberal feminist strategies for improving the situation of women in the world of work, although they have been important, have had limited impact. An example which illustrates shortcomings both in the liberal construction of the problem, and in the strategy liberalism engenders, is that of specific anti-discrimination legislation. The idea of promoting sexual equality by proscribing sex discrimination can be interpreted as a centrally liberal approach for a number of reasons. In the first place, it constructs the problem of unfair sex inequality in terms of individuals' and corporations' discriminatory actions; the implicit understanding is that if individually discriminatory actions and practices are removed, gender justice will automatically follow. It has difficulty in accommodating the insight that sex inequality is 'institutional', that is, it inheres in social practices and structures which are not susceptible of analysis in terms of cumulations of individually discriminatory acts. It also constructs labour market inequality in terms of a kind of irrational and inefficient prejudice, which must be removed so as to facilitate the proper operation of the market on the basis of free, informed, rational individual choices. And finally it assumes the tractability of sexism through the direct influence of public policy, as conventionally construed, failing to advert to broader social factors which may affect the impact of political strategies.

The United Kingdom Sex Discrimination Act was passed in 1975. This legislation also implemented the Equal Pay Act, nominally of 1970, and was enacted largely because of the UK's need to comply with the EEC Equal Treatment Directive on its accession to the Treaty of Rome. It defines and proscribes two forms of discrimination. Direct discrimination is defined as less favourable treatment on grounds of sex and is prohibited in most employment decisions.[8] Enforcement, however, generally depends on individual litigation, in which the burden of proof is extremely difficult to discharge.[9] This is partly for technical reasons, but also importantly because the individualisation of the issue decontextualises it and the focus is inevitably on a single act or series of events. Evidence, for example, of general employment patterns in a workplace, or of an employer's behaviour on other occasions, may be inadmissible as irrelevant to the precise case at issue. This often makes it hard for a litigant to convince a tribunal, whose focus on the single incident makes the various explanations which an employer may give in defence of this particular behaviour more plausible. It may be difficult for a litigant to persuade a tribunal, for example, that her employer's general record of failure to promote women is relevant to his decision not to promote her. For whilst this technically constitutes evidence from which inferences may be drawn, the inference which has to be made is itself about an individually discriminatory act on a specific occasion.

The Sex Discrimination Act's second conception is that of 'indirect' discrimination. This exists where a woman (or man) is held to the same requirement as a man (or woman), but in circumstances where a disproportionate number of the complainant's, as compared with the opposite, sex cannot comply with the requirement. This inability to comply must be to the detriment of the complainant, and the requirement itself must not be justifiable irrespective of sex.[10] This was conceived as the answer to 'institutional' discrimination in the workplace and elsewhere. The notion of indirectly discriminatory practices would, it was hoped, have a critical edge in tackling sources of gender inequality which could not be reduced to a series of individually prejudiced actions. Yet not only is the structure of the specific legal remedy – individual litigation – inadequate to the task, but also the principled acknowledgement of the injustice associated with indirect discrimination has posed intractable problems for liberal commentators.

To take the practical issue first, the starting point for an indirect discrimination case is, inevitably, the experience of an individual, and requires proof of a causal link between practice and individual detriment – a truly indirect way of addressing a problematic social structure! This gives rise to practical difficulties where, for example, a candidate for a promotion can establish that an indirectly discriminatory requirement was being used, but where it is possible for the employer to suggest that they would not have received the promotion even had the discriminatory requirement not been applied. Furthermore, tribunals inevitably apply the 'justifiability' defence in terms of their own reading of the appropriateness of the outcome, that is, in terms of whether they think that what the complainant is complaining of was really unreasonable. The legal test is therefore filtered through the sexist attitudes it was meant to challenge.[11]

The tensions of principle associated with liberal approaches to institutional discrimination are suggested by the fact that claimants cannot recover damages for indirect discrimination, unless they can prove an 'intention to discriminate'. This implicitly constructs indirect discrimination as penumbral to the focal concept of direct discrimination. For whilst indirect discrimination takes a step forward in recognising and responding to patterns of gender (or racial) inequality, the principle behind this recognition is obscure. Clearly, the conception falls short of any commitment to equality of outcome as such; rather, unequal outcomes are being used, in certain contexts, as prima facie proof of unfair inequalities of opportunity.

Putting one's finger, analytically, on just what constitutes the unfairness from the liberal point of view has proved to be tricky. Some commentators have argued that indirect discrimination can be seen as a kind of culpable negligence on the part of the discriminator. The employer has a positive duty to scrutinise hiring and promotion policies for their potential gender impact.[12] This analysis moves a step away from a direct recognition of institutional, structural discrimination, and back to the idea of a culpable individual action. If the goal is to move towards a straightforward recognition of the injustice of institutional discrimination, the question remains as to just why the liberal should have to be concerned with gender-patterned outcomes. In principle, the answer must be, because the liberal can only explain his or her concern with gender-patterned outcomes if those outcomes are evidence of genuine unfairness. But this begs the very question being asked, leaving everything to rest on the interpretation of justifiability. It is perhaps not surprising to find that some liberals have argued that the idea of indirect discrimination puts undue burdens on 'innocent' employers. It has been argued that the real basis for the proscription of indirect discrimination is a 'positive-action' rationale which is problematic for liberalism in that it aims for an egalitarian end-state.[13] On this liberal view, the patterns interpreted as evidence of indirect discrimination cannot in themselves even prima facie be regarded as problematic because they may just as easily be explained in terms of autonomous individual choices, or even biological differences, as in terms of unfairness.

The crucial notion of justifiability, however, is under explained in both the legislation and the commentaries on it. To what standards can the justifiability defence refer? These must be either current social conventions, or some full-blooded notion of equality. If it is the latter, there is strong reason to think such a conception must give rise to tensions within liberalism, as indeed we shall try to illustrate in our discussion of affirmative action below. If it is rather the former, the critical edge of the conception is blunt. A thorough notion of institutional discrimination presupposes an analysis of the role of structures and institutions in the social world, and of the political-ethical questions these give rise to, which individualist liberalism seems unlikely to be able to deliver. It also seems to be informed by more substantively egalitarian ideals than liberalism espouses.

Further practical limitations of the legislation can also be associated with liberal individualism. The Sex Discrimination Act is symmetrical; it applies equally to sex discrimination against women and against men. Hence it expresses the liberal value of formal equality and gender neutrality and delivers the message that the real social problem to which the legislation responds is discrimination on grounds of sex, rather than discrimination against women specifically. From even a moderately feminist point of view this seems a travesty of the actual situation. A further problem with the notion of direct discrimination (which also applies in an attenuated form to indirect discrimination) is that the relevant standard of comparison for cases brought by women tends to be a norm set by and/or for men. The essence of the complaint is of unequal treatment relative to a given norm. This limits the critical perspective of anti-discrimination policy in that it excludes consideration of the adequacy of the standard itself, particularly in terms of its possible gender bias. The resonance with arguments about gender and models of ethical reasoning discussed in Chapter 2 is clear. Radically unequal effects can be legitimated within a liberal world-view via assumptions about what free individuals have rationally chosen, these assumptions themselves often being tinged with naturalistic sexist presuppositions. Inevitably, the liberal legal model individualises and pathologises acts of discrimination and is unable to focus its attention on sexism in its structural form.

Liberal legal attempts to get to grips with structural gender disadvantage, for example via the guarantee, foisted upon UK law by the European Court and Commission, that women and men be paid equally for work of equal value, certainly generate some successes. But, once again, their potential has been limited not only by practical considerations but also by the difficulties of accommodating the strong, equal pay principle within liberal theory. For example, legislature and courts have insisted on the availability of a defence to employers that market forces dictate differential pay. This is evidently a core liberal argument, but equally evidently one which will in practice ride a coach and horses through the pursuit of the equal value conception of equal pay in a labour market which has historically awarded low pay and low status to jobs predominantly done by women. Furthermore, this pervasive and structural undervaluation of certain kinds of work, historically performed by women in our culture, is simply reproduced in many of the job evaluation studies on which equal value cases are based.[14] The framework of liberal political thought gives us no critical tools with which to challenge this market-constructed undervaluation. It is utterly unclear how a liberal individualist analysis can begin to construct a political critique of this kind of social fact.

The ambit of anti-discrimination and protective statutes is also circumscribed by limitations (periods of eligibility for pregnancy protection, exclusions of very small employers from sex discrimination rules) which express the assertion of a 'private' sphere where discrimination is politically irrelevant (and where work is not recognised as such). The absence of state intervention, as we have argued, need not necessarily carry this message. But it can only be prevented from doing so if the general political analysis, reflected in political discourse and other aspects of social policy, explicitly recognises private discrimination as politically significant even if not susceptible of proper or effective direct state interference. At the level of political response, advocacy of the primacy of the economic interests of employers is widespread, while if we take the viewpoint of 'rational economic man' women are undesirable employees because they are more expensive. So protective legislation such as that on pregnancy effectively continues to disadvantage women in the labour market.[15]

Beyond the legal sphere there have, of course, been genuine attempts in particular industries, often with the involvement of the Equal Opportunities Commission created by the Sex Discrimination Act, to overcome gender hierarchy by means of equal opportunities training and policies. Yet gender patterns in the labour market have changed very slowly, and most often in response to pragmatic demands for female labour in times of shortage. In the UK the material conditions such as provision of adequate child care and the restructuring of employment conditions such as working hours which would facilitate women's full participation in the world of paid work, are still lacking. A graphic illustration of the relative valuation of women's participation and economic expediency is represented by the East German government's immediate closure of state nurseries as the prospect of unification with West Germany gave rise to a surplus of labour. Given the predominance of ideas of formal equality and the gender-neutrality of citizenship, it is hard to establish any priority for gender issues within liberal politics.

Similarly, it has been difficult for liberal feminists to find the arguments for reaching beyond these kinds of policies within liberal political doctrine. The difficulty liberalism encounters in attempting a convincing account of affirmative action is particularly instructive in this respect. As suggested in Chapter 2, all affirmative action programmes must proceed from a vision of the good. Ronald Dworkin's sophisticated defence of affirmative action, although it predates his elaboration of a theory of equality of resources, clearly depends on such a notion.[16] He argues for affirmative action programmes as promoting a valued social goal and hence as ethically distinct from 'prejudiced' discrimination. Dworkin has powerful arguments to demonstrate that his postulate of a basic right to equal respect and concern does not entail that, for example, citizens have a right that jobs be distributed *only* on the basis of merit. But his argument crucially depends on the idea that a particular end-state, that is, a substantively less inegalitarian one in terms of the distribution of certain kinds of valuable resources, can be a genuine liberal ideal. What exactly does this mean? Are we to take it that any patterned inequality of outcome is to be taken as an example of unfair inequality in resources, and hence that affirmative action programmes must continue as long as any significant degree of race or gender patterning remains? This seems to go well beyond the idea of even Dworkin's relatively robust conception of equality.

At other points in Dworkin's work the suggestion is that this is a necessary condition for the realisation of the fundamental value of treating individuals with equal respect and concern. If this is so, the argument for affirmative action seems to be question-begging. What precisely is it about patterned gender and racial inequalities with respect to valued social goods such as jobs that constitutes a denial of equality in this more fundamental sense? If the relevant question is to do with the link between patterns and access to goods, we seem to be closer to a theory of equality of opportunity than to the robust vision of equality of resources which Dworkin takes himself to be defending. This brings us back to problems we have already discussed. How are we to distinguish between vicious and virtuous patterns if we take the notion of individual choice seriously, as Dworkin must?

These are precisely the questions feminist theory puts to liberalism, and it is a great merit of Dworkin's work that it unearths them. What is unclear is how he could address them adequately whilst still holding to an individualist liberal framework. Why should a liberal individualist value as such end states which are not patterned on gender lines? An argument, for example, in terms of the incompatibility of patterns with the liberal value of self respect itself draws on a more sophisticated conception of social structure than any which can be generated by the social theory implicit in Rawls' or Dworkin's liberal political theory. Ultimately, within a liberal legal structure which constructs and adjudicates upon an essentially liberal world it is hard to find a real purchase for feminist arguments which attend to the hierarchical gender order.

Sexuality

Similar problems in accommodating feminist analysis emerge in liberal constructions of and debates about sexuality. The problem is that liberals will tend to agree in the first instance that sexual harassment and other forms of sexual abuse are wrong, and that sexual practices are susceptible to liberal-political and moral analysis. However, when liberal arguments and concepts are brought to bear on issues of sexuality in general and sexual abuse in particular, it turns out that they do not capture the wrong that is experienced and understood, and even render it unclear that in liberal terms, any wrong has occurred at all.

Sexual harassment
Liberalism has a purchase on sexual harassment – the subjection of women and men to unwelcome and oppressive sexual attentions – so long as it can be incorporated within the notion of sexual discrimination. The notion of sexual discrimination is symmetrical, but in recognition of the social fact that sexual harassment is overwhelmingly

directed by men towards women we refer in this discussion to perpetrators and victims as men and women respectively. So long as a particular victim can claim that she has suffered a legally recognised harm by means of harassment, and so long as it is clear that she has been detrimentally treated in sexual ways to an extent that a man would not have been, or has had some requirement made of her that would not have been made of a man, she has a foothold to complain of sexual harassment. Indeed, as the liberal establishment has taken on board feminist demands to respond to sexual harassment, the model of sex discrimination has been found the most convenient response.[17] However the 'so long as' clauses are a major qualification, for many forms of sexual harassment cannot be accommodated easily within a discrimination model. Quite apart from the general problems with that model which have already been touched on, sexual harassment can only be dealt with in gender symmetrical terms by grossly distorting its social meaning, as constructed in feminist discourse.

The essence of the oppression of harassment is not that women are treated differently from and less favourably than men: it is that it is a sexually specific form of the exploitation of power practised by the relatively powerful on the relatively powerless. Further, it is *normal*, and does not require malice on the part of the perpetrator. The meaning of individual acts of sexual harassment cannot be grasped in isolation: their power consists in their relation to a social structure. The essence of sexual harassment is the sexual objectification of women in contexts in which male as opposed to female sexuality would be regarded as totally irrelevant. It is against the background of a *particular* set of power relations, structured along gender lines, in which power itself is sexualised, that sexual harassment can be understood as peculiarly demeaning. If the problem of sexual harassment had to do with individually sexist men, rather than a sexist culture, liberal analysis would be adequate. As it is, liberal individualism's failure to develop any sophisticated notion of culture obstructs its response to sexual harassment. Indeed, it is questionable whether liberal analysis could ever have got as far as recognising and naming sexual harassment in the first place.

The ambivalence of the liberal position on sexual harassment is reflected in the pervasive concern in liberal debates with the protection of the harasser's freedom, not just in the sense of his procedural rights but also his right to free personal and sexual expression. In so far as liberalism is capable of recognising women as persons and of seeing the importance of positive freedom, sexual harassment must be seen as a major problem. Yet the notion that personhood is essentially disembodied and hence not gendered marginalises the idea of sexually-oriented, gender specific harms which undermine personhood by inscribing the female body, whenever it appears, with sexual meanings. The pre-eminence of negative as opposed to positive conceptions of freedom is significant here.[18] The harasser's loss of freedom in being prohibited from harassing, that is, from doing what he wants to do because it may be construed as doing harm to another, is perceived as of overriding concern. It is not so obviously the case that the woman who is the object of harassment is being prevented from *acting as she wishes*, or in other words is being deprived of freedom in any sense. If we are to construe her as suffering a 'loss of freedom' then freedom must be understood in more subtle terms – she is being prevented from enjoyment and appreciation of herself as an actor. From a liberal point of view which emphasises negative freedom there are practical and theoretical difficulties in recognising this. Given that 'freedom' is the prime liberal value, the man's loss of freedom will inevitably be of greater moral significance than the woman's problem (whatever that is).

Feminist critique of liberalism points out that in a liberal world men enjoy the power and pleasure of a freely expressed sexuality by imposing themselves, sexually speaking, on women, but that this process of domination is made invisible by virtue of common sense understandings and sexual practices. Some philosophers suggest that the very idea of liberal subjecthood and freedom presupposes the status of object and unfreedom on the part of another: one can only have a concept of the experience of existential freedom, of subjectivity, by virtue of objectifying and dominating an 'other'. In the western tradition subjecthood is implicitly or explicitly equated with masculinity, and objecthood with femininity.[19] And sexuality, with its culturally given meanings of transcendence of social norms and mundane bodily experience, of struggle, surrender and domination, has in the modern era been seen by many theorists as a sphere of being with peculiar significance.[20] This is why feminists see the practice of sexual harassment as so important in maintaining sexual power relations. The equation of subjectivity and masculinity means that sexuality is a crucial site on which men can affirm their subjecthood, and the constitution of women as sexual objects is a necessary part of this process. In other words, liberalism is disabled from dealing properly with sexual harassment precisely because such harassment is functional to one form of subjectivity which is central to recent liberalism, and which feminist theory argues to be essentially a male subjectivity.

The fact that liberals have traditionally constructed sexuality as within the private sphere and hence insulated not only from state intervention but also political analysis further hinders an adequate analysis of sexual harassment, which is often seen as a problem which the parties ought to sort out between themselves. This is the case even when it occurs in areas like the workplace, which liberalism otherwise sees as public. A political theory which starts out from the disembodied, atomistic individual, which depoliticises sexuality as private and which privileges a negative conception of human freedom is unable to deal with as pervasive and embedded a social practice as sexual harassment. The social gains which we have seen in terms of the recognition of and struggles against sexual harassment have issued from an uneasy compromise between liberalism and post-liberal feminism rather than from liberal feminism itself. But the feminist campaign around sexual harassment has further significance as an excellent example of the power of political deconstruction and critique. Over the last two decades, our world has been changed by the feminist construction of sexual harassment. The change has come about through a transformation of consciousness, rather than by penalising transgression. Yet this source of social change tends to be defined as outwith the boundaries of liberal political theory.

Rape
Similar difficulties have arisen with the liberal approach to the concept and practice of rape. Rape is defined in British law, for example, as unlawful sexual intercourse with a woman who does not consent, the perpetrator being aware of, or perhaps indifferent to, the woman's lack of consent.[21] Predictably, consent is the crucial issue in most rape cases, either its existence or otherwise, or the perpetrator's belief or lack of belief in its existence. The liberal legal construction of rape focuses on an individual act, with only heavily circumscribed contextual factors being relevant, according to the rules of evidence. These rules are themselves notoriously sexist: judges have a (frequently exercised) discretion to admit evidence of the victim's past experience with men other than the defendant when they deem it necessary for the fair disposal of the case, whereas the perpetrator's

general sexual experience would almost never be admissible as evidence. An active sexual life is thus explicitly constructed as casting doubt on a woman's credibility as a witness.[22]

But the most evident shortcoming in the liberal analysis of rape has to do with the notion of consent itself. Can the reality of consent be assessed on the basis of the limited evidence admitted? Is it appropriate to rule out of court, literally and metaphorically, background social factors about the power of women both to withhold their consent, and effectively to communicate that refusal, in a culture in which men hold power over women in the sexual sphere, and in which women's expressed refusal is frequently constructed as consent? As recently as 1983 a leading textbook of criminal law used psychoanalytic reports of women's rape and seduction *fantasies* as material 'evidence' that a woman resisting a rapist might nevertheless be construed as 'welcoming a masterful advance'. It also opined that false allegations of rape may be made by adolescent girls to 'placate their parents', by 'a girl who is ashamed of her part in the affair and perhaps fears that she is pregnant', and 'out of spite, when the man was in fact a lover who jilted the woman or slighted her in some way, or for obscure psychological reasons'.[23]

Not only feminist theorists and activists, but also many practising lawyers are convinced that rape law operates oppressively to rape victims, but without an analysis of the culture which sexualises power and disempowers women partly through its construction of their sexuality as a paradoxical mixture of the capricious and the passive, political theory cannot begin to transform this area of social practice. Nobody would decry liberalism's proper concern with fairness to men accused of rape, but the inability of liberal analysis to articulate adequately the point of view of rape victims must be accounted a serious shortcoming.

Pornography

Feminist theorists have argued that the sexual objectification of women expressed in and consolidated by pornography genuinely and seriously harms all women. Yet feminist campaigns around this issue illustrate both the pitfalls of attempting to accommodate a feminist interpretation of pornography within a quasi-liberal framework, and the dangers of the kind of simplistic application of the public–private critique to which we adverted earlier. Catharine MacKinnon's and Andrea Dworkin's campaign against pornography, like the work of many other feminist writers in this area, has had the inestimable merit of rendering vivid the iniquity and injustice of pornography by exposing previously under-recognised aspects of its social meaning in our culture.[24] The exposure of the way pornography constructs women as sexual objects, as powerless, as bodies inevitably and constantly inscribed with sexual meaning, and ultimately as victims, has radically changed and sharpened our consciousness of this political and social phenomenon.[25] Equally, MacKinnon's and Dworkin's critique of central aspects of the liberal arguments against the proscription of pornography is astute.

In particular, Dworkin and MacKinnon assert that the argument that pornography is a valuable exercise of freedom of expression by both producers and consumers, fails to advert to what should be the central question, that is, what is the *value* of their freedom of expression to different members of the community. This hits a crucially important anti-liberal nail firmly on the head, for if, as they argue, pornography is an important means whereby women's freedom of expression is systematically constructed as of less value than men's, because it both silences women in certain contexts and changes the meaning of women's speech by sexualising it, the straightforward liberal argument from freedom of expression simply fails to go through in defence of pornography. Here we confront yet again the failure of liberal theory to focus on questions of substance, of access, of power, as opposed to questions of formal holdings of rights and freedoms.

However, the anti-pornography legislation which followed this critique is instructive as to the dangers of simplistic inference from the public–private critique, and of participation in quasi-liberal reform. In order to have any hope of successfully legislating against pornography, Dworkin and MacKinnon had to overcome the potential constitutional challenge to an anti-pornography law, based on its restriction of freedom of speech, for free speech is protected in virtually absolute terms by the First Amendment to the US Constitution as interpreted by the Supreme Court. MacKinnon and Dworkin addressed this problem in two ways. In the first place they conceptualised pornography as itself the kind of harm, or causing the kind of harm, which liberal theory would recognise and justify proscribing. Second, they did so in terms of harm to an interest which had the kind of constitutional protection which might counterbalance the argument from freedom of speech. This they did by conceptualising pornography, defined as particular kinds of material representing the sexual objectification of women, as *sex discrimination*, and by giving individual women the right to sue for damages for the harm done to them by pornography. This strategy cleverly sidesteps the intractable problem of establishing a causal link between pornography and sexual violence encountered by many critical analyses.[26] It also appeared to offer the hope of counterbalancing the free speech challenge. In the event, the attempt failed and the ordinance was held to be unconstitutional.[27]

Yet it is far from clear that feminist opponents of pornography should feel unambiguously sorry about that failure. In the first place, important questions arise about the kinds of political alliances which had to be made if the anti-pornography ordinance was to be passed by more than one or two unusually progressive legislative bodies. After all, the New Right and evangelical movements might well have supported it for reasons very different to those of the framers themselves. Following on from this, questions arise about what the fate of the ordinance would have been once it was subject to interpretation by judges. We have already seen that in order to participate in this legal reform project Dworkin and MacKinnon had to frame the notion of pornography in terms which were consonant with the liberal notion of harm caused to individuals. Certainly their conceptualisation deploys the liberal framework in a startlingly imaginative and tactically clever way. But their ordinance, in the hand of judges, might have been interpreted in very different ways from those they envisaged, and might well have been used to suppress, as degrading of women's citizenship status, kinds of literature (such as literature dealing with lesbian sexuality, or women's health) which feminists among others would be horrified to see proscribed. It is a serious and recurrent question whether any specific post-liberal vision can remain intact once one has entered into liberal legal reform. The subsequent processes of interpretation and enforcement involve the imposition of liberal categories and arguments which inevitably distort analysis of the situation or phenomenon which is to be ameliorated.

Furthermore, Dworkin's and MacKinnon's reform tactic seems to engage in precisely the kind of inference from the public–private critique which we criticised earlier.[28] They move from a subtle and sophisticated feminist critique of pornography and a deconstruction of the liberal political analysis of it, to the conclusion that the remedy lies in legal regulation (albeit civil) – in the regulation, that is, of the 'private'. They do not sufficiently consider all the complex issues of principle and strategy involved. In their eagerness to advance their radical view of the meaning of pornography, they tread a path which is both strategically uncertain, and which risks doing serious damage to the feminist cause by representing feminism as a political doctrine which is conservative, authoritarian and unconcerned with free expression. Moreover, their reform campaign arguably participates in liberalism's own rather undifferentiated view of the sources of social change, that is, in its optimism about the power of state politics. Feminism has reason to reject both liberalism's conception of the political, and its faith in the power of traditional political institutions to change the world; feminism also has grounds to criticise its blindness to the way public policy plugs into and interacts with wider aspects of culture.

In so far as Dworkin's and MacKinnon's argument concentrates on the opening up of our understanding of pornography and its implications in terms of women's citizenship and the value of women's expression, it is an immensely valuable contribution to the feminist critique of the liberal analysis of sexuality and of liberalism's construction of the political. Of course, the deconstruction of pornography and sexuality has been of interest to, and further developed by, feminist writers many of whom do not share Dworkin's and MacKinnon's views about the pre-eminent importance of sexuality as the site, symptom and cause of women's oppression. And feminist critique has focused on many other issues of sexuality – marital rape, violence against women, child sexual abuse, prostitution, and so on.[29] The three examples we have selected merely suffice to illustrate the power of feminist critique to identify issues to which liberal analysis is insensitive or which it misconstrues, and to suggest some pitfalls of certain ways of applying the feminist critique.

Political representation and participation

Finally, we shall consider liberal individualist contributions to questions of women's role in the political sphere. It is a commonplace of contemporary western political science that women are under-represented in the sphere of state politics. In Britain, for example, only 6.6 per cent of Members of Parliament elected in 1987 were women, and in 1992 8.9 per cent. And whilst this under-participation is less marked in quasi-public bodies such as trade union councils and in local and regional politics, in practically no area of political life except voting do women constitute anything approaching fifty per cent of political actors. Nor is the UK peculiar in the respect. Of western developed nations only the Nordic countries have made real progress in encouraging and achieving the political participation of women in government.[30]

The question of women's representation and participation in elective and non-elective political life is, however, one which has received remarkably little attention from political theorists. In the case of the liberal tradition, as we have seen, the constitution of the subject as a degendered individual (the basic gender neutrality of liberal political thought) means that once again a fundamental problem is obscured. For, on a gender neutral theory which assumes some form of representative democracy it is quite unclear whether the under-representation of women among political representatives raises any genuine issue about the proper political representation of female citizens.

Indeed, the idea that proper representation requires proportionate representation of women by number is deeply problematic. Whilst no legislature can constitute an exact microcosm of society in every respect, attributes or characteristics which are of deep importance to the position of particular groups in a social and political power structure, which are related to their access to political power, for example, would seem to justify a call for roughly proportionate representation in political institutions. For whilst most elected political actors are called upon to represent a range of interests, a failure in any political body to include people with a diversity of social experience is likely to make for decision-making which, albeit unconsciously, reflects certain kinds of viewpoint and experience. Exactly this claim can be made not only about gender but also, most obviously, about class and race.

It is unclear, however, whether this argument would appeal or even occur to a thoroughgoing liberal individualist. For, as we have already seen, liberal individualism lacks the conceptual tools which could identify structural factors such as gender or race as important determinants of political position in the way the argument requires if we are to distinguish these factors from, for example, eye colour or height. Of course, eye colour and height, along with almost any other human characteristic *might* potentially mark and divide social groups by lines of exploitation and oppression. In western liberal democracies at present they do not. An adequate answer to the question 'why not?'

presupposes exactly what liberalism does not have – an account of how features of culture and social institutions such as gender systematically structure citizens' political positions.

Indeed, from a feminist perspective, the question of the numbers of women participating in democratic practices and institutions, and taking up the role of representative, is connected with a wider series of questions about women's citizenship status. The problematic nature of citizenship for women is revealed in the differential impact on women and men of a wide range of social welfare rules and practices. Women are more likely to be poor, and more likely to undertake negotiations with welfare state agencies on their own and their families' behalf, but, as we have seen, less likely to participate in legislation, policy making, or in the higher echelons of the executive agencies.[31] In a political tradition in which citizenship has been conceptualised in terms of freedom and independence, women's citizenship status is thereby impugned both practically and theoretically.[32]

However, we must be wary of making too quick a move from these considerations to conclusions about women's political outlook and policy preferences (and therefore putting forward certain consequentialist arguments for an increase in women's political participation). As the recent British experience of a female prime minister illustrates, we cannot assume that all women Members of Parliament will express in their political practice the kinds of concerns which we might expect the social experience of femininity in our culture to generate. Indeed, to assume that they would necessarily do so would be to participate in the very kind of biologistic sexual determinism which the constructionist feminist movement has consistently rejected. Social constructionists acknowledge that women can behave and indeed see the world in ways which are, as MacKinnon neatly puts it, 'socially male'. The structure of gender is part of what constitutes the social world, but it is not a monolithic structure which dichotomises male and female rigidly. No person is untouched by the discourse of gender, but its effect in terms of their sense of themselves, their world view, their political sympathies, will be realised in different ways in different persons, at different times, according to their personal psychology, history and social situation. The proportionate representation of women in the public political sphere would not necessarily, in and of itself, engender woman-friendly or woman-sensitive politics. For similar reasons, because the diversity of women's experience makes it inappropriate to generalise about women's point of view, we have to be aware that the very idea of women's concerns and interests as a basis for claims of fair representation by and for women is problematic.[33]

This counter-argument can itself be pushed to a *reductio ad absurdum*, however, for if we were to follow it through absolutely, it would deconstruct the very notion of representative politics. Altruistic despotism by a highly educated elite would have nothing against it were there not an irreducibly important kernel to the idea of representation not just as a metaphor, but as a genuine political value. In the modern history of democratic theory, the ideal of representation has been intimately linked with the anti-elitist idea that government should, in some sense, be 'by the people'. The principle of free elections alone, it has increasingly come to be recognised, is insufficient to realise this ideal if the candidates practically available for election are drawn from a narrow social band. And this is not just an argument about genuine representation of the people in the sense of the limits of empathy of representatives. There also arises a question of justice to those who might represent. In so far as prejudice, lack of education, lack of resources and so on, hamper certain people's chances of becoming political representatives, this constitutes a genuine failure in the workings of the democratic process, and one which raises central questions of political justice. In our culture, the factors which are so important to access to politics are clearly structured along class, race and gender lines. Once again we return to the kind of structural, cultural analysis which liberalism is unable to generate. Whilst liberalism may offer superficial solutions, its analysis of the nature of the problem is flawed by its conceptual framework.

Feminist discussions of political theory have been concerned not only with the substantive realisation of an ideal of representation, but also with the idea of participation. Feminist political theorists like Carole Pateman and Anne Phillips have been developing aspects of democratic theory which attempt to realise a more substantive model of citizen participation whilst being realistic about the kinds of time commitments and expertise involved in the political process in any relatively developed society.[34] We shall return to these ideas in our later discussion of what has become known as dialogic or participation-ary communitarianism.[35] What is striking here about the feminist as opposed to the liberal response to questions of political participation is the focus on substance as opposed to form. The emphasis is on access to meaningful participation, on valuable representation, rather than consisting in a formal or tokenistic approach. And feminists point out the importance, not only of women's under-representation in the formal organs of government, but also of their partial exclusion from or marginalisation within other institutions and networks which either themselves wield political power or increase the power of particular actors in the political process. Once again, the focus on the specific constitution of the political sphere is central to the feminist critique of liberalism. Since it maintains a gender neutral individualist position and since it constructs as politically irrelevant those traditionally 'private' factors which are influential in inhibiting women's access to political power and representation (that is, their real access to wealth, waged work, just social welfare benefits and education) liberal theory is incapable of identifying and tackling gender inequalities of political power.

Conclusion

This chapter has traced the influence of certain core aspects of liberal individualist doctrine in terms of the construction of and response to the central political questions identified by feminist critique. Three themes have emerged as of particular importance in inhibiting liberal theory's identification of and response to questions of gender justice.

First we have identified particular doctrines of ontological and ethical individualism within the modern liberal tradition. This individualism generates a tendency to decontextualise political issues and brings with it a commitment to gender neutrality. This, combined with the associated absence of attention to the embodied and collective aspects of social life – to culture, social structures and institutions – systematically incapacitates liberal individualism from recognising and attending to questions of gender in the thoroughgoing way feminist critique suggests to be necessary. Second, liberal individualism, at least partly because of its reliance on abstracted, transcendent features of personhood as the moral basis for political theory, tends to focus on questions of form rather than substance: the status of citizenship, the holding of rights, rather than access to power or the worth of political rights to particular persons and groups of persons. This means that the questions central to feminist politics, questions of political substance which relate to gender patterns, are decentred in liberal analysis. Finally, the particular contours of the liberal distinction between the public and private, and its construction as a dichotomy, issue in a conception of the political which excludes both central feminist issues and many of the factors which would help explain why the formal rights and equalities offered to citizens by liberalism cash out in the substantive inequalities and gender patterns which characterise the modern western political world.

In each of these three areas of practice, then, the inadequacies of the liberal theoretical framework are felt. The perception of gender relations as a social structure is beyond the individualistic vision of liberalism; the adequate political analysis of gender is precluded by the public–private distinction; the emphasis on negative freedom and formal equality renders politically invisible significant aspects of women's oppression; the liberal paradigms of subjectivity and rationality are implicitly gendered and substantively oppressive. The ideals of liberalism are too easily met without real gender progress, the ideals of feminism impossible to explain in terms of liberal discourse. Liberalism has made an important and distinctive contribution to the cause of women's liberation, but from where we stand at the moment liberal analysis, critique and vision seem exhausted from a feminist point of view.

The major target of feminist criticism has been liberal *individualism*. By contrast, and in response, feminists emphasise the collective, or communitarian nature of social life, of values, of the processes which disadvantage women and other groups in liberal societies. The elaborated feminist answer to liberalism emphasises the necessity of public goods, the forging of a public political culture. It emphasises the ways we are connected with each other, so raising doubts about traditional liberal conceptions of 'altruism'. All these themes occur in the work of the communitarian critics of liberalism too. However, our discussion in this chapter and the last has also begun to identify potential difficulties with these themes. We have met problems about the limits of state intervention, the constitution of human identity, and the possibility of critical consciousness. We now turn our attention to a more detailed consideration of communitarian themes.

4

□

The communitarian critique of liberalism

This chapter falls into two main parts. In the first we consider the context of the present communitarian debate, and then offer a characterisation of communitarianism. In the second we discuss the affinity between communitarianism and some dominant themes and currents in feminist theory and politics. In the course of our analysis certain problems with communitarianism as it is currently conceived in political theory begin to emerge. The next chapter consists of a critical discussion of communitarianism from a feminist perspective.

The context of the debate

In Chapter 2 we saw that liberalism as a political doctrine is difficult to characterise accurately, because of the immense variety comprehended within the tradition. The same problem applies to 'communitarianism', but in an aggravated form, for communitarianism is not a tradition which has been crystallised (no matter how ambiguously) in a political movement or set of programmes. Indeed, it is very difficult to see it as a unified tradition at all. Communitarian themes appear in many kinds of political thought from Aristotle to the present day. They have formed a more or less important part of the thinking of authors who take up opposed positions on the political spectrum: liberals, feminists, Marxists, conservatives, socialists, republicans, greens and social democrats.

In recent debates, communitarianism has crystallised in the form of a critique of liberalism or, rather, a critique of the individualism and the universalism which are central to recent liberal political theory. Communitarianism rejects liberal individualism in favour of a theory of the social construction both of the self and of social reality – culture, values, institutions and relations. Persons are fundamentally connected, with each other and with the world they inhabit. Communitarians also emphasise the importance of intersubjective, collective or public goods. These two strands of communitarian thought – social constructionism and value-communitarianism – do not logically entail one another, but typically run together. And, as we shall argue, this critique of liberalism is connected with a broader theme of dissatisfaction with modernity.[1]

These themes are not, however, unique to the position of those who are identified as belonging in the communitarian camp.[2] The substantive political vision that emerges from communitarianism has a great deal in common with that which emerges from the work of the new civic republicans, and theorists of the 'new public law'.[3] In the realm of method, communitarianism resonates strongly with the hermeneutic tradition, which has generated certain specific methods of research in social science, and with the tradition of interpretivism in legal theory.[4] Recent interventions into the liberalism–communitarianism debate have begun to draw more explicitly on elements of European philosophy, particularly the critical theory of the Frankfurt School and Habermas's development of this into the conception of communicative ethics.[5] Another current evident in the debate is pragmatist philosophy, most clearly developed in the work of Richard Rorty.[6] And the most important resonance for our purposes is with the tradition of socialist and cultural feminism which has emerged as a critique of and in political opposition to liberal feminism in the last twenty years.[7]

It should also be remarked at this stage that there is variation in the extent to which communitarian thinkers construct a positive alternative to the substantive political vision offered by the liberal tradition. Sandel's work exemplifies the 'negative' nature of the communitarian critique, consisting as it does in a series of rejections of aspects of liberalism.[8] Of those we identify as communitarians, Walzer and Unger come closest to the construction of a positive alternative to the famous recent individualist texts by writers such as Rawls, Dworkin and Nozick.[9]

In substantive political terms communitarianism is indeterminate. For example, Alasdair MacIntyre advocates an approach to ethics which explicitly rejects the Enlightenment themes and methods. He locates himself in the Aristotelian tradition, and can be read as a conservative.[10] On the other hand, Roberto Unger's social constructionism is accompanied by a commitment to visionary political theory, to ideals of solidarity and the value of reciprocity, and to a reinterpretation of modernism. This has been dubbed 'super-liberalism' by Unger himself, yet it moves in many respects well beyond the kind of liberalism Rorty or Rawls would be happy to defend.[11] It has, of course, traditionally been taken that socialists are communitarians; but the extent to which this must be so is contested.[12]

The variation in substantive political commitment underlines the distinction drawn by Charles Taylor between the 'ontology' and the 'advocacy' aspects of social and political theory.[13] In Chapter 2 we argued that there is a link between ontology and advocacy in the sense of normative politics, and we shall be taking this line in the analysis of communitarianism that follows. Briefly, we shall argue that some combinations of ontology and advocacy positions are more viable than others, while some are so riven with tension as to be unviable if not strictly illogical. Furthermore, we shall continue to identify the ways in which advocacy and ontology have in fact reinforced one another in recent developments in liberal theory.

So a wide variety of projects contribute to 'communitarianism'. Further, most of the arguments made under the heading of communitarianism have been made before (often long before). In this case, we must obviously ask whether it is valid to treat communitarianism as a distinctive position at all. We do consider that the recent debates are distinctive, notwithstanding their complicated provenance. They have arisen in a particular intellectual and political context, not only when the weaknesses of liberal theory were becoming increasingly apparent, but when the ground for a resurgence of what we might call romantic thought in political theory was extremely fertile. Partly this is probably a matter of sheer chronology. Immediately after the Second World War the apparent dangers of nationalism and collectivism were at the forefront of popular and academic consciousness. Hence, political theories like those of Isaiah Berlin and F. A. Hayek, which emphasise individual rights against the state and society, were influential and set the agenda for political thought.[14] The cold war had an obvious negative effect on the credibility in mainstream political thought of Marxism, with its powerful anti-individualist critique, its scepticism about rights and its emphasis on the role of social structures. These factors were crucial inhibitors of the development of any utopian conceptions of community. They also militated against the success of critical analyses of the social structures which protected human rights and equality (no matter how oppressive these liberating social structures could also be said to be).

The important place which the communitarian challenge to liberalism has occupied in political theory of the last decade can be attributed in part to the fading of these historical experiences. It can also, as we shall argue, be explained in terms of its resonance with the resurgent uncertainties about modernity.[15] We now want to describe and discuss this context, by surveying the currents in social and political thought that we have identified as relevant and contributory to communitarianism.

Civic republicanism and the new public law

It is in the literature on civic republicanism and the 'new public law' that the link btween communitarian concerns and the critique of modernity is most apparent.[16] This literature is instructive in reminding us that fear about the degeneration of modern politics is not a phenomenon peculiar to the last twenty years. The work of Hannah Arendt and John Dewey, to name but two of the most influential contributors, raised similar issues, and the recent republican movement has drawn explicitly and productively on their ideas.[17]

The motivating idea informing the new republicanism is a sense of the way in which our political life and our conception of citizenship have become so diluted that the majority of the population feels alienated from the political process and identifies only weakly with the political society of which it is a part. The specific diagnosis varies. Some are inclined to blame centralisation and the dominance of representative as opposed to participatory forms of democracy. Others point the finger at the idea that an adequate constitutional framework can be understood in procedural as opposed to substantive terms. Some point to the diffusion of governmental power into institutions which lack accountability. Others deplore the ideological individualism and selfishness of the prevailing culture and the decline of political debate in non-state public forums. Many subscribe to some combination of these ideas. The basic message, however, is clear: unless we can revive the idea of a substantial common life, unless we can design political (state and non-state) institutions which enable each of us to feel empowered and involved as citizens, our society may disintegrate, either literally or in the sense that it will be governable only by authoritarian means.

This debate is tied to a particular political context; that is, the contemporary United States of America. Not only are contributors concerned with the design of democratic institutions, but they are concerned with specific problems in the interpretation of the US Constitution. This means that the debate has a quite concrete tone which is in marked contrast to the abstractions we encounter in the liberal–communitarian debate in political theory.

Interpretivism in legal theory

This position also has a peculiarly American dimension in the work of Dworkin, Fish, and many of the writers associated with the 'new public law'.[18] Here, law is conceptualised as an interpretive practice, as opposed to a series of laid-down principles which can be straightforwardly discovered and applied, so analogies are drawn between legal and literary interpretation. The hermeneutic tradition, which we discuss next, is drawn on somewhat pragmatically by participants in the current debate.

Hermeneutics

The hermeneutic tradition in social theory and social science has stood in opposition to empiricism and positivism.[19] Whereas empiricism takes it that social facts are to be observed and described objectively by the scientist, the hermeneuticist stresses that facts are constructed out of a process of interpretation. In this process discourse (and metaphor particularly) are deeply implicated – our perception and interpretation of the facts will be discursively shaped. This means that methods of social science must be reflexive (the scientist must scrutinise her own processes of interpretation), and that social reality is itself understood as built out of the interpretations of participants.[20]

Pragmatism

Contemporary pragmatic philosophy, which again is typically a product of the United States, resonates with the interpretivism and social constructionism of the hermeneutic tradition.[21] Pragmatists deny that reality, or the facts about reality, are straightforwardly 'out there' and knowable by us. Instead our concepts, and especially our interests, shape our knowledge of and relationship with the world. The work of John Dewey is particularly important here, especially in the political thought produced by contemporary pragmatists. On a pragmatist view, rather than speculating about the metaphysics of reality, philosophers should discuss our immediate world, and our concerns, about education, about political institutions and so on. For Dewey our reasons for doing what we do lie in our practices, not in any objective truths about the world.

Dewey's work has been taken up in contrasting ways. The new republicans, as we have seen, emphasise the necessity of re-building values which are positively assented to and which guide the actions of all citizens. Richard Rorty's pragmatic philosophy would view this project as being far too authoritarian. Instead, Rorty's scepticism about truth leads him to argue that all values and practices are contingent, and that we cannot fix these. That is to say, everything is made, and is constantly being re-made.[22]

Critical theory and discourse ethics
The Frankfurt School developed a series of theoretical and practical criticisms of capitalist society which they saw as a false reality. These critical challenges were intellectually important; they set out to reveal the ideological functions of liberal individualism and the poverty of industrial life.[23] But, as we discussed earlier, in the cold war era these assaults on liberal institutions could not attain any dominant position, either in the academy or in mainstream politics. However, more recently, Jurgen Habermas's communicative ethics has increasingly been drawn on in developing models of active citizenship and democratic institutions. Habermas moves on from earlier analyses of ideology to explore how rational judgement, and therefore a rational political process, can emerge when, and only when, communication between citizens is undistorted. Undistorted communication is possible only when all citizens have rights to speak, and are heard respectfully by others, when we speak truthfully and relevantly, and without the intention to manipulate.[24]

Habermas's work has been influential in the recent developments of explicitly critical theories of politics, theories which attempt to see how the world might be transformed (rather than devising detailed blueprints and policy proposals). These theories in turn connect with the communitarian principle that political theory is an interpretive enterprise. Obviously, his emphasis on the ideal speech community supports the classification of Habermas as a kind of communitarian. In recent political theory, too, Habermas's theory has been compared, favourably, with Rawls' conception of the original positon.[25]

Feminism

In previous chapters we have set out the main points of contention and ambiguity within feminism, and discussed the main points of the feminist critique of liberalism. The shortcomings of liberalism from a feminist perspective point to the necessity for a coherent feminist theory to include both social constructionism and a value commitment to public goods and to human solidarity (rather than individualism). Both of these enable and further the critical understanding of gender relations and the possibilities for their transformation. This conception of feminism is closer to what has been labelled 'socialist feminism' than to other varieties.[26] It is also close to what has been referred to as cultural feminism, where 'cultural' serves to emphasise that the explanation of women's subordination and the experience of femininity cannot be reduced to biology, economics, psychic drives or ir-rationality, but is institutionalised in values, practices and discourses.[27] There are obvious parallels with communitarian themes here, and in turn the insights from cultural feminism have undoubtedly made a prominent and important contribution to the communitarian critique of liberalism.

Characterising communitarianism

The variety of communitarian positions, and the complexity of the related and background debates and traditions, obviously threatens to muddy any attempt at critical or comparative analysis. We shall therefore begin with a relatively simple model of communitarianism which will serve to highlight some relevant problems and pave the way for a more differentiated analysis later.

Social constructionism

Communitarians reject the liberal view of the self, and develop a theory of the social construction both of the self and of social reality – culture, values, institutions and relations. This view entails, of course, not only that *conceptions* of selfhood, personhood and agency are socially produced and specific, but also that actual persons are too. There is great variation between communitarian writers as to how radically socially situated their conceptions of the human self turn out to be, and hence between their different ideas about the human capacity for self-reflection and agency.[28] However, one idea common to all communitarians is that the self is *situated* and *embodied*.

Sandel has set out a particularly vivid social constructionist theory in his development of the strong notion of 'constitutive communitarianism', which he contrasts with 'sentimental' or 'instrumental' communitarianism.[29] Sentimental communitarianism recognises that a person might well desire to further the interests of his or her community and other people generally, to promote values, principles and cultures which achieve this end. In other words, the individual might have altruistic impulses and sentiments. 'Instrumental' communitarianism is the view that utility will generally be maximised by fostering altruism, community values or a collective culture. This doctrine, which recommends that individuals should have altruistic or other-oriented attachments, is, like the previous one, compatible with the liberal theory of human nature and liberal politics.

Against this, Sandel argues that communitarianism is not optional: we cannot conceptualise the individual apart from his or her community, its practices, culture and values. The community *constitutes* the person. Social processes and institutions, the family, churches, political and educational systems, shape the infant into a social being who experiences emotion, who desires, who has understanding of and attitudes towards the social world and her place in it. Indeed, in this regard, although psychoanalytic accounts of human drives and desires as originating in the family drama are themselves social-constructionist, and psychoanalytic thought has been one of the most influential movements in constructionist social thought this century, it might be argued that it is inadequately social. For it takes too little account of the extent to which different social arrangements might fundamentally alter the plot and cast of characters of the drama, and thereby alter the drives and desires human beings have.

Contemporary political theory provides many versions of strong, constitutive communitarianism.[30] The idea of human consciousness and identity as contextual and intersubjective is, of course, not new[31] but in the contemporary literature distinctive implications are being drawn for *politics* from a social constructionist metaphysics of personhood and empirical facts about human existence. Contrary to the liberal arguments, many communitarians assert or imply that their approach to the social construction of human nature and identity leads naturally if not necessarily into both a constructionist approach to political and moral value, and a substantive notion of political value which gives a central place to what we shall call for the moment public goods.

If persons develop their identities in a social context, and in the context of prevailing social values, it is none the less also the case that they act upon the world in constructive ways. Social contexts are themselves historically contingent, socially constructed, and subject to change. There is thus an easy although not a necessary move to be made from one constructionist thesis to the other: that is, from the socially constructed and contingent nature of social structure to the socially constructed and contingent nature of ethical and political values. The multi-directional causal movements between the world, agents and values once again raise questions about freedom and agency.[32] For the moment we need merely to note the importance of this in communitarian, as compared with liberal, thought.

On the strongest communitarian view there simply is no a-historical, transcendent reality to be grasped in the sphere of value or anywhere else. This of course raises the issue of relativism. At one end of a spectrum of responses to this issue is Rorty's radical pragmatism. This rejects the very charge of relativism as misplaced. The impossibility of a 'view from nowhere', and the infinity of possible viewpoints should lead us to reject the very idea of meta-narratives (by which Rorty means second-order theories, theories which purport to ground first-order claims) or truth claims. So far as there is any truth to be had it is that of the inevitability of perspectivalism, which is to say that our knowledge of reality is contingent upon our point of view.[33] This is not to say that there is no place for visionary, critical or utopian political thought. This should simply be recognised, however, as an exercise in imagination and persuasion, not grounded in any independent validating practice or set of criteria.[34] At the other end of the spectrum is Taylor's interpretive approach which, whilst it recognises moral and political argument as being historically and socially grounded, does not abandon the notion of independent criteria which enable us to identify errors, irrationalities, or incoherences, in our evaluative positions.[35]

Taylor's position leaves open the possibility of what in some real sense counts as moral progress or regress, whilst maintaining an important place for the human construction of values. On this kind of view, neither 'objectivism' nor 'subjectivism' is the appropriate posture for ethics, which is conceived instead in interpretivist terms.

Value-communitarianism

In the second major strand of communitarian thought the kinds of values which tend to be the object of visionary communitarian politics are emphasised. Concomitantly, the lack of these in other political theories, especially liberalism, attracts critical attention. Communitarian discussion often speaks rather indiscriminately of collective goods, community values, the value of 'community', and even public virtues. We want to draw attention here to several distinctions which are not made clear in the literature we are discussing.[36]

'Community values' can be taken as referring to both what *kind* of values are at issue, and *whose* values they are: where they proceed from, their status and identity. This latter aspect is more properly a part of social constructionism than of value-communitarianism. It is simply the claim, already discussed, that values themselves necessarily proceed from and belong to particular communities, and are created and validated by community practices. In this sense, even the most individualistic and egoistic values (such as those of nineteenth-century capitalism) are community values, and do not, contrary to liberal capitalist theory, proceed naturally from universal human nature and rationality.

Distinct from this is the communitarian emphasis on the importance of what we shall call intersubjective, collective or public goods – value-communitarianism proper. Clearly, a commitment to such collective goods can be made without espousing a social constructionist stance, but in the work of many communitarian authors, the two themes run together. Social constructionism's ontological claims, along with empirical facts about human interdependence, are assumed to have some substantive political implications. A vision of humans as primarily social beings conduces to putting the emphasis on values which express the mutually supportive aspects of human life. This in turn conduces to the promotion of cultural practices and institutions which recognise, reaffirm and develop the communal and mutually supportive aspects of human life to the top of the political agenda. Thus reciprocity, solidarity, fraternity and community itself take the place of the liberal priorities such as fulfilment of individual rights and respect for individual freedom in the sphere of political value.

Here a further distinction must be made between collective values and public goods. Reciprocity, solidarity and community all exemplify what we call collective values. These are values which can only be realised in the context of a communal life in which members share a certain threshold recognition of both mutual dependence and each others' humanity and moral claims. They cannot be enjoyed by individuals as such – each person's enjoyment depends on others' enjoyment. These values, in other words, depend on a threshold recognition of 'intersubjectivity', although the degree to which this is taken to be so (and what exactly is meant by inter-subjectivity) turns out to be a matter of fundamental political importance. Public goods are rather different. They are institutional, and the link between them and collective values is that a commitment to these kinds of collective framework values would typically engender a political practice which realised a range of public goods in the sense of facilities and practices designed to help members of the community to develop their common and hence their personal lives.

Public goods would therefore encompass a range of things from concrete institutions such as sports and cultural facilities through education systems and political institutions, to practices such as honour systems and offices. But among goods legitimately thought of as public there are important differences in terms of whether they represent goods which are conceptually collective or intersubjective – goods such as conversation, democratic debate, or humour – or those which are not. Some, such as national security, should instead be thought of as realising the cumulative interests of individual members of the community, as aggregative rather than collective. Furthermore, whether we think of some public goods as collective or cumulative depends on our political conception of them. For example, education is a public good which can be seen in either way, with substantive political differences hingeing on the perspective. To what extent, for example, do we see the value of education in terms of its inculcation in its subjects of a common life, tradition or culture? This is important, because it will affect whether we think that public goods can be given an adequate place within liberal theory, on the basis of Sandel's instrumental or sentimental communitarianism.

Another complication in thinking about public goods should be mentioned here, as it will be important to our argument later. Public goods are defined as those from the consumption or enjoyment of which other persons cannot be excluded, so fresh air, street lighting, public transport and road cleaning services all count. But some public goods are not quite as public as that. Club goods are those shared goods from the consumption or enjoyment of which other members of the club cannot be excluded.[37] Crucially, one has to be a member of 'the club' to secure enjoyment of them. Public transport could be defined as a club good if it is so expensive that some people cannot afford it; street lighting could be defined as a club good if some people cannot be, for one reason or another, out on the streets after dark.[38]

Party and policy commitments

Value-communitarianism, and particularly the commitment to collective values, has of course been a central feature of Marxist or socialist politics. However, at the level of abstraction at which it can plausibly be linked with social constructionism, its substantive political implications are very weak. Social constructionism militates in favour of value-communitarianism, but it tells us little about the *kinds* of collective values or public goods which we should espouse or develop. It may militate in favour of reciprocity or solidarity, but how should these be interpreted, and through what kinds of institutions should they be realised? This indeterminacy can easily be seen by reflecting on the range of theories in which value-communitarianism and social constructionism, together or separately, have found a place.

Value-communitarianism, for example, has recently formed the basis for Sandel's critique of liberalism's impoverished conception of our common life and for Walzer's discussion of communal provision.[38] It engenders Unger's emphasis on community, and the place accorded by Rorty (notwithstanding his liberal commitments) to the value of solidarity.[39] It is an important theme in feminist thought, for example, in the 'ethic of care' suggested by Gilligan and others.[40] Each of these theories occupies a position towards the left of the political spectrum. Significantly, though, forms of value-communitarianism have been central to conservative visions such as Devlin's view that each society is entitled, and indeed obliged, to enforce its own morality.[41]

Some communitarian theory is best seen as a reinterpretation of and renewal of commitment to liberalism. Rorty's radical pragmatist social constructionism, for example, is accompanied by a clear identification with liberal politics. Paradoxically, he also espouses the view that the traditional framework of political philosophy – the commitment to the objectivity of reality, the universalism of truth and value – must be abandoned, thereby attempting to pull apart liberalism and modernity.[42] Another strategy is exemplified by Sandel, who develops what we might call an immanent critique of liberalism. He argues that if theorists like Dworkin and Rawls are to realise their professed ideals they must embrace social constructionism.[43] In their most recent work Taylor and Walzer clearly identify themselves as liberals.[44]

The new civic republicans analyse the shortcomings of a primarily procedural understanding of the normative framework for constitutional arguments which has predominated in liberal legal theory. They argue instead for a more substantive conception of common good and civic virtue, and for a broader conception of politics as involving the selection of values. This leads in turn to an enriched conception of active citizenship as a basic component of the human good, ideally realised through public dialogue and participation. The expanded public or political sphere becomes one in which we realise our good as citizens in the recreation or recollection of a shared normative context for our common life. This theory is difficult to locate on the traditional left-right spectrum. It can be seen as conservative in the sense of advocating a return to older, pre-modern political forms and values. On the other hand it shares a great deal with many socialist political visions.

In civic republicanism we have a good example of the links between a focus on collective values and public goods and a refusal to draw on absolute distinction between the right and the good. In contrast to the liberal priority of the right over the good, in which the former only is the business of politics, the communitarian recognition of the importance of common life and collective provision sits uneasily with the notion of justice as the primary virtue of social institutions and the sole concern of the state. If the good for individuals is intrinsically linked to that of the collective, a rigid separation of the right from the good is inappropriate and even incoherent. There is a parallel link between a rejection of the separation of the right from the good and social constructionism. Once we see human identity and value as produced and grounded in specific social contexts, traditions and ways of life, the politically relevant realm of life becomes extremely wide. The implications in terms of weakening liberal distinctions between public and private are obvious. We should also note that acceptance of an expanded political sphere with politics encompassing debates about the good, sits unhappily with the kind of division between reason and emotion, the rational and the affective, which characterises liberal thought. Once we see values as being things which are reasoned about, we are clearly employing a notion broader than that of instrumental reason. Again we must note the diversity of communitarian and liberal positions. Sandel and Taylor, possibly the most sympathetic of the communitarians to some aspects of liberal values and conceptions of agency, are none the less the most forthright critics of the separation of the right from the good. Conversely the separation is weakened, if not abandoned, in Raz's avowedly liberal theory, which rejects the idea of the state's neutrality as between conceptions of the good. As our discussion in Chapter 2 began to reveal, recent developments in liberal theory have responded positively to aspects of the communitarian critique in ways which have blurred the lines between liberal and communitarian approaches.

Rawls' recent work makes significant moves towards social constructionism, and at least pays lip service to value-communitarianism by arguing that justice as fairness is compatible with collective as much as with individualist conceptions of the good.[45] On the other hand, he does not develop a full account of collective values or public goods, nor does he in any way weaken his commitment to the separation of the right and the good. Rawls argues that his position is compatible with civic republicanism, which he defines as seeing active citizenship as simply a necessary means of realising liberal democratic values. This he distinguishes from civic humanism, which sees active citizenship as part of the *good* for human beings, and hence with which justice as fairness is incompatible. We have already set out our view that these developments in Rawls' position give rise to internal tensions which it is not clear that his theory can resolve. But we should note that Rorty, included in our discussion of communitarianism because of the central role a radical form of social constructionism plays in his work, defends Rawls' current position as a distinctively liberal one which is justified in maintaining the separation of the right and the good, and dismisses communitarianism as unrealistic neo-romanticism.[46]

Dworkin, too, has identified himself as a constructionist and gives a central place to the idea of community in his recent work. However, the idea of constructionism he develops finds its roots in the common acceptance of the liberal idea that each individual has a right to equal respect and concern from his (sic) fellow citizens.[47] Hence, even in his most recent affirmation of the importance of community, Dworkin's is still a position in which the value of community is ultimately driven by and dependent on its value for individuals. It also embraces a paradoxically traditionalist, backward-looking (and hence potentially conservative) conception of the community.[48] Kymlicka intends to push liberalism in a somewhat value-communitarian direction. He, however, disagrees with Sandel's reading of Rawls, and defends Rawls' ability to satisfactorily accommodate a concept of cultural membership. If Kymlicka were right the communitarian critique of the priority of the right over the good would be undermined.[49] However, Kymlicka does not meet the communitarian case. For him, cultural membership is an individual right.

The point of noting all this variety is to underline the importance of recognising that our models of communitarianism and liberalism provide a framework for examining some central questions of and debates within contemporary political and social theory, and are not means of attaching rigid labels to particular writers.

Communitarianism and the status of political theory
Finally, we must consider what is widely held to be a methodological implication of the social constructionist aspect of communitarian thought. This is its entailment of an 'interpretivist' approach to political and social theory. The social construction of human identity and value suggests that there is no transcendent, objective viewpoint from which the theorist can speak. She speaks, rather, from within a culture, and from the standpoint of certain intellectual, political and affective commitments. According to this approach, the boundaries between subjective and objective, between descriptive and prescriptive aspects of political theory begin to blur.

We can illustrate the point with an example. In conventional political theoretical terms, the communitarian critique of liberalism has both descriptive and prescriptive aspects. On the one hand, liberalism is criticised as being untrue as a description of human beings and societies. Communitarians argue that people are socially constructed in particular political and cultural contexts, that is, they are embedded in networks of social relations. If liberal individualism has any validity, according to communitarian constructionism, it is because social constructionism is true: the liberal individual is a social product. On the other hand, at least some forms of communitarianism (those committed to value-communitarianism as well as constructionism) propose a normative theory. We must put in place the kinds of social institutions, practices, policies, norms and values which will bring proper community life about. The strongest versions of communitarianism are engaged in advocacy as well as ontology, and though the former is not straightforwardly entailed by the latter, the two are linked. This way of looking at communitarian theory, however, makes two methodological and epistemological assumptions which are questioned, to a greater or lesser extent, by the interpretive approach. In the first place, the idea that communitarianism makes descriptive claims implies a quasi-scientific appeal to the 'facts of the matter' about human nature. Second, the normative aspects of value-communitarian prescription could be understood as claiming some kind of objective or universal truth or validity. But beyond the framework truth claim about the validity of social constructionism itself, the espousal of a thoroughly constructionist position seems to entail the deconstruction of each of these projects. The only 'fact of the matter' about human nature is its openness and contingency, and since values are similarly contingent, there is no Archimedean point from which to prescribe with any kind of objectivity or universal validity about either political or ethical values. The idea of social theory as interpretive seeks to capture the sense in which its judgements are inevitably grounded (not transcendent) and are context dependent.[50]

Once again, we have to be aware of the variety of views on this subject among communitarians. At one extreme, Rorty rejects the ideas of truth and objective knowledge in such a way as to render the very category of 'interpretation' uninteresting. On his view, there simply is nothing in which interpretation could be grounded, other than contingent selves, conceived as networks of belief and desire, and their practices. Hence he applauds Rawls' assertion that metaphysical conceptions of selfhood are irrelevant to political theory.[51] For Rorty, as for the later Rawls, political theory is independent of both philosophy and social theory: it is simply the project of explicating the grounds for consensus about political arrangements in particular societies.[52] Other theorists would rejoin that the very insight that all judgement is socially grounded reveals precisely that the conceptions of human nature and personhood which inevitably inform, implicitly if not explicitly, theories such as Rawls', are of *substantive* and *political* rather than only metaphysical significance.

At the other end of the spectrum, Taylor wants to push an interpretive approach as far towards a realist epistemology as possible without losing sight of the idea that all claims and judgements are inevitably historically and socially grounded. For him, the idea of social and political theory as interpretive therefore represents an adequate recognition of constructionism whilst avoiding the dangerous slide into total relativism.[53] Similarly, for Habermas, the dialogic process of undistorted communication *constructs* value, but according to conversational constraints which are not themselves contingent (although on Benhabib's reading they must themselves be subject to critical assessment).[54] Walzer sits between the radical pragmatists and the minimalist objectivists with his notion of limited necessity of critical distance.[55]

The possibility of treading an acceptable path between what might be characterised as 'modernist' and 'post-modernist' approaches here will be a major concern of the following chapters. In the meantime it is important merely to note the shared constructionist communitarian rejection of the universalist, transcendental view of political theory. On the interpretivist view which seems to be shared in some form by all communitarians, a political theory's analysis of society, like its critique of the 'descriptive' inadequacies of any other political theory, are informed by the historical, social and political position which the theorist occupies. Our ideas of what should and could be are rooted in our experience of what is, and could be seen as a 'recollective imagination' of what might have been.[56] Similarly, the theorist's utopias are grounded in her interpretation of the culture within which she lives and works. The ideas of 'representing the world as it is' and of 'speaking from nowhere' become deeply problematic, just as the distinction between 'is' and 'ought' becomes blurred.

The feminist attraction to communitarianism

Feminist politics, as we have tried to make clear, is not a simple object of analysis. There have been significant divisions between the liberal feminists who have spearheaded the legislative reform process we discussed in Chapter 3, and a wide variety of feminist groups and campaigns which have taken up a broadly counter-cultural position, from which they have tried to challenge orthodox conceptions of the political process while bringing about social change. There have been tensions and problems of political strategy – about whether to run single-issue campaigns or broad ones, whether to try to organise nationally or to concentrate on local activism, about what kind of organisation can be both politically successful and distinctively feminist.[57]

In the remainder of this chapter we want to examine the ways in which feminist politics must be to some degree communitarian politics. We think that liberal feminists, too, must be committed to some extent to communitarian ideas. This is in light of the undoubted limits to liberalism we explored in Chapter 3. It is also because, as we shall go on to argue, the logic of feminist demands entails the recognition of social groups, of socially constructed identities and structures which can be altered. This suggests the need for the further recognition that purely rational argument will be inadequate, on its own, to bring about political change. Furthermore, in a society in which women do not enjoy fully fledged citizenship status, successful feminist political action relies on community-based political organisation.

Community politics

In practical political terms, for many activists the current wave of feminism was born out of dissatisfaction with socialist and left parties and organisations generally. This dissatisfaction developed into a dissatisfaction with the theories and programmes of socialism and the left. Women's experience in left politics led them to see authoritarianism and hierarchy in what traditional political activists understood as perfectly innocent and taken-for-granted political practices and arrangements. Good examples include committee procedures, policy-making processes, and the division of labour in political organisations.

In subsequent developments in feminist politics there has been an emphatic aversion to hierarchical and authoritarian organisation. There has also been an aversion to rigid divisions of labour. Practically, this translates into a commitment to the constant scrutiny of habits and established ways of doing things in organisations, and the relations between members to see whether power is becoming sedimented. The basis for and the success of these practices is a matter of dispute. Some commentators, for example, have interpreted them as a sign that feminists are pursuing a (chimerical) harmonious equality and have an unreasonable aversion to power as such.[58] Anne Phillips argues that the commitment to equal participation has often had the effect of forging a false (and effectively authoritarian) consensus.[59] Where this happens, of course, splintering or the disintegration of groups is a probability.[60] But equally, feminist politics has many successes in help-lines, campaigning groups and other enterprises where conflict which would be straightforwardly suppressed in conventional organisations is dealt with more openly. This is not, of course, to say that in such groups all is equal sweetness and light. But this is not an argument for suppressing conflict by the institutionalisation of hierarchies, standing orders, points of order and all other conventional means – rather it is an argument for finding more constructive ways of practising conflict.

The aversion to hierarchy and a fixed division of labour is connected with women's refusal to try to set up feminist political parties. Feminism is seen by political sociologists as a social movement, and as such as a very different kind of political organisation from a party. It is fair to say that feminists have adopted this stance self-consciously.[61] This stance is connected with the distinctive conception of politics developed by feminists, especially the challenge to 'public–private' distinctions and the insistence that changes in mundane practices can count as political changes. Specifically, feminist activists are critical of the two dominant models of social and political change, that is Marxist revolution and liberal reform. (We are aware that at the time of writing it is becoming more and more odd to count Marxist revolution among the dominant models! Nevertheless, these are the two models feminists have had to negotiate with in the last twenty five years).

We discussed the feminist unhappiness with liberal reform in Chapter 3. The Marxist theory of revolution is of the seizure of power by a conscious acting class who are irremediably oppressed by and alienated from the dominant class. There are several reasons why this model is unsatisfactory for feminism. First, the history of Marxist revolutions is sadly a dismal one, and many radicals are suspicious that the Marxist overthrow of power structures can only result in the immediate erection of new, equally monolithic, ones. Second, there are obvious problems with the incorporation of specifically feminist struggles into the class struggle.[62] Third, apart from the obvious difference in the strategic position of women *vis-à-vis* men and the Marxian proletariat *vis-à-vis* the bourgeoisie (that is, many women live with men), there is doubt (among Marxists themselves too, of course) that the means of production, or indeed any one set of goods or phenomena, hold the key to power in a society. A clear theoretical upshot of feminist experience is the view that the possibilities for revolution lie in living our utopias in the here and now. In this connection, personal struggles for a transformation in sexual relations are relevant; feminists are clear that alteration of our desires and behaviours is possible now. These personal struggles entail concerted attacks on social norms, institutional rules, cultural discourses, laws; and, of course, they bring women into collision with men and each other.

These rejections locate feminism, on the face of it, in much the same spot as communitarianism. But there is a further clear affinity between feminism and community. Feminist political campaigns have centred on childcare; rape; battering; norms of heterosexuality; the representations of women in popular culture and pornography; and women's health. When women first tried to raise these issues in traditional political forums they met with blank incredulity. Of course, many women have persisted, with the result that there has been accommodation of feminist concerns in some of the political parties, in unions, and institutions of government.[63] But where there have been successes in traditional politics it is certainly by virtue of links with alternative, community-based, feminist projects such as rape crisis centres, refuges, community health campaigns, pickets against sex shops and so on. On the whole feminists have opted for community as opposed to national or regional organisation, although loose affiliations and umbrella groups do exist at national and international levels. And, of course, the nation state is a relevant category when feminists organise internationally – it makes some sense to talk of British, Chilean and Zimbabwean feminists.[64] But it is an outcome of feminist theory and practice that the community (although loosely and problematically defined) is the proper locus of politics. Feminist scepticism about strategies of legislative reform, which necessitate national organisation, and specifically organisation in the capital, is obviously relevant here.[65]

The ideal of community also has an attractive ring to it, given feminist concern to transform models of association developed and utilised in conventional politics. The traditional family, for example, constructed as a 'haven in a heartless world' in capitalist theory, as the realm of personal freedom in liberal theory, has for the most part been identified in feminist theory and practice as the location of much of women's misery, and a significant source of and context for sexual violence.[66] The state, from a critical feminist perspective, is potentially oppressive as well as inefficient, and has failed to deliver the means of women's liberation. By contrast, 'community' conjures up a vision of secure and committed networks of people, to an extent like-minded, rooted in a geographical area, offering fluidity and flexibility, unconstrained by biological kinship or marriage.

Beyond these considerations in favour of the ideal of community, and the strategic and theoretical considerations in favour of political organisation at the community level, feminist politics also requires a specifically communitarian analysis in many respects. The argument is that neither liberalism, nor Marxism nor social democracy in its dominant European form, can deliver the solutions to problems of childcare, sexual violence, the ideologies of popular culture and pornography, or the legal regulation of sexuality and gender.

Anti-individualism

Feminism is a project for the transformation of relations between the sexes. This means that any feminist (including anyone who considers herself to be a liberal feminist) must accept that these relations could be transformed, and that involves accepting that dominant definitions and practices of masculinity and femininity are not absolutely fixed, either biologically or metaphysically, but are socially contructed. The very idea of social construction threatens any crystal-clear distinction, such as that played on in much liberal theory, between the individual and the society. In liberal thought this clear distinction is connected, as we discussed in Chapter 2 with the definition of rationality as self-interested instrumentality, and the perception of society as unavoidably a threat to the individual. As Taylor has put it, the communitarian target is a shift in the burden of justification which emerged with a certain enlightenment conception of the individual, whereby person-hood itself became the moral *source*, and the community, formerly taken for granted as a social necessity, became reconstructed as a threat to individual autonomy.[67]

The social construction of gender, of sexual practice and so on, turns our theoretical attention immediately to the realm of meaning and value. In communitarian and in feminist thought an intersubjective conception of the self feeds into an intersubjective conception of value. In a somewhat romantic vision, the pooling of talents and sharing of responsibility is assumed to be justifiable, instead of seen as the trammelling of individual rights. The ideal of human autonomy is understood in a way which dissolves the liberal dichotomy between individualism and solidarity. Self-fulfilment and the social good are seen as working in the same rather than in different directions.

Communitarianism is committed, too, to the significance of traditions and practices in building up cultures, and this analysis finds a deep echo in feminist politics. The liberal conception of 'sexism', as a particular set of attitudes, and a particular way of treating women and men, is found to be inadequate. Feminist analysis is based on women's practical experience of the power of rules, of structures, of taken-for-granted ways of doing things. Feminists have experienced the transformation of taken-for-granted practices and the painful building of alternatives in their own political organisations. The way things are done in groups, meetings and campaigns is problematised. The rules which govern group processes are subject to scrutiny and argument. For example, in many feminist groups 'honesty' as a central political commitment is valued, as is acceptance of other people's experience, equality of participation and access to the floor, supportive listening and so on.

That is, the collective nature of feminist discourse and practice is acknowledged. This is politically important. Many jokes and complaints are made about feminists who try to make changes in other, more conventional, groups of which they are members, such as altering how the furniture is arranged in the room, challenging sexist language, questioning how meetings are chaired and so on.[68] But the degree of discomfort and even moral outrage revealed by these jokes and complaints is testimony to how very *un*trivial these matters are. Social and political power is at stake. Democracy can be enhanced if standards of communication are raised. An ideal speech community relies on a particular arrangement of the chairs! Yet in many forums discourses and practices are so taken for granted, so settled, that their disruption is unthinkable (and profoundly disturbing when it does occur) and their collective and conventional nature is concealed.

Practices and discourses are constitutive of political and social reality. They are the stuff out of which positive and progressive relations, institutions and actions are built as well as being the stuff of oppressive social phenomena like rape, sexual harassment and inequality in parenting and childrearing. This explains why these things are not susceptible of easy alteration or reform. They are rooted in taken-for-granted definitions and norms, in settled social identities, maintained in ingrained habits and in the routine exercise of power. But it is the essence of feminist politics that these practices might be altered.

Communitarian values

The ideals of solidarity and reciprocity fostered by value-com-munitarianism resonate with significant themes in feminist ethics and politics, themes which stress mutuality, interdependence, collective values of sharing, responsibility and care.[69] Those caring for children, for example, need baby-sitting circles and trusted others who will meet children from school. In communitarian theory our relations to others and our affective ties are incorporated in the political realm in a way which is welcome to feminists. Both social constructionism and value-communitarianism push us towards just the contextualised, concretised model of rationality and reflection presupposed by this approach to ethics. That is, our affective ties and embodied experience feed into our ethical and rational decisions.

Similarly, feminist politics cannot proceed without a commitment to public goods. Campaigns for women's safety call for adequate street lighting and safe public transport. Children need nurseries and playgrounds, safe streets, clean air. Of course, it has been argued recently that market mechanisms, rather than public provision as such, can take care of such needs perfectly well. This argument is obviously rather difficult to put in the cases of clean air and safe streets. Leaving that aside, it will be useful to look at a more plausible candidate for market provision: the example of childcare. It is argued by some liberals that parents should make economic decisions about whether to stay at home and care for children, or buy nursery space, the services of nannies and so on. That is, women are free to make choices, and this is seen as compatible with feminist aspirations. We argue that this 'liberal capitalist feminism' is fundamentally flawed.[70] To begin with, all childcare, whether done by isolated and disadvantaged biological parents, by professional nannies, or by carers who are able to participate in local community networks, definitely calls for and relies on sharing and reciprocity (if a child is not to be fatally neglected when its carer falls ill, for example). So the standard categories of a political theory, such as liberalism, which fails to put these kinds of values at its centre, are already wanting.

Even beyond the provision of childcare, the practice of parenting requires public goods proper. The thoroughgoing capitalist feminist would argue that women should make individual contracts with men for support while they mother. But anyone who comes out of the conventional labour market for the period of time required to look after children is thereafter disadvantaged in that market. This disadvantage must be made good – by training or other forms of compensation – and this requires the provision of public goods. The theorist who rejects public goods at the outset has two alternatives. Either women's bargain with men must be for a lifetime, which is to say the current discourse and practice of marriage remains intact. This cannot by any stretch of the definition of terms count as a *feminist* solution. Or there will be a *systematically* disadvantaged group in the labour market, which is in contravention of free market theory (the 'capitalist' half of capitalist feminism). This argument also holds, of course, in the case where sometimes men and sometimes women take on the full-time parenting role, for there would still be a systematically disadvantaged group in the labour market, namely parents and carers. Of course, a further alternative is that women and men, or groups of committed parents, share childcare. But this cannot be done without fundamental alterations in the labour market, to conventional career structures, with respect to the remuneration and conditions of part-time work and so on, which cannot be accommodated within existing capitalist discourse and practice. The political values and institutions needed to generate and maintain such collective solutions, in other words, also seem to gesture towards communitarianism.

The embodied subject

Communitarianism issues in a political theory which recognises the embodied nature of human subjectivity. Feminists have long argued that the disembodied conception of human selfhood is implicitly male. Liberal individualism abstracts away from the body – humanity, after all, is not determined by one's bodily characteristics. Of course, the progressive and humane implications of this are not to be underestimated in a world in which disabled people have been denied human rights in many societies, and in which skin colour and other indicators of 'race' are signals for oppression and violence. However, the downside of this progressive philosophy is that a pretence is maintained that the body is not at issue, while in fact male (and indeed white, and able-bodied) bodily experience is taken for granted, so that other bodily experiences are constructed as problematic, abnormal, or outwith the realm of politics. As our discussion of sexual harassment showed, male sexuality as constructed in modern western culture is taken for granted, and women's experience of this and protests against it considered bizarre and inappropriate. Women's bodily experience in particular, because it is not identical to men's, is construed as a barrier to citizenship and to ethical reason. Strong social currents as well as concrete institutional practices prevent it from being straightforwardly admitted to the realm of political discussion. Menstruation, pregnancy, lactation, menopause and so on define women as *abnormal*.

In rejecting the liberal dualisms of mind and body, rationality and emotion, communitarianism resonates with feminist politics, which are of course concerned to construct social relations and institutions within which women are normal and full members, notwithstanding menstruation, pregnancy, lactation and menopause. Concomitantly, feminist politics also is concerned to clarify and establish the political implications of male bodily matters, such as sexual desire, hypertension, and businessmen's lunches! That is to say that bodily experience and the bodily aspects of practices are politically and ethically relevant and subject to critique.

Public–private dichotomies

Communitarianism also opens up the possibility of either abandoning or radically weakening the liberal distinction between public and private spheres. *Social groups*, not just individuals, or the monolithic state and society, which confront the liberal individual, can be accommodated as a central category in communitarianism. If the individual, state, desires, values and practices are all social products, the metaphysical basis for the liberal distinction between the public and private spheres is weakened. If human subjectivity is in an important sense a product of, for example, the family, rather than vice versa, the public–private distinction loses its integrity. Individual identity, desire and value all become objects of political critique, challenge and social transformation. In other words the scope of the political realm is enormously increased in a way which echoes the feminist slogan 'the personal is political'.

We discussed in Chapter 3 the way the theoretical and practical public–private distinction is of crucial significance in feminist politics, especially in marriage relations, domestic violence, sexual violence more generally, and, of course, the relations between parents or carers and children. We discussed there the power of the feminist argument that the pretence that the private realm is unregulated is ideological. If police do not intervene on a woman's behalf in a case of domestic battering, that is precisely equivalent to an intervention of the state (on the man's side). The state of affairs in which police policy is 'non-intervention' is a direct result of marriage law and associated practices.

This argument is connected with arguments that personal matters are political. After all, sexuality and domestic relations are exemplary personal matters. So are decisions about consumption, for example, consumption of pornography. Feminist analysis insists upon the political relevance of these matters (although not, it is important to note, on the invariable appropriateness of state regulation). This is both on grounds of the interdependence argument (that private oppression leads to public disadvantage), and because the definitions of such matters as private can themselves be shown to be disingenuous. For the analysis which defines pornography as a matter of private preference in one breath constructs it as a matter of public rights to free expression in the next. Thus both sides of the public–private, political–personal divide are manipulated in ways which exclude certain arguments.

This analysis of the personal and the political is also revealed in certain aspects of feminist political organisation. Women's movement members have tended to speak for themselves and to decline to speak for or on behalf of the organisation as a whole, or for other members. This is connected with the rejection of hierarchy, and of conventional models of representation, which we discussed earlier. It has also been a frankly counter-cultural strategy for upsetting journalists, police officers, magistrates and other representatives of 'the Establishment'.[71] But it also underlines the idea that as individuals we are political beings, and that our individual social lives are genuinely political – we don't need a party or a tight organisation to validate our political speech and action.

The blurring of a particular conception of public and private is, of course, further advanced by the rejection of the priority of the right over the good. Another implication here is a weakening of the opposition between reason and emotion central to pre-modern and enlightenment thought alike. If we can be rational in our choices of the good and of values, affectivity becomes a part of, rather than oppositional to, rational thought, choice and action. Hence one common way of marginalising women, particularly in political terms – their identification with emotion, and the view that they are defective in terms of reason – is undermined. On the one hand, the ideal of the purely rational man is shown to be a fiction; on the other, the emotion that women are identified with (at the moment, to their detriment) is shown to be an indispensable factor in ethical life.

Finally, as well as challenging clear distinctions between public and private, feminists, like communitarians, have been sceptical of the coherence of liberal conceptions of 'the public' as a body of people. The public, in liberal thought, is made up of the body of citizens and members of society. This is understood as a mass of individuals each of whom has the same relation with the state. Further, they have formally equal relations with each other. They are able to enter into economic and other social exchanges in which their legal rights are equally protected.[72] As we have seen in what has gone before feminists argue that this picture of formal equality systematically conceals substantive, structural inequality and difference. So-called public goods, for example, may be unavailable to some because of their membership of a group or community (like an ethnic group) which makes an effective difference to their identity as members of 'the public'.

Interpretivism

The development of an interpretivist model of political theory, along with the blurring of the prescription/description divide, also chimes with many currents in feminist theory. To begin with, this methodology rules out of court the idea of an objectively valid, natural political order (which just happens to issue in a highly gendered world). That is, perspectivalism or constructionism in knowledge is systematically connected with the idea that reality itself is socially constructed. Feminists, perhaps more than any other political and intellectual movement, have had plenty of reason to be suspicious of 'objective' scientific facts. On some accounts, the job of feminism must be straightforwardly to correct bias, and substitute for partial knowledge the whole truth. This is the 'add women and stir' strategy in social science.[73] But most feminist researchers would accept that the very idea of objective facts in this traditional sense is problematic and that feminists are not well advised to pretend that their version of reality is the final one. The principle that the standpoint from which knowledge is constructed must be made clear in any presentation of that knowledge is widely accepted.[74]

More than this, though, some theorists have recently argued that the standpoint of the oppressed should be privileged in our interpretive processes. In one version, this is a matter of political strategy. The presumption is that the perspective of the oppressed is the correct one from which to judge a practice or a law.[75] There are also stronger versions of this kind of argument. One concentrates on skills and knowledge. It is argued that oppressed persons know much more about the world than those who oppress. Think how much more highly developed than her husband's a woman's social skills must be if she is in the kind of marriage in which his comforts are paramount. She and he rely on her implicitly understanding his mood and anticipating his wishes. This is a matter of power, not a matter of gender. The same is true of other oppressed people. For example, it has often been observed that slaves (as for example in the southern states of America) depended for their physical survival on reacting precisely to the mood of overseers.[76]

Another argument concentrates on the reality different people inhabit. Women, who typically are the ones who look after children and other people's bodily needs, are in a much better position to understand reality than a person (man) who has never, for example, cleaned a lavatory and who can play the part of a purely rational, disembodied subject.[77] This argument puts a sociological gloss on liberal values. Transcendence of our embodied state is a role that some people can play. Given the sociological facts about the division of labour some men can, it seems, play it without even realising they are playing a role; for they are effectively able not to know the work that goes into reproducing their bodies daily – cooking for it, cleaning it and cleaning up after it, clothing it. Thus, such people's knowledge of the world is fatally flawed.

These arguments also overturn the traditional emphasis on the need for disinterestedness, detachment and objectivity if genuine knowledge is to be attained. All knowledge is the upshot of interpretation from some standpoint or another. Traditionally, knowledge from the 'objective' standpoint has been privileged. Now that judgement is challenged, and the argument put that knowledge which derives from the embodied, socially concrete, position should be privileged. We do not have to accept this reversal of traditional conceptions of what sort of knowledge is best. But we do, it seems, have to accept that producers of knowledge should be reflexive and honest about the standpoint from which their knowledge is produced. If this standpoint is concealed or erased then the knowledge is the less valid.

Conclusion

We have now laid out the affinities between communitarianism and feminism. Indeed, in many ways the relationship is closer than an affinity, for feminist arguments against liberalism have been an important ingredient in the development of the communitarian critique. We have, however, already begun to hint at some weaknesses in the communitarian literature, notably its blurring of some important distinctions in the area of public goods and collective values. We now turn to a more critical assessment of communitarianism, to see whether the affinity is really one which feminists should be concerned to foster.

5

☐

Communitarianism: a feminist critique

In the last chapter we saw that several of the themes developed in communitarian political theory are ones with which feminist theorists have also allied themselves or which are implicitly sympathetic to the direction of feminist thought. Despite this resonance, however, we shall argue that in several respects communitarian theories should be regarded as deeply unsatisfactory by any feminist, including those of us who endorse the feminist critique of liberalism. Indeed, we shall suggest that one could sometimes be forgiven for forgetting that communitarianism is really engaged in *political* theory at all.

Romanticism and conservatism

We have argued that the resurgence of communitarian ideas in political theory is partly to be explained in relation to contemporary fears about the disintegration and alienation of the modern world. These fears are felt on both the left and the right of the political spectrum. Yet the main and most frequently voiced objection to communitarianism is that it is, at least potentially, politically conservative. Communitarianism has been thought to be conservative in a number of ways, notably in the senses that it appeals to a romantic and unrealistic vision of the past and that it provides no critical basis for assessing or trying to modify the status quo. We now want to assess this common charge.

From a feminist point of view, the suggestion that communitarianism is conservative is of particular concern. This is because feminism has usually conceived itself as politically radical. However, the phenomenon of conservative feminism has become a significant feature of the political scene in both the UK and the USA, and the resonance between some feminist arguments and certain conservative positions has been a recurring feature of feminist politics. Particularly over the last decade, feminist writers and activists have frequently been concerned with issues which have also preoccupied those on the right of the political spectrum. Pornography, prostitution, sexual violence, contraception policy (particularly the use of the contraceptive pill), the valuation of motherhood: these are just a few obvious areas in which feminist and right-wing campaigns have sometimes found themselves, to their mutual surprise, sharing certain conclusions and even political strategies.[1] The links between feminism, conservatism and moralism in these areas are both interesting and problematic: they have been widely commented upon, and cannot be dealt with in detail here.[2] But we do need to attend to some of the features of feminist thought which help to explain the link.

Several factors have been of particular importance. In the first place, a substantial amount of recent feminist theory places emphasis on ideas such as a distinctively 'women's point of view', 'women's voice', or 'feminine morality'.[3] Indeed, particularly through the work of Carol Gilligan, these are among the very few feminist ideas which are regularly referred to in 'mainstream' political theory.[4] Yet the idea that women have a distinctive morality or viewpoint is easily (though not necessarily) read as a biologically essentialist claim. Any such essentialist reading is inimical to feminism, given its resonance with conservative discourse assuming the appropriateness of distinctive roles for men and women, and even of separate spheres.

We need to pause here to distinguish between two issues often equated with each other under the heading of 'essentialism'. As we saw in Chapter 1, 'the' question of essentialism has become one of the most contested of feminist theory. A challenging literature, much of it written by African-American women, has pointed out not only the dangers of biological essentialism but also the essentialism which lurks in any claim about 'women', as if we constituted a homogeneous group.[5] Some have taken this to mean that the very enterprise of feminist theory is deeply problematic: if to speak of 'women' is to engage in illegitimate essentialism, how is feminist theory to articulate its claims?[6] In our view, although the obligation to attend to difference is among the most important for any critical analysis, the problems which this kind of 'essentialism' pose for feminist theory have been exaggerated. As we suggested in Chapter 1, we must recognise both that a woman's subject position is as importantly determined by, for example, her race and class as by her gender, and that race, class and gender oppression cannot simply be regarded as cumulative as opposed to transformative of experience.[7] But, in the societies about which we are writing, social reality is structured in such a way that gender is *always one* influential factor in determining lived experience.[8] This modest claim is all that is necessary to make the category 'women', and hence feminist discourse and politics, legitimate, so long as it is used with an appropriate awareness of the diversity of women's experiences and situations.

The attempt to derive *one* distinctive ethical or epistemological stance from feminine embodiment, on the other hand, raises the problem of essentialism in a genuinely dangerous form, for it directly suppresses any recognition of differences among women. Furthermore, this kind of essentialist argument tends to proceed from highly questionable, often ahistorical, empirical generalisations, such as the claim that 'all' or 'most' women live their lives predominantly in the 'private sphere'[9] or construe ethical dilemmas in terms of 'responsibilities' rather than 'rights'.[10] These empirical assumptions then form part of the basis for normative conclusions which are of similarly dubious validity. What is more, the inference from oppression to distinctive epistemology can serve to disguise the discontinuities between gender oppression and subordination based on other factors such as cultural identity. The idea that women, like aboriginal Australians or native Americans, for example, want recognition for a distinctive culture which is in some meaningful sense their own has a pleasing simplicity. This has sometimes made it attractive to the few political theorists who acknowledge the importance of gender. But it suppresses the difficult questions feminists need to raise about the oppression inherent in that 'culture'. For even if we were to concede that it is possible to identify shared features of women's experience in terms of a 'culture', it is incontrovertible that this is a culture which has been in many respects imposed on women and whose shape must now be up for reassessment.[11]

There can be little doubt that feminist arguments touched by these damaging kinds of essentialism tend to lead in a conservative direction.

For example, feminist attempts to re-order the social valuation of traditionally female roles such as motherhood are double-edged, particularly where the prevailing political discourse is committed to gender neutrality. Feminists have argued convincingly that policies based on gender neutrality perpetuate ancient disadvantages and evade the task of re-evaluating the status and allocation of certain kinds of work or role. The real point here is to expand the basis for a critique of the way in which the status quo realises gender hierarchy rather than to revalue (without challenging the construction of) femininity.

But there is a plausible conservative reading of what sets out as a distinctively feminist campaign. This conservative reading sees the undervaluation of, for example, mothering as itself a *consequence* of the inappropriate extension of equal treatment ideology. In a way which is reminiscent of some late-nineteenth-century feminist literature, conservatives seek to justify something like the status quo by glorifying women's distinctive contribution. Although the analyses are very different, not only in terms of historical context but also in terms of political goals, both the statement of the problem and the conclusions often look deceptively similar. As Gisela Kaplan shows in relation to the women's movements of the 1920s, feminist embrace of such arguments is often a symptom of political discouragement: when the political climate is particularly hostile to real change for women, the 'retreat into virtue' seems attractive to feminists.[12]

Another important issue is the relationship between feminism and moralism. The emphasis on the importance of sexuality in radical feminist literature can be read as resonating with conservative preoccupations both in its occasionally moralistic tone when applied to issues such as pornography or prostitution and in its tendency to construct male sexuality as inevitably and essentially aggressive.[13] The line between the radical feminist position on male sexuality and the view of it to be found in conservative literature which affirms the ideal of the 'total woman' who has to tame essentially dangerous male nature has occasionally seemed to be blurred. Clearly, the strategic conclusions drawn by conservatives and by radical feminists are poles apart: whilst conservatives basically favour a form of appeasement which leaves the male domain intact, radical feminists are committed to what amounts to a (sex-based) class struggle.[14] But features of certain political campaigns which have attracted a great deal of publicity (the best known being that of the evangelical right's alliance with feminist groups to pass the Dworkin and MacKinnon anti-pornography ordinance in several cities in the United States) have helped to create a certain resonance between feminism and moralism in contemporary political discourse.[15] Whilst this resonance is justified neither by shared historical origins nor by any genuine political common cause, its existence inevitably gives rise to important strategic and theoretical complexities for contemporary feminist politics.

It is perhaps not surprising, then, to find the phenomenon of conservative feminism as a significant feature of the contemporary political scene. On the surface, the idea of conservative feminism looks like an oxymoron, yet a substantial number of conservative female politicians in Britain and the US now identify themselves as feminist and become actively involved in campaigning around feminist issues such as the provision of child care, equal opportunities legislation, political participation of women and so on. This phenomenon is important from our point of view because, in so far as 'conservative feminists' draw on communitarian discourse, it seems to undercut the argument made in Chapter 4 about the resonance between communitarianism, public goods and socialist feminist politics.[16]

Modern forms of conservative feminism are caught in inescapable tensions of principle which relate to contradictions within modern conservatism more generally. British and American conservative ideology has become markedly more economically libertarian over the last fifteen years, applauding the market as the principal organising and legitimating device in the political economy. At the same time, however, it seeks to appeal to 'traditional' values and ways of life. Conservative feminism shares this dual strategy, and involves itself in some spectacular contortions in the process. Intervention in the market is clearly necessary if women's subordination is to be tackled by government. Structural inequalities call for special measures for women, yet how can these be reconciled with market thinking? The kinds of public goods and social provision (genuinely comprehensive childcare, to name only the most obvious example) which would be necessary for women's equal participation in the market go beyond anything which could be legitimated by market ideology.

In other words, whilst the libertarian strand in modern conservatism has provided a foothold for some feminist ideas, it simultaneously rules out effective policies in pursuit of those feminist ideals. Conservative feminism is therefore incapable of producing a politics which integrates women rather than glorifying their role in their separate sphere. Conservative feminist rhetoric is constantly being pulled back to the more literally 'conservative' project of reinstating separate spheres, notably the family, along with the project (resonant with radical feminism) of effecting a revaluation of those sexually-marked roles and activities. This is a project whose recommendations for feminism, we argued above, are highly questionable. In short, the phenomenon of 'conservative feminism' raises questions about the resonance between communitarianism in political theory and contemporary political practice, and makes the suggestion that communitarian ideas are potentially conservative particularly troubling.

Feminists, then, have particular reason to be concerned at the suggestion that communitarianism is conservatve. But is there any evidence that communitarian ideas have contributed to or expressed themselves in contemporary conservative politics? Even the briefest survey of political discourse shows the extraordinary degree to which the rhetoric of community was exploited, to great effect, by right-wing governments such as those of Ronald Reagan and Margaret Thatcher.[17] These regimes combined ideologies (though not always practices) of deregulation with appeals to the value of community: punishment 'in the community' for offenders[18]; 'care in the community' for the mentally ill; and the need to get 'the community' to take responsibility for a whole range of social provision thought of in the post-Second World War era as part of the state's domain.

The cosiness of 'community' was, of course, only rhetorical. The relevant 'communities' were often fragmented or non-existent, as former prisoners, victims of mental illness and other homeless people now sleeping on the streets of American and British cities can readily testify. But as political strategy, the rhetoric was inspired. By playing on the slippage between sociological and ideological senses of community, it appealed to people's ideals in the same breath as it played on our fears. We like to think that we live in 'communities' which evince the values of 'community' – which are capable of providing support, solidarity, reciprocity, love. But we fear – indeed, we know – that in many respects we do not live in such communities. Even the 'communities' which approximate most closely to the cosy image – the family, the club – fall short of the ideal.

Furthermore, as members of more or less liberal–individualist cultures, we are fundamentally ambivalent about how much of our lives we *want* to live in such communities. In the increasingly individualised and differentiated modern world, the question of how to generate a degree of social integration adequate to sustain peaceable and mutually supportive coexistence without unduly curtailing hallowed individual freedom has become a central political concern. And one way of responding to this concern is to evoke a past era in which stable, integrative, identity-generating communities were a dominant feature of social organisation. So, despite the fact that many of us on reflection find the idea of the 'unoppressive city' plausible and attractive as a political ideal,[19] the fear of loss of community, and with it identity, lies deep in some cultural vein in the UK and USA. It is this vein which the fear of disintegration captured by the critique of modernity has tapped, and this is an important clue to both the salience and the potential conservatism of communitarian thinking in recent Anglo-American political and legal theory.[20]

Is the coincidence between conservative political appeals to the idea of community and the theoretical resurgence of communitarianism merely a historical accident? Although this is an appealing thought to anyone sympathetic to communitarianism, we doubt that it is the case. For the weaknesses of liberal theory do not provide a complete explanation of the extraordinary degree to which the central themes of Sandel's *Liberalism and the Limits of Justice* were taken up and debated. In the first place, many of these weaknesses were already well-known and had been analysed in Marxist and other radical political philosophy long before the 1980s.[21] And, as subsequent developments have shown, liberal theory is sufficiently elastic to accommodate at least some aspects of the communitarian critique.[22] As our discussion of the prevailing intellectual climate suggests, a more plausible explanation for the attention given to Sandel's book is the fact that the ground for a resurgence of communitarian and romantic thought in political theory was extremely fertile. The romantic strain in communitarian thought has been widely commented upon and is to be found in the all too often vague appeals to 'community' in a wide range of communitarian literature – appeals which both echo and prefigure those of contemporary political discourse and practice. In the work of MacIntyre in particular, dissatisfaction with modernity is explicit and is expressed in terms of an attempt to recover an essentially pre-modern or perhaps anti-modern world. We now need to return to the communitarian theories themselves to look for more concrete evidence that they are (potentially) conservative and to consider how any such relationship works at a conceptual level.

In thinking about communitarianism and conservatism, one is met by an initial difficulty which is highly significant. This is that although communitarians take on board a critique of liberal individualism and purport to recognise the constitutive role of the social in our identity, they have so far stopped short of any genuinely political analysis or critique of the very community institutions whose importance they acknowledge. Indeed, they manage this in part by maintaining their arguments at a high level of abstraction (Walzer being an honourable exception). This seems paradoxical given the contextualist slant of the communitarian framework.[23] The problem is exacerbated by a pervasive vagueness in communitarian discourse of the ideas of 'community', 'tradition', and 'culture', which leaves the communitarian analysis of both society and the specific ideals purportedly affirmed opaque.[24] Even in the absence of any overtly conservative orientation, this lack of substantive argument opens communitarianism to the charge of conservatism, for as we shall show, it inevitably favours the status quo.

One possible way of understanding why communitarians fail to generate a *political* critique is that this failure is an inevitable side effect of a thoroughgoing social constructionist approach to moral and political value. As we have seen, this approach issues in an essentially interpretive conception of political theory (although several of the communitarian authors do not deem themselves to have abandoned entirely the aspiration to universality of the kind subjected to feminist critique in Chapters 2 and 3). One way of diagnosing the problem of communitarianism's blunted political edge is to see it as a negative consequence of the blurring, entailed by interpretivism, of the description/prescription divide. The communitarian approach provides no means of making the move from a *description* of a community in which women learn, for example, to expect certain kinds of sexually-oriented behaviour from men in every context and in which men regard such behaviour as usual and legitimate, to the *critical* judgement that such practices are coercive, demeaning, abusive and damaging, that is, to the political construction of sexual harassment. What, on a communitarian view, is to tell us that there is anything *problematic* about a gender-segregated labour force or a general sexual division of labour?

At the very least, it seems that communitarian analysis has to be supplemented with some substantive political vision such as Walzer's principle of complex equality to generate a critique of gender hierarchy. But it is not clear how complex equality or any other critical principle emerges from constructionist or interpretivist communitarian method. As we have seen, it is an advantage of communitarianism in this context that it escapes any rigid distinction between public and private spheres, and thus opens up the possibility of political critique of women's subordination in the 'private sphere'. However, it fails to deliver the critique which it makes possible. For, in some versions of communitarianism, we have slid from the extreme of the radically disembodied subject to the other extreme of the radically embodied subject, from the search for transcendence in political value to complete relativism. We are facing what Bernstein has called the 'Cartesian anxiety'[25]: the fear that once we let go of an account which claims an objectively true or valid status, we will slide into the incoherence of total relativism in which our claims lack any grounding whatsoever. Without a fuller analysis of the relationship of human agency to social structure, the interpretive approach to political theory threatens to collapse into mere conservatism, conventionalism and rationalisation.

The extent to which this danger exists varies among the communitarians. Perhaps the best example of how a conservative tendency manifests itself in communitarian literature is MacIntyre's work, which arguably constructs the theoretical project as a form of social history. For MacIntyre, man's moral nature and moral practice are tied up with his sociality, his membership of a tradition and his participation in practices.[26] On MacIntyre's view, practices are:

> any coherent and complex form of socially established co-operative human activity through which goods internal to that form of activity are realised in the course of trying to achieve those standards of excellence which are appropriate to, and partially definitive of, that form of activity.[27]

If virtue is the exercise of what is necessary to attain goods internal to practices, a question arises about how one could ever come to perceive a practice as evil or otherwise morally unacceptable.

Asking himself this question, MacIntyre simply doubts whether the examples he cites (torture and sado–masochism) really 'count' as practices. But it is far from clear how his theory can generate criteria to exclude them. And the problem begins to look acute when one thinks of widespread practices in the modern world whose ethical status is more controversial – heterosexuality, to name but one.[28] Even more disturbing, on MacIntyre's conception of value-generating practice, there seems to be no reason, within a society characterised by gender hierarchy, why rape, or sexual harassment, should not count as such a practice. If feminism is to be a merely 'internal' critique, we need to know much more about where the sources of critical insight emerge within dominant traditions and practices. The explanatory and descriptive aspects of MacIntyre's project may on occasion be useful for feminism, but the foothold needed by critical and utopian feminist projects seems to be unavailable. We shall have to return to consider whether communitarianisms (such as Taylor's) which do give more attention to this question, or (like Unger's) do have more explicit commitment to utopian or visionary politics, throw any light on the problem via an account of the acquisition of critical consciousness.

So far we have been exploring the extent to which the conservative implications of communitarianism are a feature of its social construc- tionist stance on identity and its interpretivist methodological orienta- tion. Another way of looking at the problem is to consider the nature of the communities which the communitarian approach promises to accommodate. As we saw in the last chapter, the idea of 'community' plays a double role – in generating and grounding moral judgement, and in providing a source of inspiration for at least some forms of value-communitarian commitment. By thinking through some gender examples, we can see how far the appeal of each of these ideas depends on the lack of specificity with which they are put. Women are indeed often thought of – and think of ourselves – as members of groups – as women, as mothers, as wives. The attitude of feminism to these roles has been understandably ambivalent given their involvement in stereotyping and controlling women in a variety of disadvantaging ways. We would argue with Rorty's assertion that one feminist complaint has been the impossibility of constructing an identity 'as a woman'; rather, it is the shape of the possible identity which has been subject to critique.[29]

Communitarianism holds out the hope of recognising the sig- nificance of these and other roles and attachments in constructing our identity. But what of critique? A moment's look at the *content* of the communitarian models on which we have to build – the family, to take the most obvious – shows that, as one would expect, they tend to exemplify the salient features of women's oppression – the reproduc- tion and reinforcement of a coercive heterosexist culture, the sexual division of labour, the objectification of women as property, sexual harassment of women by men. These communitarian models in themselves hold out little hope in the project of political reconstruction. And whilst the loosening of any rigid public–private distinction may open oppressive practices up for feminist political critique, we nevertheless return to the question of whether communitarianism can provide any source of prescriptive and critical insight. If the communities which generate meanings are not themselves susceptible of critique, progressive politics becomes impossible. From a feminist point of view, there is a crucial difference between communities, practices or traditions of which critical evaluation is a *part* and those of which it is not.[30] And the question of whether association with any particular community is genuinely voluntary or not, raised but inadequately dealt with by liberal theory, appears to be another highly relevant issue which communitarianism is ill-equipped to address.[31]

Similarly, the collective values on which value-communitarianism allows us to focus are themselves in need of reconstruction from a feminist point of view. The exclusion of women is historically and linguistically embedded in the notion of 'fraternity'. Part of the resonance of 'solidarity' comes from predominantly male forms of association such as early trades unionism; the term 'reciprocity' is susceptible of an individualist interpretation.[32] The mere switch of focus from individual to collective values and public goods does not guarantee progress towards the ending of women's subordination. Indeed, although it represents an important switch of focus from earlier liberal theories, its substantive political implications are relatively weak. Most communitarian writers are extremely vague when it comes to the details of the substantive value-communitarianism they advocate.[33] As we have seen, communitarianism improves on liberal individualism in moving beyond the conception of society as a mere aggregation of individuals and hence by accommodating the idea of genuinely public goods. But it treats the idea of public goods in an undifferentiated and uncritical fashion.

For example, communitarians have been insensitive to the distinction between public goods in the sense of those such as clean air from which (at least within a given space) no one can be excluded, and what have been called 'club goods', that is, goods which operate in the same way as public goods but only in respect to those who have membership of a certain 'club' or community.[34] Technically, club goods are instances of an 'impure' public goods – those from which it is in fact possible to exclude certain people. In political terms, the distinction between club goods and genuinely public goods is of fundamental importance, for, on a broad notion of what constitutes a club, it is very often the case that what are thought of as public goods in fact turn out on closer inspection to be club goods. This is because membership of a certain club or community – in the case of clean air, the community of those rich enough to live in areas free from pollution – is a pre-condition for access to the goods themselves. From a socialist point of view, unequal access to 'clubs', and the construction of club goods as public goods, is one of the main ways in which social injustice is perpetrated and disguised. Communitarianism, as we shall see, puts 'clubs' on the political landscape, but stops short of generating an adequate critical analysis of club membership.

Furthermore, much communitarian discussion is characterised by a disturbing slippage between sociological ideas of community and community as an *ideal*. Whilst sociology and ontology provide the framework within which the plausibility of ideals must be assessed, they do not *determine* which ideals we should adopt: prescription and analysis are different from one another.[35] Yet the communitarians offer little by way of *reconstruction* of value-communitarianism, relying instead on appeals to what seem to be (themselves inadequate) sociological conceptions. For a satisfactory reconstruction of value-communitarianism, political theory needs critical tools which it appears that communitarianism lacks.

What these arguments amount to is the claim that communitarianism may experience difficulty in distinguishing itself from mere sexist conservatism. Whilst many communitarian arguments are themselves politically indeterminate, the lack of critical foothold in communitarian analysis will tend to the rationalisation of the status quo, whatever it happens to be. Communitarianism purports to engage explicitly with substantive values and judgements, moving beyond the liberal emphasis on procedures. Yet the source from which it draws the values and from which it claims to legitimate them, thus escaping the dilemma of the apparent need to choose between extremes of relativism and objectivism, seem unpromising from a feminist perspective. If the basic communitarian claim is that moral and political argument is validated within particular cultural discourses and practices, whose role in constructing human identity must be recognised, it is difficult to see how one is to attain the critical capacity to judge the sexism, patriarchy or any other feature of the culture in question. Deeply embedded practices such as sexual harassment or the hierarchical, gendered organisation of labour, which may be regarded as an expression of certain fundamentally important features of culture, will remain immune from critique. Whilst feminism seemed to be in accord with the communitarian approach to human nature, it finds itself uncomfortable with the approach to politics which communitarianism has issued in.

Membership and power

Another way of developing the feminist critique of communitarianism is by using some concrete examples of relevant (and potentially embarassing) questions which the communitarians fail to address. The first issue which calls for attention concerns membership and the power which goes with it. This is an issue which scarcely arises for liberal political theory given the scant attention it gives to concepts such as groups and other collectivities. For a feminist analysis of communitarianism, two questions about membership and power arise. In the first place, we need to ask whether women can even be regarded as genuine members of the communities whose traditions ground the communitarian approach to political action and judgement.[36] How are women and members of other subordinated groups to gain access to the powerful, value-defining communities – those whose understandings become 'common sense' – or the 'clubs' whose membership ensures valuable benefits, if they are currently excluded? How is the standpoint of those who are excluded from such communities to attain any measure of political power? Second, there is an issue about the relative power of different communities. We shall address each of these in turn.

Most advocates of a communitarian approach recognise the significance of the issue of membership, yet they are naive about the feminist questions the issue raises. For example, in Walzer's work membership occupies a whole chapter (as well as receiving attention in several others), yet in none of these contexts is the issue of women's position in the communities considered addressed. He gives one example of a debate about women's education in medieval Jewish communities, but makes no reference to gender issues and struggles in other relevant areas, such as in his chapter on education. While he recognises the contemporary exclusion of women from full membership in society, his general analysis offers little argument about how progress might be made in this particular egalitarian direction. As Okin has argued, once we get to the stage of recognising monopolies of power distributed on gender lines as a problem, the theory of complex equality gives us a critical edge – although one which is sharper in the cases of actual monopolies than of widespread inequalities across many spheres such as the generalised but not absolute divisions which characterise labour markets in countries like the UK and USA.[37] But how, on Walzer's view as expounded in *Spheres of Justice*,[38] do we get to the point of recognising gender division as problematic, as opposed to socially apt? We need an account of how the community of feminists gets off the ground in the first place.

This point emerges even more clearly in the context of a concrete example. Sexual harassment proceeds from the community which in a gendered society has the power to define value and meanings, that is, it is part of our social tradition. Women, like men, are socialised into the sexist culture. Sexual harassment helps to exclude women from full membership of, and participation in, sub-communities such as workplaces which might give us a voice in criticising the dominant practices and so give our standpoint a measure of power. It does so by sexualising women in a way which either makes it difficult for us to speak or changes the meaning of our speech in a way which renders it less effective. In so far as communitarianism, like liberal social contract theory, lacks a theory of power and remains silent on the relevance of gender in constructing social relations, it too will prove an unpromising basis for analysis and critique of deeply embedded and indeed 'traditional' practices such as sexual harassment. For it will be unable to see the ways in which they are legitimated and depoliticised by the prevailing culture. The status of sexual harassment as an institution which, in Pateman's words,[39] 'helps maintain men's patriarchal right in the public world' and which flows from the fact that '(s)exual domination is part of the structure of subordination in the workplace' can only become visible once a critical stance which is sensitive to the importance of power relations is adopted.

The same applies to other 'traditionally' gendered social practices. What could make the participants in MacIntyre's favoured Aristotelian practices get to the point of recognising women's exclusion, or the exclusion of slaves, as a political issue? In so far as MacIntyre is committed to reversing the exclusion of women, this must be at least in part on the basis of values external to those practices. For whilst traditions may be sustained and advanced, as MacIntyre suggests, by their own internal arguments and conflicts,[40] it cannot be *assumed* that where, for example, sexism is a feature of the prevailing culture, a degree of conflict or innovation sufficient to reverse women's exclusion will emerge from within the tradition. In other words, not only internal but also external critique – that generated by debate across traditions and on the basis of values external to prevailing cultures – needs to be part of any theory which aspires to account for the kind of radical reconstruction of gender relations MacIntyre assumes to be desirable.

Similar difficulties arise in relation to Rorty's suggested solution to the problems of membership. In the context of women's exclusion from powerful communities, Rorty argues[41] that the relevant (and only possible) project for feminism is the imaginative construction of a different vocabulary, generating new meanings and ways of speaking about and looking at social practices. In the early stages, Rorty suggests, such political thinking has to go on in separate spheres among people with common commitments and visions. Only once the vocabulary – what we would call the feminist discourse – is securely established among this group can it begin to enter the general political fray, persuading members of the dominant group to see things differently, to attach new meanings to established practices. Commentators have noted that Rorty's account of the extent to which debate 'across vocabularies' is possible is somewhat opaque, and have even questioned whether his analysis can accommodate the development of oppositional political discourses.[42] He insists that the advocate of a particular political position inevitably speaks from *within* his or her own vocabulary: she may seek to stir and persuade, but she can make no claim to any criteria independent of her own framework. This, as much as other communitarian approaches, seems either to expand the concept of 'a tradition' so far that it loses any analytic integrity, or to insulate particular traditions from the critique of others, and in particular from excluded others' claims to membership.

For Rorty, women's representation (and, possibly, participation – there is no mention of anything so concrete) is part of the tradition of liberalism from which 'we' speak. But we are given few reasons as to why we *should* speak from this position, and to the extent that we are, this can only, consistently with his position, be an argument from within the tradition. Rorty (in a way which evokes Taylor's account) emphasises the contrastive nature of political argument. Political argument is essentially persuasive; it proceeds by presenting alternative visions and, by differentiating them from current states of affairs, uses them to mark up deficiencies in the status quo. But advocates of one way of life can never be sure of speaking to advocates of another in terms which they will find in the least bit persuasive. There is simply no foothold for critical argument across traditions.

This is particularly significant when we think of the meaning of women's participation. We need to ask what guarantees that the different moral vocabularies which women might seek to introduce to the political arena, such as the 'ethic of care', would be *heard*. Many feminists will share Lovibond's discomfort with a position which reduces arguments about women's subordination to the level of interest-group politics, with no greater moral credentials than racist doctrine.[43] Among the communitarians, Rorty's position raises in sharpest focus the central question of the status of feminist politics. For Rorty, feminist politics has to be regarded as essentially engaged in a power struggle, with no grounding other than in feminist practice itself. This entails that feminism's understanding of itself as giving voice to claims of *justice* is merely an expressive or tactical feature of feminist discourse.

Not all communitarians, of course, share Rorty's pragmatism. Towards the other end of this particular spectrum, for example, we find Taylor and Habermas. Yet they too, have so far failed to make significant contributions on questions of membership and power. Habermas's theory of communicative action provides little analysis of the question of the systematic domination of certain groups such as women. What is more, it hardly begins to address the *political* problem of overcoming the domination and inequalities which deprive certain groups of a voice, or give their voices systematically lower status. In the non-ideal community of discourse which is the political world, who has the power, not only to speak, but to be heard?[44] Taylor's historical and interpretive project in *Sources of the Self* is, implicitly, an eloquent testimony to the male-domination of the intellectual and cultural traditions which he analyses, but although here and in his other work he suggests the existence of criteria of 'error' and 'coherence' external to particular practices and traditions, he has given no explicit account of how these might be used by or developed in a direction useful to feminism.[45]

For Taylor, perhaps, the modern moral sources of autonomy and dignity could provide the kind of critical framework needed by feminism. Indeed, in his recent work on multiculturalism he asserts his belief in the possibility of, and commitment to, a non-atomistic and perfectionist liberalism.[46] His account appears to be informed by a (somewhat inchoate) teleological faith in human progress towards less error-ridden moral frameworks, but the bases for these judgements about moral error are gestured at rather than spelled out. We shall return in Chapter 6 to consider whether the sort of position defended by Taylor can be developed so as to generate an adequate *political* analysis of dominance and of the possibilities for change, and whether such a developed account is properly described as either liberal or communitarian.

In recent years, several of the writers associated with communitarianism have asserted or (in some cases) re-asserted their commitment to liberalism or to significant features of liberal doctrine (indeed, the same is true, in reverse, of some of the best-known liberals[47]). This may give us some clues as to why, as will be clear from what has been said so far, several of the problems encountered by communitarian theories in addressing questions of membership are parallel to those encountered by liberal theories. The feminist critique of social contract theory, discussed in Chapter 2, demonstrates that, despite the alleged gender-neutrality of liberal theory, serious doubts exist about whether women are genuinely to be regarded as parties to the initial, hypothetical agreement. A similar point can be made about communitarian assumptions about accession to membership of linguistic and political communities. Given facts such as the history of women's exclusion from many spheres and the importance of male bonding in exclusive and powerful clubs and associations in many cultures, obvious doubts arise about the implications for women of a theory which takes 'our' membership of 'communities' as its starting point. Just what are these 'communities', and why should they be valued? Given that the notion of membership entails non-membership, exclusion from the private or impure public goods to which the club gives access is an implicit part of the meaning and indeed *value* of membership.[48] This raises a fundamental question hardly addressed by communitarians. Who, in the relevant context, are *we*?

We need to ask, in other words, whether communitarianism has really escaped the implicitly male individualism of liberal theories. Are the people who enjoy membership in fact the very same liberal individuals whose existence the theory denies or at least constructs as contingent? Of course, in a liberal culture, this is precisely what the social constructionist would teach us to expect, but feminists will expect a political theory to offer a critical toehold from which we can recognise such political issues and struggle for political progress. While acknowledging the social construction of male as much as of female identity and sexuality, an adequate political theory would have to provide a basis for critique of the gendered nature of practices such as sexual harassment. This would have to include an analysis of the ways in which such practices relate to roles produced and legitimated by particular kinds of communities – among them, of course, communities developed in the context of the dominance of liberal ideology. Similarly, communitarians' failure to develop an adequate account of power means that women's over-representation in occupations which lack both socio-economic and cultural power is not necessarily seen as problematic. Even more fundamentally, it disables communitarians from generating any critique of the hierarchical division of labour in general.

This brings us to the second question identified at the beginning of the section, that of political power as between different communities. Communitarian theory has the advantage of giving a central place to the fact that we live our lives within and across a number of identity-forming and meaning-generating communities. But this multiplicity and fragmentation gives rise to a new set of questions. How should we assess the significance of the fact that some 'communities within communities' are joined by the exercise of 'choice' at some level, whereas others simply cannot be escaped? To what extent is women's oppression a product of our coerced identification with certain kinds of communities?[49] Furthermore, membership of some communities confers or entails power to a far greater extent than is the case for others. Quite apart from the question this raises about access to membership, communitarianism needs an analysis of the power relations which must exist between competing or coexisting communities. It also needs an account of how certain communities come to have the power to define meaning, objectivity and right in particular places at particular times.

Again, these are questions about power. They are confronted by communitarian writers in different ways and to different degrees, but they are rarely given the attention for which we would argue they call. A brief survey of the indices of major communitarian books shows that the probability of even finding that power has been identified as a significant concept is no greater here than in the case of liberal writers who have not taken up communitarian ideas. There is some recognition but no analysis in Walzer's work[50]; in so far as he does address the problem of power, his focus is on problems of power and membership *within* particular communities. Habermas's theory of communicative action fails to generate an adequate critical purchase on the possible development of hierarchies and domination within the speech community, let alone across competing speech communities.[51] Rorty simply embraces the conception of politics as power struggle – he has neither a sophisticated analytical account nor a normative theory of power. Taylor has a much more sophisticated account of how particular meanings come to be dominant but, as we have seen, the normative framework at which he gestures is under-developed. Furthermore, his account of the importance of respect for cultural diversity as a precondition for the realisation of equal citizenship is arguably inapt to accommodate the political concerns of women and other groups whose oppression and exclusion from full citizenship is not centrally associated with the refusal to recognise their distinctive 'culture'.[52] Issues raised by the multiplicity of values entailed by communitarian analysis are often adverted to by Sandel but never really confronted.[53] He does not advert to the concept of power and hence does not see the questions about power and its distribution which the multiplicity of value-generating communities raises. MacIntyre is only able to minimise the problems to which the diversity and fragmentation implied by his theory give rise by presupposing an unrealistically homogeneous society in which certain roles and combinations of roles become 'nested'.

None of these writers asks the questions about the *materiality* of the meanings or values generated by non-powerful communities which we would argue must be central to political theory. In other words, they give us theories of meaning-generating communities yet no account of their *power*, no account of the political 'meaningfulness' of the 'meanings' they generate. In the absence of any analysis of these and other *political* questions, the degree of fragmentation which communitarianism entails seems fundamentally to undermine any pretensions it might have to be a critical as opposed to a merely explanatory theory. This gives rise to further doubts about whether the tenuous critical foothold of interpretive political theory can be maintained.

Despite the theory's emphasis on the importance of communities, then, communitarian analysis of the issues raised by its reliance on the concept of community is inadequate. In terms of the question of membership, communitarians have failed to provide the kind of critical analysis which would be capable of addressing issues about access to and the power that comes with membership. They also ignore the liberal individualistic resonance of the concept of membership. Without a more critical analysis, the avowedly distinct constitutive communitarianism threatens to run into instrumental or sentimental communitarianisms which can easily be embraced by liberalism itself. Communitarian analysis is similarly defective in terms of the relationship between the different communities whose importance it insists upon. In this context the failure of communitarian theorists, like their liberal counterparts, to develop and use an adequate theory of power is a fundamental flaw in their analysis.

The self and society

In terms of the conceptual framework of communitarian theory, three interrelated aspects of communitarianism's social ontology contribute to the problems we have so far identified. These are the communitarian account of critical consciousness; the communitarian conception of the subject; and the communitarian conception of society/community. Despite their apparently abstract nature, these are intimately connected with issues of central concern to feminist politics; issues such as the possibility and power of political campaigns, the acquisition of a political voice, and the prospects for social change. Each of these questions therefore needs to be addressed.

If communitarianism seems unsatisfactory in explaining how feminist critique is to be validated at the level of political theory, what are we to make of its approach to the question of how women achieve critical consciousness in the first place? To assess this, we need to focus specifically on the communitarian approach to human nature. Once again, we encounter serious difficulties. For here communitarianism seems to be in a position which is equally poor to, or possibly even worse than, that of liberalism. On a classical liberal view, the exclusion of women from the social contract reflected our general exclusion from the political sphere on biological grounds related to a fixed, pre-political view of women's 'nature'. On this view, there could be little hope of explaining how it is that women, from our 'natural' and appropriate position, come to a critical appraisal of our situation, define it as imposed and oppressive and begin to struggle against it.

Early liberalism's commitment to an atomistic conception of personhood and its individualistic social ontology hampered it from explaining how individual citizens could come to a critical appreciation of the systematically oppressive operation of social structures. It is stretching matters to say that, on a strictly liberal view, practices such as wife-beating or sexual harassment would be seen as either politically legitimate or politically irrelevant. Because this kind of liberal analysis is myopic when it comes to the structural aspects of social life which impact in a patterned way on particular *groups*, it is rather the case that they would not be seen at all. A notable feature of this 'loony liberal' ontology is its obvious disproval by the facts of women's movements through the ages. Conversely, the great difficulty of our struggle to recognise, name and fight against sexual harassment or the marginalisation of women's work testifies to the powerful hold a liberal perspective enjoys in our culture. The pre-eminence of liberal discourse survives the fact that, as Pateman points out, liberalism is self-contradictory in implicitly denying women's participation in the sexual and social contracts yet acknowledging our contracting power by conceptualising marriage in terms of contract.[54]

Of course, most modern liberals attempt to resolve the contradictions and ambiguities in classical texts in favour of regarding women as full liberal individuals. And in doing so, liberalism provides liberal feminism, for all its inadequacies, with a model of woman's subjectivity which is consonant with our coming to an understanding of, and beginning to struggle against, oppression. For liberal feminism, women are free and choosing subjects who have been discriminated against. They exercise their individual subjectivity by asserting their rights and pointing out the injustices of their situation. Liberal feminism, indeed, has operated as a powerful critique internal to liberalism, constantly drawing attention to the faulty logic, the irrationality, of discrimination against women.[55] Certainly, as we saw in Chapter 3, the liberal feminist's critique is limited by her inability to identify the harms of sexism as part of a social structure of subordination as opposed to an aggregation of individually discriminatory actions. But to the extent that, for example, job segregation, low pay or sexual harassment constitute discrimination, in the sense of adverse and differential treatment of women on sexual grounds, the liberal feminist can identify and oppose these phenomena.

For a communitarian, on the other hand, the subject is the product, rather than the generator, of social reality. 'Communities' comprise persons in social relations. In modern western industrial societies the persons who comprise the community are 'individuals', related by ties of economic exchange, the values of the market economy, the modern bureaucratic rule of law and so on. These individuals do not have any irreducible ontological status – they are not in any sense 'pre-social'. Political theorists are rarely explicit about the processes that construct biological beings into individuals or persons. The one that seems to fit most readily with the picture painted by MacIntyre and some other communitarians is a socialisation model – babies are born into a particular cultural formation of roles, rules, norms, values and practices, and grow into persons whose psychological, even physical features are shaped by the culture.[56]

On this communitarian view of personhood, the woman who lives in a sexist and patriarchal culture is peculiarly powerless. For she cannot find any jumping-off point for a critique of the dominant conception of value: her position as a socially constructed being seems to render her a helpless victim of her situation. By what means, through what subjectivity, can she begin to comprehend her situation in critical terms? How is she to attain any measure of critical consciousness, so as to move towards the formation of alternative communities, alternative definitions, towards the reconstruction of chivalry as sexism, of flattering attention as sexual harassment?[57] On a communitarian view, it is difficult to see where the community of feminists emerges from, let alone, once it has emerged, how it attains the power to be heard, to have its values and social meanings adopted more widely in the culture. It is not clear, for example, how or why the sexual division of labour or the under-representation of women among elected politicians would be seen as problematic. While liberal analysis can legitimise gendered patterns on the basis of hypotheses about individual choice, communitarian analysis may be similarly uncritical in that it can see them as the products of sexist socialisation, of which it has no critique. In other words, all communitarianism can say is that women as persons are constructed in terms of a gendered culture, and live our lives accordingly. Within a communitarian framework, who is to say that a community with gender segregation and hierarchy in its labour market is not preferable to one without such a hierarchy, and how are they going to get to the stage of saying it?

Two important kinds of problems are implicit in this discussion of the attainment of critical consciousness: first, the fragmentation of the communitarian subject and second, the inadequacy of the communitarian model of society. There can be no doubt that the communitarian subject is, at least *potentially*, 'fragmented' in a radical way. Communitarians and many feminists abandon the disembodied, liberal, choosing self as both theoretically flawed and patriarchally constructed. But in doing so, we risk finding ourselves in the arms of the radically embodied communitarian self, a determined product of her or his circumstances, social conditioning and community culture. The situation of a being whose consciousness is determined by structure, communities, and institutions seems to be that of a helpless subscriber to the dominant conception of value. Arguably, the communitarian conception of personhood hardly deserves the name. At least in the context of a complex or pluralist society, it seems that the unity or even identity of the communitarian subject would break down as she is subsumed within a complexity of meaning-generating communities. If there is no self prior to or independent of its social constitution, it might be argued that the very idea of personhood becomes incoherent.

This might be seen as yet another 'Cartesian anxiety', a false dilemma posed by liberalism and to be rejected at all costs. Doubtless we all feel and acknowledge the importance of our community ties, experiences and upbringing in shaping our identities, as well as pressures generated by our culture to live, think and behave in particular ways. Yet we also experience a resistance to dominant, conventional roles and definitions, a resistance which for many of us takes the form of feminist activism and self-definition. Our experience is neither of total self-determination nor of total determinism. Why should we accept the 'logic' of a philosophical tradition which tells us that we must choose between the two? We certainly think that the Cartesian anxiety can and should be resisted but we also think that there is a real problem lurking here for communitarianism. To see why, we have to advert to the second issue referred to above, that of communitarian assumptions about the structure of society.

Clearly, any adequate political theory has to acknowledge the sociological facts of plurality and complexity in modern societies. The radically situated communitarian subject can and does belong to specific 'communities within communities'. These generate judgements which compete with those of dominant social groups. Thus a communitarianism which is plausible in the modern context entails not only a fragmentation of the human subject, but also a fragmentation of political and moral value. The culture, values and traditions of the nation-state are not homogeneous but rather complex and to some extent contradictory. The discourses and practices of these multiple traditions and communities generate values and overlapping identities. Communitarianism refers to the judgements emerging from groups more various than merely the obvious candidates, nation-states. Indeed, it might be seen as a kind of compromise between liberal individualism on the one hand and tory nationalism and paternalism on the other. In any society, a heterogeneous plurality of communities – clubs, families, political parties, churches, women's groups – are generating judgements and ascribing meanings in a variety of areas of life. Political theory has to come to terms with a welter of linguistic, spatial, functional and moral communities generating a multiplicity of roles and norms to be adopted, negotiated or imposed.

Yet, despite the central role of the concept (perhaps we should say concepts) of community in communitarian thought, neither the idea of community itself nor its relation to the social order more generally is analysed in any rigorous way by communitarian writers. A number of different ideas can be conveyed by the concept of 'community'.[58] We could distinguish, to start with, between '*a*' or '*the*' community, on the one hand, and the *idea* of 'community' on the other, that is, between communities as entities and community as an ideal. Communities as entities can be identified in a variety of ways: as geographical entities; as groups constituted by ties of kinship; or as collectivities bound by common values and/or a shared history. We might want to emphasise, as some social theorists have, the significance of a group characterised by shared values, and a *society* in the sense of a less integrated group of individuals.[59] This distinction might prompt us to consider the implications of such a characterisation in terms of degrees of respect for or tolerance of diversity within the group. Among communities in the restricted sense, that is, opposed to societies, we could distinguish on the basis of the shared values themselves: conservative communities, Christian communities, Islamic communities, and so on.

Additionally or alternatively we might identify communities in terms of some *specific* shared purpose or practice. Particular discourses and practices, ranging from complex, open-ended activities through to the institutionalised production and distribution of particular benefits, can be thought of as marking distinctive 'communities'. Hence we might speak, for example, of 'linguistic communities', of 'interpretive communities', of 'communities' based around clubs or associations, all of these cutting across other lines of community membership and identification. *Conceptual* differentiations, in each of these cases, can serve to mark out *political* questions. Hence, as we saw in the case of the failure to distinguish between public goods and club goods, the lack of sophistication of communitarians' conceptual apparatus gives rise to difficulties for its production of an adequate political analysis.

Turning to the *ideal* of 'community', once again a cluster of related ideas have been influential in the history of political thought: cooperation, fraternity, sisterhood, solidarity, reciprocity, to name just the most obvious. Each of these is open-textured and raises complicated but crucially important questions about appropriate political and social institutions, relations between persons and, perhaps most obviously, the accommodation of diversity. The elaboration of these ideas is of central importance to communitarian theories. For one of their main claims to our attention flows from their critique of the poverty of modern liberalism's account of both the ideals of community and the institutional practices necessary to their realisation. Yet communitarians themselves have devoted scarcely more attention to the analysis of value-communitarian ideas than have liberals, and their institutional analysis (mainly found in the work of Walzer and MacIntyre) tends to focus on historical examples rather than contemporary practices. From a feminist point of view, this is particularly worrying. For, as we have already suggested, some of the available communitarian ideals (most obviously fraternity) and institutional models (unions, mutual assistance societies) are themselves historically associated with the exclusion of women. Furthermore, the means by which communitarian ideals might be realised, in terms of public goods and institutional mechanisms such as those of the welfare state, receive little attention in communitarian analyses.

In communitarian literature, then, no real attempt is made to specify which of these senses of community is being referred to at any given time. Nor is any systematic attempt made to assess the relative importance of different kinds of communities in the production of dominant meanings. Thus we have no way of assessing what it is that communitarians regard as analytically definitive of, or ideally important to, the notion of community on which they rely. Earlier, we identified a rhetorically powerful slippage between sociological and normative conceptions of community within communitarian discourse. Similarly, the failure to specify an analytic notion of community and its relation to the social order has allowed communitarians to switch between different conceptions, evoking that which is most suitable to the particular argument at hand. Of course, this kind of rhetorical displacement characterises much political theoretical argument. It is none the less important to identify its operation and to assess its implications. For in this context there is reason to think that it not only obscures questions about whether different claims are consistent with each other but also disguises communitarianism's failure to provide the analysis of social structure on which the validity of its claims depends.

It is clear, at least, that most communitarians assume the importance of a number of overlapping meaning-generating communities within social orders. The contradictions and possibilities for challenge generated by the diversity of communities within social orders must, of course, constitute an important occasion for the acquisition of critical consciousness – the communitarian subject is exposed not just to one predominant cultural discourse but to multiple discourses. But whilst the fragmentation of value suggests a possible source for critical consciousness and social change, the accompanying fragmentation of the subject seems to deprive that consciousness of any being in which it could inhere in an effective or coherent way. Without a heavily modified version of fragmented subjectivity, the fragmentation of value threatens to collapse the subject into total incoherence. Unless the communitarian conception of the subject is revised, the only hope of retaining a necessary baseline of coherence lies in violating the requirement that political theory proceed from realistic sociological assumptions, that is, by assuming the world to be far more homogeneous than it is.

Communitarians such as MacIntyre preserve the unity of the subject by evoking a pre-modern world of relative simplicity and homogeneity, but even if we allow the propriety of evoking a political world which no longer exists, MacIntyre's approach is problematic. For he is able to represent that world as homogeneous only by suppressing diversities which did exist – for example, by ignoring the exclusion of women or slaves from citizenship and hence from political theory.[60] The only realistically envisagable world which is sufficiently homogeneous to keep the communitarian subject together is an authoritarian one – yet another reason to be wary of the political implications of communitarian thought. The analysis of critical consciousness, the subject and society turn out to be inextricably linked, and the form which their analysis has taken in communitarian thought gives rise to a number of related problems in communitarianism's capacity to give an adequate political analysis.

The degree of recognition of questions about the fragmentation of both the subject and society varies enormously among the communitarian writers we have mentioned. Unger, for example, retains a central place for a strong conception of human agency and will: indeed, this is an important reason why he calls himself a 'super-liberal'.[61] On his view, the formative contexts of social life leave room for conflicts which are transformative; the assertion of will over structure takes place when context-preserving routines are brought closer to structure-transforming conflict by critical political practice which fixes on disputes within stabilising routines. For example, the division of labour is a part of the context-preserving routine of British society. But feminist consciousness has led many women and men to question the routine sexual division of labour, for instance by arguing for a redistribution of labour (that is, 'housework', which feminism has reconstructed as 'labour' and hence as of economic value) within the home or for access to jobs in the labour market which have traditionally been held by men. This kind of political practice is disruptive, causing conflict in homes, workplaces, unions, and legislatures. It prevents the routine from being taken for granted: it gradually creates a pressure which destabilises, often *via* social conflict, and which ultimately facilitates structural change. This account does not entirely explain the relationship of agency to the social constitution of identity, but it is one of the most plausible models available.

Rorty, by contrast, says little about the sources of the visionary ideas which find expression in literature or social theory and which sharpen our awareness of cruelty or provide new languages in which to express the aspirations and judgements of a particular age.[62] Indeed, as we have seen, Rorty speaks of the self as nothing more than a network of beliefs and desires. Yet if the self is entirely engulfed in her circumstances, how can she have anything approaching the kind of agency presupposed not only by liberal but also by feminist (or indeed any) politics?[63]

Walzer recognises the potential difficulty raised by the fragmentation of value[64] but does not advert to the fragmentation of subjectivity in his main communitarian work. Sandel, however, does confront the issue, and argues that:

> Even an enlarged self, conceived as a community, has its bounds, however provisional its contours may be. The bounds between the self

and (some) others are thus relaxed on the intersubjective account, but not so completely relaxed as to give way to a radically situated subject. The bounds that remain are not given by the physical, bodily differences between individual human beings, but by the capacity of the self through reflection to participate in the constitution of its identity, and where circumstances permit, to arrive at an expansive self-understanding.[65]

He also speaks of our being:

subjects constituted in part by our central aspirations and attachments, always open, indeed vulnerable, to growth and transformation in the light of revised self-understandings. And in so far as our constitutive self-understandings comprehend a wider subject than the individual alone, whether a family or tribe or city or class or nation or people, to this extent they define a community in the constitutive sense.[66]

These passages make clear Sandel's commitment to a meaningful conception of subjectivity, encompassing a subject with the capacity for both reflexion (critical contemplation of its own identity and commitments) and reflection (critical contemplation of its social context, understood broadly to include prevailing norms and social institutions).[67] But they leave opaque the precise source and nature of that subjectivity, and the *extent* of the influence of social factors both in constructing personhood, and in identifying the boundaries between the reflective subject and its social constitution. If the reflective subject can resist all social construction, it looks very much like a liberal individual; if it cannot, what are the limits of its powers? Can the logic of radical constructionism be resisted? A communitarian might plausibly suggest that the very notion of reflexion and self-creation on which a strong notion of subjectivity depends is itself culturally grounded in particular practices such as psychoanalysis and religion. What does this imply in terms of the basis for a sufficiently distanced account of subjectivity to generate radical politics?

Taylor suggests a slightly different exit from this particular dilemma. His wide-ranging survey of the history of the emergence of the modern identity pays painstaking attention to historical and social contingencies – the arts, philosophy, religion, politics.[68] Yet the project itself proceeds from certain framework assumptions about the human condition which are not themselves supposed to be socially contingent, however importantly particular contexts influence our perceptions of that condition. For Taylor, the human constant is our status as self-interpreting animals – as beings who seek to make sense of our own lives.[69] This we do in terms of moral frameworks and sources through the practice of 'strong evaluation'. Our sense of our selves is hence inextricably linked with our conceptions of the good – identity and the good, ethics and epistemology cannot be separated in the way writers like Rorty or the later Rawls favour.

Taylor's moral sources and frameworks are historically grounded in specific texts and/or intepretive practices (religious traditions would be one example), but are not impervious to critique in terms of 'canons' of rationality-error-identifying arguments which, whilst intelligible across frameworks, are not themselves internal to particular frameworks. For Taylor, unlike Rorty (and in our view MacIntyre), it is not a question of 'contexts all the way down'. Though some goods clearly emerge internally to practices, this is not exhaustive of relevant criteria for moral and political judgement. Taylor's view is, therefore, genuinely interpretive: it is grounded in particular social contexts, but conceives the self as having the capacity for reflection and hence some measure of distancing, as well as access to insights which are not exclusively internal to dominant social practices.[70] Unfortunately, however, the basis for and shape of what we might call the 'universalist remnant' in Taylor's interpretivism is only sketchily set out.[71]

An important divide therefore emerges between different communitarian and constructionist writers along the axis of their conception of selfhood. Whilst Sandel and Taylor leave room for the reflective subject, MacIntyre and Rorty have little place for any conception of subjectivity beyond the radically embodied, while Walzer lies somewhere in between.[72] The problems which we have identified with communitarianism seem likely only to be susceptible of resolution on something like the Taylor/Sandel view.

The invisibility of gender

Finally, we have the fact that, like liberal theorists, advocates of communitarianism have had little to say about women or women's oppression. Gender remains a conceptual irrelevance for communitarian political theory: it is either ignored, or gestured at in a way which assumes that gender issues can be incorporated without conceptual modification. This is true even of the small number of communitarians who have acknowledged the existence of or engaged with feminist theory. Our analysis so far has suggested that this has to do not (just) with failings of political commitment on the part of individual theorists but with conceptual, structural features of communitarian theory. It is worth adverting to some of the specific implications of gender-invisibility in communitarian theory.

Communitarians have not begun to analyse the male-dominated nature of existing political communities (or indeed to acknowledge the importance of such a project). For example, MacIntyre's discussion of the 'traditions' within which certain criteria of judgement emerge and are validated proceeds without reference to the issue of gender (or indeed to those of race or class).[73] Indeed, he adds insult to injury by using sex-inclusive language in discussing traditions (such as that of the Greek *polis*) which excluded women, whilst simply noting the exclusion as if it could be reversed in a modern return to the tradition. It seems not to occur to him that the exclusion of women constituted part of the conception of the good – of virtue – realised in the practices of that particular tradition.

Despite his effective critique of liberal social contract theory, Sandel's communitarian claims are similarly 'gender-blind' and naive to questions of structural disadvantage and disparities of power more generally. This is perhaps particularly surprising given Sandel's focus on the interpersonal conception of subjectivity and his critique of the liberal conception of the disembodied subject: the gendered meaning of bodies nevertheless calls forth no comment from him. Unger, despite his generally radical orientation, accords no place to the analysis of gender in *Politics*, occasionally adverting to gender patterns without pausing to offer any critical comment. Indeed Unger is in many ways as individualistic in his analysis, and hence as blind to structural issues, as more traditional liberals.[74] The family and questions of reproduction are as conspicuously absent from most communitarian theory as they are from liberal analysis.[75]

Taylor adverts regularly to gender issues but gives a number of isolated (if perceptive) comments rather than any systematic treatment.[76] Habermas's social theory is similarly silent on gender issues. He constructs a dichotomy between symbolic and material reproduction, that is, between on the one hand the reproduction of the ideas and norms which characterise and hold a society together, and on the other the production of the material means of a society's survival and development. Habermas locates 'lifeworld' activities such as human reproduction in the sphere of symbolic reproduction.[77] This constitutes yet another form of reified, albeit sophisticated, public–private division. It obscures the multiple significance of women's work in the home, which certainly consists in material as well as symbolic reproduction. Conversely, it underplays the symbolically reproductive functions of systems-world institutions such as labour market workplaces.[78] Certainly, Habermas's critique of the inner colonisation of the lifeworld would meet with approval from many feminists because of its criticism of the extended dominance of instrumental reason – a characteristic culturally associated with men and one in which in western culture women have all too often been assumed to be deficient. But his critique carries with it the risk of obscuring the extent to which the developing interpenetration of lifeworld and systems associated with the blurring of lines between 'public' and 'private' spheres has produced opportunities for struggle and progress for women.[79]

Of the communitarians, only Walzer and Rorty have reached beyond the use of non-sexist language to address gender issues explicitly. In *Spheres of Justice*, Walzer specifically discusses 'The Woman Question' in the chapter on 'Kinship and Love'. Walzer transcends the public–private divide by having such a chapter, but why do women appear *only* here? Women's issues are, as usual, confined to the private sphere, and questions of women's political representation or participation, or their office-holding, for example, are not discussed.[80] There is no systematic incorporation of gender issues within his overall framework, nor any appraisal of the implications of complex equality for a structural site of disadvantage and domination such as gender.[81]

The only contributor to the liberal–communitarian debate who has, to our knowledge, explicitly engaged with feminist theory is Rorty. In a recent paper,[82] he has suggested that his 'pragmatist' theory is just the kind of social theory which feminists need. Its radical embrace of contingency can accommodate the kind of thoroughgoing visionary, constructive politics which feminism espouses – it can comprehend the feminist struggle for new vocabularies as well as new practices. We have already mentioned and will return in the next chapter to the implications of Rorty's pragmatist method for feminist politics. As far as the substance of his theory is concerned, however, it is far from clear that Rorty's brand of liberal individualism would prove any more satisfactory from a feminist point of view than any other. This doubt is not rebutted by any substantive analysis of gender or other issues of structural disadvantage in Rorty's work. In particular, despite his explicit enthusiasm for feminism, he has not thought fit to respond to feminist critique of the public–private distinction, to which he adheres in a particularly strong form.[83]

In earlier chapters we saw how feminist theorists have subjected the implications of the invisibility of gender in political theory to a powerful critique. These arguments apply with equal force against the communitarians. In so far as communitarianism, like liberal social contract theory, remains silent on the relevance of gender in constructing social relations, it too will prove an unpromising basis for analysis and critique of deeply embedded and indeed 'traditional' practices such as the gendered division of labour and sexual harassment, which are legitimated and depoliticised by the prevailing culture. The absence of discussions of gender from communitarian theory suggests that communitarianism has yet to develop an adequately critical stance.

Conclusion

The foregoing discussion shows that, although communitarians take on board a critique of liberal individualism and purport to recognise the constitutive role of the social in our identity, they stop short of any genuinely *political* analysis or critique of the very community institutions whose importance they acknowledge. We have considered a variety of problems: they concern the substantive vision of value-communitarianism, the communitarian approach to the grounding of political value, the social constructionist approach to human nature, and the communitarian analysis of society. Communitarianism fails to give gender the central place in political theory which we have argued it needs. It has not acknowledged, let alone escaped, the gender bias in our structures of thought, and in some of its forms it exemplifies the worst of gender invisibility and blindness in political theory.

Communitarianism lacks a theory of power. It presupposes a model of the self and society which is either radically post-modern – so fragmented as to be incoherent and chaotic – or neo-romantic – unrealistically homogeneous and static, allowing for the possibility of only the most modest, incremental social change. Largely as a consequence of these features, in so far as any substantive political implications flow from communitarianism, they tend to be conservative ones. Although feminist thought is sympathetic to the insights of 'constitutive communitarianism' in its acknowledgement of the significance of the social construction of human nature and value, as well as its advocacy of a greater valuation of genuinely inter-subjective values, the communitarian alternative to liberalism is far from qualifying as a potentially feminist political theory.

However, we have also begun to see some significant differences opening up between communitarians. This suggests the need for a more sophisticated characterisation of the communitarian position and a more careful linking of these issues to wider debates in philosophy and social theory. Furthermore, the feminist exploration of communitarianism has not been a wasted effort. For feminism encounters just the same problems of political and social theory as those we have encountered in this chapter. The difficulties we have identified with communitarian approaches serve as a warning about the drawbacks of too uncritical a feminist espousal of the doctrines of social constructionism and value-communitarianism. We can draw the preliminary conclusion that these broad categories now need to be refined, to see just which elements within them feminist theory can retain, without abandoning its political commitments and critical edge. We have also opened the path to a fuller consideration of the links between these issues in communitarian political theory and wider questions in social theory.

6

□

Beyond the liberal–communitarian debate

Our discussion so far has focused on the significant debate between those espousing liberal and communitarian positions in political theory. We have used feminist and other critical arguments to expose or emphasise the ways in which each position is inadequate. We argued that the currently influential North American brand of liberalism is flawed by both its universalism, its individualism and its circumscribed conception of the political, and that it is incapable of confronting and accommodating oppression and injustice flowing from structural features of social organisation such as gender. But we suggested that the communitarian position which puts itself forward as an alternative to Rawlsian liberalism is flawed by a conception of the self and of society which is incapable of explicating radical politics. In this respect communitarianism turns out to be potentially conservative, as well as sharing with modern liberal theory a lack of attention to gender and the absence of a theory of power.

We also suggested that the liberal–communitarian debate in Anglo-American political theory is best understood as located within a broader set of cultural debates about modernity and the atomistic disintegration of modern societies. Corresponding to our discussion in Chapter 1, three main impulses can be identified as characterising the distinctive way in which particular writers respond to the sense of a crisis in liberalism as the dominant political discourse of modernity. Locating contributors to the liberal–communitarian debate within these three tendencies helps to illuminate the important differences *among* those sympathetic to communitarianism which we began to encounter in the last chapter.

The first impulse, particularly evident in the work of MacIntyre, is to respond to the perceived crisis in modernity by rejecting modernity in favour of a pre-modern or anti-modern conception of the political world. Typically, this involves evoking purportedly more integrated societies of the past in which small, homogeneous communities provided a stable set of social identities. This romantic impulse, which was discussed and criticised in Chapter 5, turned out to be one of the main ways in which the conservative potential of communitarianism manifested itself.

The second impulse is to stick with liberalism as a genuinely progressive political discourse, but to modify it in the light of certain anxieties about the problems of modernity which form part of the communitarian critique. This 'welfarist' impulse is, as we saw in Chapters 2 and 4, common to a number of liberal and communitarian writers. We saw that Rawls has revised his statement of his own position in a way which emphasises the central place of social constructionist themes.[1] Similarly, Dworkin now explicitly accommodates a distinctive conception of community[2]; Rosenblum emphasises the advantages of pluralism whilst acknowledging the need to accommodate notions of the affective aspects of political life within liberalism[3]; and Raz rejects anti-perfectionism and embraces a positive conception of freedom which recognises the importance of a public culture.[4] Indeed, these kinds of developments might be regarded as attempts to re-orient modern Anglo-American liberal theory in a way more resonant with the more social democratic version of liberalism espoused in the early twentieth century by writers such as Hobhouse.[5] This version was influential in the development of European thinking about the welfare state yet, as we saw in Chapter 2, it has been submerged in more recent political theory by the deontological version of liberalism, the roots of which reach back to Kant and to natural rights theory.

The preference expressed in this second impulse to stay within liberal discourse is strengthened by a sense of the dangers (canvassed in Chapter 5) of giving up any pretension to the kind of grounding associated with modernism, particularly of losing a critical foothold. It is also prompted, politically, by the move to the right in the complexion of governments in the USA and the UK during the 1980s. This move has helped to emphasise both the progressiveness of liberalism and the dangers of the potential conservatism of communitarianism. The later Rawls' notion of liberal politics as the best possible interpretation of the conception of the common life embedded in 'our' political practices seeks a middle position between universalism and subjectivism. It also seems to promise a path between the certainties of pre-modernism and the uncertainties of post-modernism. The attractions of this middle way are felt not only by liberals who do not identify themselves as communitarians, but also among what we might call the 'optimistic communitarians'. They would include writers like Sandel, Taylor and Walzer, who are reluctant to abandon the philosophical discourse of modernity and whose (explicit or implicit) conception of the critically reflective subject opens up the possibility of imaginative reinterpretation of traditions and ways of life. These writers' recent assertions of their continuing commitment to liberalism are further evidence of the attractions of a rapprochement between liberal and communitarian positions.[6] The welfare liberal impulse, then, assumes such a rapprochement to be both possible and desirable.

The third impulse which can be identified in current debates about modernity is the embrace of 'post-modernism' and the fragmentation of meaning and value. This is in many respects the most radical reaction to the perceived crisis of modernity. What is meant by post-modernism is, of course, as deeply contested as its intellectual and political recommendations. Among the themes of relevance to political and social theory discussed in Chapter 1, we shall focus here on the renunciation of 'meta-narratives', 'grand' theories which purport to ground and legitimate claims to 'Truth' (post-modernists often use the capital 'T' to denote universal claims to 'objective' truths as distinct from the (supposedly trivial) claim to truth which can be said to be part of the logic of a wide range of linguistic utterances). Unlike 'welfare liberals' or critical theorists like Habermas, who seek to rescue enlightenment ideals by recapturing the appeals to rationality and values (such as justice) which transcend particular contexts, but in ways that can accommodate difference, post-modernists and pragmatists like Rorty reject the idea of universally valid ethical and political principles. They tend to focus instead on the analysis or 'deconstruction' of specific discourses and practices. Rather than seeking order and certainty, the post-modernist sees the way to liberation (if any is to be had) through the opening up of our consciousness to the 'play of difference' implicit in language. The attempt of 'meta-narratives' to impose a generalised order on an open world is seen as an act of power: it is regarded as repressive in a sense which post-modernists often refer to as 'totalising'.

The clearest example of the post-modernist impulse in American political theory is the work of Rorty, who also identifies himself as a liberal.[7] His project is distinctively post-modern in the sense that it attempts 'to defend the institutions and practices of the rich North Atlantic Democracies without using . . . buttresses' such as 'an account of "rationality" and "morality" as transcultural and ahistorical'.[8] But Rorty is not alone among the theorists we have considered in his post-modernist leanings. Both Walzer's and Unger's work also resonate in some respects with post-modern thought (we need to be clear, of course, that we are dealing here with themes rather than absolute classifications). Some aspects of Walzer's discussion, such as his analyses of the distributive principles immanent in certain historical practices, are reminiscent of the pre-modernism of MacIntyre, whilst others are close to the welfare liberal impulse. But both his focus on the specificities of particular practices and his resistance to a universal theory of justice such as that of the early Rawls is resonant with post-modern ideas. The post-modern theme in *Spheres of Justice* is expressed in the thought that a society can be said to be just if it is faithful to the shared understanding of its members: 'Social goods have social meanings, and we find our way to distributive justice through an interpretation of those meanings. We search for principles internal to each distributive sphere'.[9]

Similar complexity characterises Unger's work. His occasional forays into imaginative reconstruction of political institutions hark back to the liberationist aspirations of modernism, and the unvarying emphasis Unger places on the importance of (individual) freedom seems thoroughly liberal. Yet his emphasis on freedom brings with it the idea of 'negative capability' – the ability to think ourselves beyond the dominant structures of the contemporary world – and the extent to which Unger not only assumes but *celebrates* the contingency of political arrangements and the 'smashing of contexts' which negative capability makes possible seems thoroughly post-modern. The same could be said of his resistance to fixing 'just' solutions in stabilising institutional frameworks such as constitutions, something which he sees as the disempowering 'entrenchment' of particular frameworks, inimical to negative capability.[10] Part of our task in this chapter is to assess the importance of this third, post-modern impulse in contemporary social theory.

We have suggested that communitarianism has to be understood in terms of two main features – social constructionism and value-communitarianism. We have also observed that a strong commitment to social constructionism in the area of values conduces to the adoption of a distinctive interpretivist methodology for political theory. But we have felt the need to differentiate this characterisation, and to do so in terms of more fundamental questions which each aspect of the characterisation raises. For the liberal–communitarian debate which has been so important in contemporary political theory turns out to be not one debate but several. This means that it is often impossible to characterise particular theorists as falling into one or the other category, because they take different positions on different issues. The underlying assumption (and at times explicit argument) of this chapter is that the variety of the issues means that the full significance of the debate cannot be understood within the bounds of political theory as conceived by its protagonists. Furthermore, we shall suggest that one important feature of the liberal–communitarian debate is that it tends to dichotomise the various points at issue. This is a tendency which, as we have seen, has been subject to feminist critique across a number of spheres of social thought. In this chapter, we shall offer a more differentiated analysis of the issues involved in the liberal–communitarian debate, and suggest the direction in which political theory needs to develop if it is to accommodate the insights generated by a critical and feminist understanding of the debate.

Beyond dichotomised analysis

Feminist and other critical discourses have often noted and deplored the extent to which western social thought tends to be carried forward in terms of dichotomised categories. Our analyses and judgements, it is argued, tend to be structured in terms of binary oppositions which find their roots deep in western culture and philosophy: subject/object; reason/emotion; individual/community; mind/body; form/substance; public/private; culture/nature; male/female.[11] Politically, this dichotomised thinking has several adverse implications. In the first place, western culture valorises one member of each pair over the other. These unequal values are so deeply embedded in our thinking that they can be appealed to in ways which have substantive consequences, without the normative arguments for those consequences ever having to be spelled out. The identification of (relatively) powerless people with the disvalued members of the pairs thus has political consequences which are difficult to reveal, because they appear neutral or normal to the gaze from within the culture. The identification of women with emotion and hence unreason, and as objects or bodies, creatures of nature in the private sphere as opposed to creators of public culture, is one of the clearest and most widely analysed aspects of this dichotomised thinking and its social implications. We have seen that these dichotomies underpin many of the features of liberal thought which are most unsatisfactory from a feminist point of view. The social constructionist stance of communitarianism promises to transcend the dichotomy between individual and society. Also, by accommodating the embodied aspects of subjectivity, it holds out hope of escaping an implicitly male conception of the individual who transcends his bodily state. But these promises can not be fulfilled, because communitarian emphasis on traditional discourses and practices inevitably reproduces the dichotomised thinking characteristic of western culture.

Second, dichotomised thinking tends to lead to unduly polarised debates in which middle positions are marginalised as mere compromises and as unprincipled. A dichotomised distinction implies not only that the two concepts in question are used to mark out phenomena which are analytically distinct, but also that they refer to opposites. That which is public cannot be private, and that which is a subject can not be an object. Crucially, these oppositions are often assumed to refer to *real* distinctions in the world. Political arguments drawing on such dichotomies inevitably reproduce the either/or opposition in terms of which they are constructed. This means that certain political positions are ruled out, without ever having been considered. For example, the attempt to understand public and private in terms of a spectrum or number of spectrums, or as a question of degree, is excluded, because the conceptual framework of the debate assumes a 'really' dichotomised world. This seems to rule out the (plausible) view that the dichotomies are not fixed but rather constructed, and hence open to competing interpretations. The implications of this kind of dualistic thinking, and its persistence even given the logical possibility of a multiplicity of positions between the two poles, are well illustrated by some aspects of the liberal–communitarian debate. Good examples of questionable dichotomies which continue to underpin the debate are polarised conceptions of embodied and disembodied subjectivity, and the dilemma posed by the apparent need (discussed further below) to choose between objectivism and subjectivism as epistemological stances. Furthermore, the construction of 'liberalism–communitarianism' as 'itself' an opposition can be shown to have obscured some of the most important substantive issues which the participants might have been trying to debate.

Third, and most importantly, however, recent critical social theory has developed arguments which suggest that dichotomised thinking is flawed at the level of meaning. Derrida and others have drawn on Saussure's relational theory of language to develop the notion of deconstruction.[12] This, it is argued, can be used to illustrate that the apparent choice offered us by the binary oppositions is itself an illusion. For, if meaning depends on the relation between linguistic signs, rather than the relation between those signs and things 'out there' in the world which they seek to represent, the meaning of each side of the pair invokes the other. Male finds its meaning only in relation to female, from which it is different; subjectivity is defined in relation to objectivity, which it is not, and so on. Moreover, within particular discourses, the two members often stand in a power relation with each other, the less powerful side being defined in relation to the more powerful – hence culturally endorsed notions such as man as 'subject' and woman as 'object' or 'other'. Deconstructionist analysis retains a notion of opposition, but changes the significance of that oppositional relation. Dichotomies purport to present us with clear choices, either/or, but our very choice evokes the other by implicit reference: meaning is never closed. Furthermore, we need to bear in mind the extent to which language is open-textured and susceptible to competing interpretations. In the very act of interpretation, of giving meaning, far from fixing that meaning, we inevitably refer to the implicit other, and hence to a different meaning which might have been. Openness and contingency are the most significant feature of our interpretations of the world and each other.

In this chapter we aim to draw explicitly the implications of the deconstructive theory of language for specific debates in political theory. In particular, we can learn from the history of deconstruction some lessons for the development of an adequate theory of the human subject. In its early manifestations, deconstruction developed out of dualist versions of structuralist philosophy and social science. This meant, inevitably, that it downplayed the importance of the subject. Structuralist dualism entailed that social reality 'was' binary and dichotomised, and this in turn seemed to entail that there was no escape from the dichotomies. On this basis, deconstruction inevitably participated in the logic of binary oppositions, and without a conception of the subject with some capacity for critical reflection and imagination, deconstruction could make no contribution to the explication of radical politics.

However, as these problems were recognised, 'post-structuralist' ideas developed further and further from structuralism and 'post-modernist' ideas became more influential. In a number of different disciplines and traditions, drawing on a variety of intellectual sources, the importance of subjectivity has been 'rediscovered'.[13] For example, Drucilla Cornell has shown how the insights of Lacanian psychoanalysis may be combined with those of some aspects of Hegelian philosophy and Derridean deconstruction to explicate a conception of the subject which neither collapses into social structure nor floats free of social context in a unrealistically transcendent way.[14] It is this strand of deconstruction generated by later post-structuralist work on which we think it is useful to draw. We shall use a similar account to show that an application of post-structuralist social theory can illuminate problems which are at the core of the liberal–communitarian debate in political theory and which traditional political philosophical techniques have dealt with unsuccessfully.

We do want to be clear, however, about our view of the limits of the enterprise of deconstructing binary oppositions. Inevitably, the method of deconstruction takes off from *within* the very hierarchical opposi-tions whose power it seeks to expose and unsettle. This raises a question about whether deconstruction can ever 'transcend' dichotomies as opposed to seeking to unearth the suppressed 'other' – the 'dangerous supplement' – and effect its re-valuation. One politically dubious implication of such a project might be its merely issuing in the reversal of a hierarchical relation that a genuinely radical politics would want to escape altogether (the subordination of men by women could hardly count as an attractive feminist ideal). More relevant to contemporary feminist politics, this theoretical problem has implications for debates such as that about a 'feminine' 'ethic of care' discussed in Chapter 5. As we argued then, a genuinely transformative politics would have to reassess the shape, content and conditions of existence of such an ethic as well as the more straightforward question of its valuation in contemporary political practice. This is a complex project, not possible given a view of the world constructed exclusively in terms of deconstructible binary oppositions. The transformative and utopian potential of deconstruction, whilst significant, is limited in so far as it comes mainly from the *re-ordering* of hierarchy. This is why a genuinely transformative deconstruction has to emphasise the openness of language and in particular metaphor, which allows for new meanings as well as new orderings to be imagined.[15]

In addition, there is, as many critical theorists have noted, a danger in placing too great a reliance on deconstruction. For it may lead us to re-erect binary oppositions – to re-envisage the world in terms of dichotomised opposites – even in areas where critical analysis has already unsettled their power.[16] Concrete examples include current debates about public and private or about masculinity and femininity, where we have begun to understand difference not as binary or oppositional but as multiple and relational. Practices such as sexuality may be seen as having both public and private aspects. Gender or sexuality may be seen as a spectrum rather than a binary opposition, and have been so reconstructed in some forms of critical social theory. Similarly, in our lived gender or sexual practice we sometimes *escape* the apparent straitjacket of masculine/feminine, homosexual/heterosexual dichotomies.[17] Deconstructive theorists might, that is, see dichotomies where ordinary social actors do not. It is therefore important to see deconstruction as just one among many useful critical tools to be employed where binary oppositions still have a strong hold on our thinking, on practice, and hence a continuing power.[18]

Binary oppositions in the liberal–communitarian debate
Among the binary oppositions which have been influential in western thought, we now want to focus on three which are of particular importance to the liberal–communitarian debate – those between agency and structure, self and other, and individual and community. In Chapter 5, we saw that one of the most important problems faced by communitarian political theory was the adequate conceptualisation of the self and society. The constructionist debate about the human subject and its relation to social structure links up with debates in a variety of disciplines about agency and personhood. These include various branches of philosophy (philosophy of the social sciences, linguistic philosophy and ethics, to name the most obvious), psychology, psychoanalysis, and perhaps most centrally, social theory. In

particular, much of the liberal–communitarian debate about the subject is reminiscent of the recent debates in social theory about empiricism, structuralism and post-structuralism which we discussed in Chapter 1. It also raises questions about freedom and determinism which have preoccupied social theorists and philosophers of mind.[19] We shall argue that the location of the liberal–communitarian debate in political theory within these debates in social theory is necessary both to a proper understanding of that debate and to a resolution of the apparent impasse. We therefore want to return to these debates to examine them in more depth.

The first opposition which is of particular relevance to the liberal–communitarian debate is that between *agency and structure*. As we saw in Chapter 1, structuralism in social theory emerged as a reaction to, and against, the empiricist views which have dominated social theory and social science during the first half of the twentieth century and beyond. Empiricist thought starts out from a conception of the unified, rational subject who acts on the basis of his preferences. This model of the rational subject has been central to much positivist social science, economics and rational choice theory.[20] Structuralists turned their attention rather to the structure of situations, societies, modes of production, taking structure to be a quasi-grammatical relation between elements, just as grammar constitutes the structure of a language. Rather than seeing the agent as cause – as acting on the world – structuralism regards agents as epiphenomenal, as merely the effects of the relevant structures. The empiricist view, as we have seen, resonated strongly with the liberal conception of society as an aggregate of autonomous individuals coming into a certain relation with each other. In structuralism, on the other hand, the pattern of relations is set.

Even on this very simplified characterisation of structuralist developments in social theory, we can see the links between the structuralist reaction to empiricism and the communitarian reaction to liberalism's focus on individual agency at the expense of social structure. And, just as commentators on the liberal–communitarian debate have pointed to the political dangers attendant on the loss of a meaningful conception of agency, similarly, attempts soon came to be made in social theory to solve the agency–structure dilemma in ways which could preserve the strengths and avoid the weaknesses of empiricism and structuralism. Berger and Luckmann, for example, of reality, showing how a dialectical relationship between subjects and social structures worked. When an individual person is born, they argued, she is born into a *real* social world with rules, norms, institutions and so on.[21] But this social world is real by virtue of the continuing actions and behaviour and projects of social subjects. The institutions and practices which make up a society are not fixed, like the wax interior of a beehive. Nevertheless they face individual subjects like a coercive force.

In similar vein, Anthony Giddens has developed the notion of 'structuration', which is intended to emphasise the processual nature of social structure and individual identity and to show the facilitative and empowering as well as the repressive and constraining aspect of social structures.[22] David Beetham's account of the legitimation of power is another good example of successful evasion of the agency/structure dichotomy. He shows how existing modes of legitimation structure agents' interests and incentives in a way which helps to perpetuate the status quo yet which falls far short of *determining* agency and hence the course of social history.[23] Structures are constantly being made by individuals and individuals are constantly being made by structures. There will therefore be change, even radical change, over time. This contrasts with the static, determinist picture drawn by structuralism, a notable weakness of which is its failure to account properly for social change.

The 'rediscovery' of the subject in the more recent development of post-structuralist thought is also associated with the later work of Foucault,[24] and with the deconstructionist and psychoanalytic work emerging in French philosophy and social, literary and psychoanalytic theory over the last twenty years.[25] Recent post-structuralist reconstruction of theories of subjectivity and freedom can be seen as a reaction to the pessimistic determinism of a structuralism which regards the subject as a mere epiphenomenon, a reflection of the social structures which are accorded theoretical priority. Here we see a kind of inversion of the liberal–communitarian debate. Yet these related debates in political and social theory have remained curiously insulated from each other. The communitarian critique is in need of a revised conception of critical, reflective and non-determined subjectivity if it is to escape the conservative implications of the simple theory of radically embodied subjectivity. In seeking such a conception, social theory is the obvious source of insight. One important element here – a discourse generally ignored by political theorists – is likely to be psychoanalysis and theories about the role of the unconscious in human subjectivity. The importance of the unconscious in psychoanalytic theory is that it undermines the notion of the unified subject, and provides insights into the possibility of dialectical, non-determined yet intimate relations between *self and other* and between *individual and community*.[26] These ideas have already been influential in feminist post-liberal theory. Yet most of the communitarian political theorists (like the liberals) are extraordinarily slow to pick up on developments in discussions of subjectivity, agency and structure in these other intellectual discourses, and this has kept the debate in political theory unduly polarised.

To most ordinary people, the news that both social theory and political philosophy have got themselves tied up to the extent that they have in the agency/structure dichotomy would probably come as something of a surprise, and might justly be the cause of some ridicule. At a common sense level, the idea that human life and social development can only be understood in terms of both aspects seems obvious. Yet the common sense view itself participates in the dichotomy. The idea that human action takes place against a backcloth of social structure, and that social structure is in some sense the product of human agency suggests a strong discontinuity between the two. As we have seen, the resolution, or at least weakening, of the agency/structure dichotomy is of first importance from a feminist perspective. For if this cannot be achieved, we are stuck with an unenviable choice. We can have a disembodied conception of selfhood which implicitly excludes or problematises women and marginalises women's experiences, and to which we can only have access at the cost of abandoning aspects of embodied existence which feminist thought has struggled to celebrate and to reveal as central to our selves. Or we can have a determined if embodied conception of the socially situated self which seems to take away with one hand the possibility of critical thinking, social struggle and radical politics just as it gives us the possibility of contextualised political theory with the other. The notion of a subjectivity which is not engulfed by its social situation seems central to the very concepts in terms of which radical politics have been constructed – struggle, liberation and so on. This dichotomy between the radically situated and the radically disembodied self will have to be escaped if the hope of a political theory adequate from feminist and other critical perspectives is not to be abandoned. The historical facts of social change suggest that the task is not beyond our reach.

Reconstructing subjectivity

We want to sketch the way in which an adequate theory of subjectivity and its relation to social structure can be understood so as to feed back into debates in political theory. In the first place, we start from the fact that, as both certain philosophical traditions and psychoanalytic theory have shown, our self-consciousness as human subjects depends on our relations with others. I only come to recognise myself as a subject by means of my recognition of you as the same, in this abstract aspect, as myself. In Hegel's famous account, this gives rise to the desire to master the other. But the impulse to mastery is self-defeating, for once I have enslaved you, you can no longer fulfil the function of helping me to recognise myself.[27] Human subjectivity is, according to this kind of view, inevitably relational, and even a form of inter-subjectivity. And in so far as it has been understood in relation to a dichotomy between self and other, it is a prime candidate for deconstruction. For the very notion of the subject takes its meaning from its relation to the suppressed other. We need not remain within the binary logic of self/other. Nor is it a question of complete connection or the dissolution of boundaries between selves. It is rather a question of mutuality – of recognition both *of* and *by* another as a pre-condition for self-consciousness. It is this insight which renders the idea of the pre-social self at once an incoherent and a disingenuous starting point for political theory.

Psychoanalytic theories provide further insights into the flaws in the notion of unified, autonomous subjectivity. They also help us to understand the ways in which human subjects' acquisition of self-consciousness both depends on the *differentiation* of, and yet undermines an *opposition* between, subject and object, self and other. The recognition of the power of the unconscious entails recognition of its potential to disrupt and unsettle conscious identity and decision-making. And that very identity is formed in an interactive process. In the earliest stages of its consciousness, the infant is not aware of itself as distinct from the other or others who care for it (usually taken in psychoanalytic theory to be the mother, in dispiritingly universalist vein). The acquisition of subjective identity therefore involves a consciousness of separation, a recognition of oneself as separate. Yet this too takes places in relation to the other from whom one separates. This moment of separation and of the acquisition of identity gives rise to a crisis which has, of course, generated a bewildering and fascinating variety of psychoanalytic theories, giving varying emphasis to biological, social and psychic elements. In all of them, however, subjectivity is achieved in relation to not only the 'other' but also to structures – language, biology, practices of parenting.

In object–relations theory, for example, it is argued that the structure of a person's subjectivity is fundamentally affected by the interaction of sex. Where mothers are primary carers of infants, the moment of separation for a girl involves a simultaneous recognition of connectedness – the other from whom I separate is like myself.[28] For a boy, the separation is a more thorough matter of differentiation and the acceptance of otherness and separateness. As many commentators have noted, this theory has the drawback that it fails to explain why the infant fixes on sexual difference as the decisive index of difference (and hence threatens to collapse into the kind of biologism it seeks to escape).[29] It lacks, in other words, the theory of social power which is needed to explain the significance of sexual distinction.[30] Furthermore, it fails to generate an account of why men and women born into these particular parenting structures would ever want to change them or come to see them as problematic except because of individual pathology. (The capacity of theories which gain a significant degree of social power to impose their views upon the world even in the face of 'common sense' – indeed to *alter* 'common sense' – should of course make us very aware of the dangers of pathologising those whose behaviour deviates from any dominant theoretical model.)

On the other hand, the strength of object–relations theory lies both in its insight into the interaction of subjectivity and social structure, and in its important supplementation of many psychoanalytic accounts which seem to rely solely on biology as the determinant of sexual difference. The insights of psychoanalysis into the dynamics of the acquisition of subjectivity point firmly to an interaction between social and psychic structures. The recognition in psychoanalysis of the importance of early experiences needs to be followed through in terms of accepting the historical contingency and tractability of the dynamics of early life in terms of parenting practices, to name only the most obviously relevant social structures. Hence a relational conception of the self, acquiring its identity in relation to both other persons and social structures, deconstructs not only the dichotomy between self and other, but also that between individual and community.

Subjectivity, of course, does not consist merely in self-consciousness. In psychoanalytic terms, there is a move from the pre-linguistic to the linguistic stage, and it is the subject's acquisition of (or 'entry into') language which provides further possibilities for both deconstructing and transcending the agency/structure dichotomy. On the view we sketched earlier, which is common to post-structuralist theory and the hermeneutic tradition in philosophy, language is inevitably constructive or interpretive. Our attempts to make sense of the world and each other are made in language, hence our experience of the world and of each other is mediated through language. As soon as we have spoken our experience, we have interpreted it. Furthermore, the categories of everyday discourse are constraining – they make it difficult to communicate, sometimes even to express, certain kinds of experience. The deconstructive argument helps us to see, however, that language is not entirely constraining: it is not fixed but open; its use inevitably evokes that which is other.[31] And the possibilities of evoking the 'other' – that which might have been – are increased by the use of metaphor and other linguistic devices. We have only to think of the importance of renaming and re-imagining in feminist and other radical discourses – pornography as 'violence', housework as 'expropriation', the personal as 'political', property as 'theft', date 'rape' – to see how these possibilities have been played out in political practice.

Subjects, then, can in a significant sense act upon as well as through language: meaning and usage can change. This account of language and the subject's relation to it subverts the agency–structure dichotomy. It moves beyond the structuralism of early deconstruction's undermining of the subject. To function as, to *be* subjects, we must enter into language. Yet language itself is a social structure, albeit a fluid, open one which is constantly (like the subject) in the process of transition and transformation. The speaking subject is a subject which is embedded in social structure, yet which acts on that structure, which is open and not fixed. This meshes with the insights of Giddens' theory of structuration, in which the empowering as well as the constraining aspects of social structure are emphasised, and the relation between agency and structure is dialectical.[32] In Unger's terms, social structures constitute the 'formative contexts' within which human consciousness and action take place, yet 'negative capability' entails that structures are constantly up for reassessment and transformation via political struggle.[33] Another important feature of this account of subjectivity is the role which it envisages for *imagination*, sometimes evoked among deconstructionists as the 'play of difference'. The positive aspect of this from a feminist point of view is the promise it holds out of further undermining the dichotomy between reason and emotion and, in contrast to the rationalist liberal conception of politics, the recapturing of a role for creativity, insight, feeling and imagination in political life.

As well as confronting the dangers presented by essentialist thinking in some forms of psychoanalytic theory, we need to advert to three further questions which might be thought to challenge the use of the conceptual framework sketched above. First, is it possible to develop a theory of the relational self which maintains a sufficient sense of distinctive selfhood to underpin not only the possibility of critical consciousness but also potential political and ethical claims to privacy and autonomy? Both Seyla Benhabib[34] and Iris Marion Young[35] have warned persuasively of feminists' too-ready acceptance of the dissolution of boundaries of selfhood in integrationist models of community which are potentially repressive of differences between subjects. For similar reasons, we prefer to use Virgina Held's terminology of the relational self[36] rather than the conception of inter-subjectivity. Certainly, we do not rule out the possibility of inter-subjective experience and consciousness in some areas of life. Nor, as a normative matter, do we want to deny the value of the kinds of empathy and mutuality which can be fostered by such consciousness. But we do think that its adoption as the central idea of what it is to be a subject would entail a dilution of the capacity for critical reflection, which implies capacity for distancing and differentiation from both other selves and social structures (including norms, conventions and practices). Such a dilution of subjectivity would be both threatening to radical politics and repressive of differences among women and other subjects.[37] The notion of the relational self, in contrast to both atomistic and inter-subjective selves, nicely captures our empirical and logical interdependence and the centrality to our identity of our relations with others and with practices and institutions, whilst retaining an idea of human uniqueness and discreteness as central to our sense of ourselves. It entails the collapse of any self/other or individual/community *dichotomy* without abandoning the idea of genuine agency and subjectivity.

Second, does a commitment to the dialectical notion of relational subjectivity derived from Hegel need to be accompanied by a recognition of the split between male and female aspects of identity which he took to be an implication of the argument? We reject any such implication. Nothing in the logic of the argument entails such a split, any more than it entails that other features of Hegel's philosophy must be accepted.[38] In emphasising the relational nature of *all* human subjectivity, we regard the feminist reading of the Hegelian tradition as potentially powerful in undermining the notion of the unified, rational subject which has been revealed by feminist social theorists as implicitly masculine.

Third, is it possible to defend the privileged position held by language in our view of subjectivity and of the agency/structure relationship? We need to clarify our view of this, given that the 'discursive' turn in social theory has been controversial. It has often been thought, and not without reason, that a focus on discourse as the object of social analysis and critique has led to an underplaying of the material aspects of social life, in particular oppressive power relations. This view assumes a strong division between the discursive and the material. This is just what theorists like Foucault have sought to undermine, by showing precisely the material implications, the *power* of discourse in human life.[39] On this view, disciplines such as law, psychiatry and medicine are seen as *normalising* and hence implicitly as *normative* discourses. By fixing subjects within their classifications, these sciences discipline us, exercise power over us, by labelling us good or bad, well or sick, sane or mad according to disciplinary 'régimes of truth'. In our view this kind of analysis is not only compatible with the kind of realist view of social structure which we shall argue for, but indeed helps to show the material reality of forms of power which have tended to be invisible to political theory. But in some forms the focus on discourse has been accompanied by an exaggerated, anti-realist view in which the intoxicating pleasure of analysing narratives and telling stories about stories seems to become an end in itself, detached from political critique which in any sense seeks to change the world.[40]

Our view of social structure is realist in the sense (to be elaborated below) that we regard structures, *including discourses*, as having material effects in the world. These effects are realised and manifested in discourse, but not exclusively so. The discourse of rape is not the same as or exhaustive of rape itself – its physical reality and the experiences of rapist and victim. The analysis of discourse has to be combined with the analysis of *practices*. Clearly, one can undermine this point by expanding the concept of discourse so as to include practically everything, in which case it loses any analytic hold. Obviously, we do not regard it as useful to collapse the experience of poverty, rape or lynching into discourse, although we recognise both their discursive elements and the power discourse has to promote and maintain material injustices. And though literary texts are certainly not politically or ethically irrelevant, we should never lose sight of the differences between literary and other kinds of interpretive project.[41]

Two important implications of the critique of the agency/structure dichotomy remain to be noted. First, whilst the argument so far has been at the level of social theory, we can once again see the way in which the theoretical argument opens certain possibilities at the substantive political level which seemed problematic within the framework of traditional political theory. The notion of the unified, rational self posited not only an ontological but a political problem about the relation between individual and society. This was most notable in its resonance with a strong dichotomy between autonomy and community at the evaluative level. Here, advocacy and ontology connect.[42] On the relational conception of subjectivity, autonomy can still claim its place as an important value, but our conception of autonomy is no longer of separateness in the sense of isolation. Rather we can see that autonomy (note the resonance with arguments about positive freedom) typically depends not only on background facilities and welfare levels but also on our relations with others. My autonomy depends not just on others' or the state's leaving me alone, but in others' acknowledgement of, respect for and support towards me, including my wishes for privacy in certain areas.

Second, the relational notion of subjectivity and the deconstruction of the agency/structure dichotomy opens political theory to the conceptual framework introduced in Chapter 1. It is here that the idea of *practice*, which captures the ways in which agents both act within and upon social structures, comes into its own as a central part of the conceptual apparatus of political theory. We have argued that practices, seen as value and meaning-generating, structured activities, roles and crafts, have to be central to any understanding of the political world which could accommodate questions of gender. Thus the extent to which the language of practice is voiced in communitarian political theory, notably that of MacIntyre, is one of the attractions of communitarian theory from a feminist point of view. As we saw in Chapter 5, however, without a reconstructed theory of the subject, MacIntyre's focus on value-generating practices is potentially conservative. Since it cannot account for the development of critical consciousness, practices are introduced only to be assessed on the basis of internally generated criteria, and this seems to be a recipe for uncritical rationalisation. This is precisely the defect which the post-structuralist account of the relation between agency and structure seeks to remedy.

Metaphysics and method

The constructionist debates within communitarianism about both human identity and value link up with fundamental debates in philosophy concerning 'realism' and 'constructivism'. These debates have themselves frequently been couched in terms of dichotomised oppositions. Of these, the supposed oppositions between 'realism' and 'anti-realism' and between 'objectivism' and 'relativism' or 'subjectivism' are of direct relevance to the liberal–communitarian debate. Whilst these questions look extremely abstract, we keep encountering them because they in fact have concrete implications for questions of political theory. Furthermore, they tie up with questions about the proper method for social and political theory, and in particular questions about the relationship between descriptive, prescriptive and 'interpretive' aspects of the political theoretical enterprise. We therefore need to address these questions, clarifying what is meant by the terms involved and, in doing so, to assess the extent to which the realism/anti-realism, objectivism/relativism dichotomies present us with a false dilemma.

In principle we can distinguish here between questions of *ontology*, of what is in the world and its status, and of *epistemology* – how we can come to know about it, and the status of our claims to knowledge or access to truth. As we saw in Chapter 1, in social science, the empiricist stance which was dominant for many years was often associated with a common-sensical ontological realism. Empiricism is *realist*, in other words, in that it assumes that there is something 'out there' whose existence is independent of our beliefs about it, and that the facts are objective.[43] In social science, this objectivism has all too often gone hand in hand with a relatively uncritical approach to questions of gender, class, racial or ethnic division. The empiricist focuses on these so-called 'facts of the matter', and not on the role of discourse and practice in the political *construction* of either these facts or other features of social organisation. Conversely, the opposite ontological pole to realism – the *anti-realist* view that nothing in the world is independent of agents' beliefs or experience – seems even more unlikely to generate the kind of critical analysis demanded by feminism. For on this approach, sometimes known as *phenomenology*, subjects and their linguistic usage become authoritative: the discourse of biologically-based racial superiority, of the contented housewife, of the happy slave, are invulnerable to critique. If the agent's viewpoint is the ultimate arbiter of 'reality', there is no space for any account of false consciousness, nor any basis for critical political discourse in general.[44]

Even if one is a realist at the ontological level, however, one *could* be an epistemological *interpretivist*. In other words, one might argue that since knowledge is mediated by language, which is irreducibly open-textured and itself an outcome of configurations of power, our knowledge of the real world is inevitably interpretive and provisional rather than straightforwardly representational. This has implications for the divide between description and prescription. To the extent that we move to an interpretivist methodology, we muddy the clear distinction between fact and value on which empiricist social science has relied.[45] It is this relationship between epistemological interpretivism and certain kinds of ontological realism which is particularly important to the liberal–communitarian debate. In Chapters 4 and 5, we showed that communitarian constructionism goes hand in hand with a rejection of the 'Cartesian anxiety' that once we let go of *universalism* and *objectivism* – the ideas that there are facts of the matter existing independently of agents' viewpoints, and that they can in principle be known – the world will collapse into the chaos of *subjectivism* or *relativism*, in which anybody's view of moral, political or even empirical questions is as valid as anyone else's, or in which knowledge and truth are taken to be contingent upon agents' situation and perspective. The possibility of interpretivism seems to transcend the universalism/subjectivism dichotomy. It embraces the insight that there is no 'Archimedean point' from which a detached observer can come to a 'True' appreciation of justice or the good for human beings, that human consciousness and subjectivity are both embodied and socially situated, and that these contexts – including linguistic structures – affect the ways in which we see the world.[46] On the other hand, by locating, or 'grounding' social judgement in context – in social structure, in language, in practices, traditions, conventions – interpretivism seemed to escape the agency/structure dichotomy and the threat of the complete subjectivism which would render meaningful political or ethical debate impossible.

As we saw in Chapter 5, however, the 'grounding' of interpretivism in 'community practices' could be seen as the Achilles Heel of much communitarian thought. For it seemed to commit communitarianism to conventionalism and hence to conservatism. Much the same could be said for the position of liberals like Rawls and Dworkin to the extent that they have moved in a communitarian direction on this point.[47] The central problem here is an anxiety that an interpretivist approach is not genuinely distinct from subjectivism. On an interpretivist position, do we lose the very sense of an ethical or political argument, as distinct from an argument about taste or the expression of any unreflective feeling? Related to this is a second fear, about the extent to which the deconstructive techniques used as part of the interpretivist methodology we have been employing can be associated with critique only in a negative sense. The fact that both interpretation and deconstruction are firmly grounded in the world we inhabit precludes them, it could be argued, from generating the kind of reconstructive, positive and even utopian politics which radical political movements such as feminism must seek to develop.[48] How can mere interpretation of a solidly sexist culture generate transformative politics? In the light of these difficulties, it is not surprising to find an interpretivist theorist like Taylor reaching for universalist props in his later work, or to find that the criteria of undistorted communication and of rationality presupposed by Habermas's communicative ethics has a special status not entirely determined by the outcome of the dialogue itself.[49]

We shall return in a moment to consider the potential of such sophisticated accounts. Before doing so, however, we want to consider the more radical position which combines epistemological with ontological anti-realism. The epistemological issues arising out of a commitment to interpretivism (sometimes referred to as 'contextualism') have had more of an airing in contemporary political and social theory than have the ontological questions. But the ontological and epistemological are not unconnected. If we take up an ontologically anti-realist, phenomenological position, that is, if we give up the idea that the world (social or physical) consists in things which are waiting 'out there' to be discovered and represented in human discourse, then inevitably we believe that knowledge and truth are human constructs. On a radically anti-realist position, the divide between description and evaluation is not muddied so much as collapsed. Indeed the notion of description seems to make no sense, and even the idea of knowledge as interpretive seems opaque: what, after all, is being interpreted?[50]

We want to make it very clear at this stage that there is a distinction between the radically anti-realist ontological position which entails the kind of epistemological pragmatism espoused by Rorty and the interpretivist position which is combined with some degree of realism or openness to the possibility of realism at the ontological level. This is because although we are not ethical realists (at least as traditionally understood), we do want to defend a particular kind of realist position (we shall call it 'modified realism') with respect to social structure and social relations. We want, in other words, to affirm a commitment to interpretivism and to resist Rorty's suggestions that we should simply accept that ethical, political and aesthetic judgements are all of a type, and that meaningful political debate across competing vocabularies is impossible.[51]

We reject Rorty's radical post-modernist pragmatism for two main reasons. In the first place, whilst he denies that it implies the inaptness of ethical commitment or discourse, he embraces, as Lovibond has shown, the implication that the status in point of legitimacy of, say, a feminist argument against sexual harassment or an anti-racist argument against slavery is just the same as that of the fascist argument for persecution of Jewish people or the mentally handicapped. Each simply competes for attention in the cacophony of human discourse.[52] This seems to us an unacceptably reductionist view. Second, Rorty's radical ontological anti-realism conflicts with what we regard as a fundamental tenet of feminist politics: the commitment to exposing, analysing and struggling against the *social reality* of women's oppression and that of other powerless and dominated groups. As we shall argue, once we give up the notion of the social reality of women's oppression (including its ideal and discursive aspects), the basis for feminist politics has been undermined, as has that for any other radical political discourse.

To state the difficulties of Rorty's position, of course, is far easier than arguing for the alternative, for his view has all the beauty of a simple argument pushed to its logical extreme. Other theorists who have tried to preserve the idea of 'strong evaluation' as opposed to mere expressivism have tended to do so in terms of limited but significant appeals back to values which transcend particular historical or cultural contexts. Notable examples include Taylor's universal criteria of error and incoherence, already discussed in Chapter 5[53]; Dworkin's 'right to equal respect and concern' and the notion that the 'communities of principle' which recognise that basic right for all their members enjoy an 'integrity' – an idea which has connotations of both procedural consistency and substantive, moral coherence[54]; Habermas's criteria of rationality and undistorted communication[55]; and many writers' commitment to the idea that certain human needs which claim our moral attention transcend particular contexts or can be said to be universal at any particular point in history.[56]

Whilst some of these approaches are undoubtedly more promising than others, we do think that an appeal to certain framework features of the human condition is both defensible and important to the ultimate deconstruction of the objectivism/relativism dichotomy. Clearly, both the persistent needs arising from technically contingent but historically persistent features of human life and the moral and political claims which they generate are open to socially specific *interpretation*. The contemporary state of social scientific, psychoanalytic and other understandings of human nature, as well as prevailing moral and political doctrines, are central to how human needs are understood. But this is not to say that the need for food, shelter or love are entirely constructed, in the sense which radical pragmatism would suggest.[57] Material and discursive products of socialisation or culture though they may be, hunger, unhappiness, loneliness, alienation, marginalisation are real, and their reality claims our moral and political attention. Unfortunately, in the literature we have referred to, these 'transcendent' features are all too often only briefly sketched, and the question of their grounding and status all but ignored. But this does not mean that such a task is beyond the scope of political theory: indeed, it might well be regarded as one of its most pressing projects.

Furthermore, whilst we accept the basic elements of Rorty's thesis that the substance of ethics is historically and culturally contingent, we would argue that his own insight entails that, within modernity conceived as a tradition, only certain kinds of arguments count as moral arguments in the first place.[58] In other words, we should, as Waldron suggests, take some aspects of the 'communitarian' (we would prefer to say 'constructionist') argument more seriously than do some of its proponents, by acknowledging that 'our' tradition includes a certain commitment to critical re-evaluation as a distinctively ethical stance.[59] In this world, an argument which is to count as a genuine contribution to ethical or political debate must be one in which both the relational and reflective subjectivity of every human being is fully recognised in terms of a claim to our attention and respect. This framework idea of the modern world (let us call it the primacy of critique) constitutes only a benchmark and includes diversity of possible views. But it serves to rule out others, albeit that it is itself subject to debate and interpretation. If the transition from modernity to post-modernity is one which entails the abandonment of this conception (a view which we doubt that Rorty really wants to defend), then we decisively do not embrace post-modernism.

Notwithstanding the fact that his avowed project is to deny the need for these kinds of second-order debates within philosophy, one of the great merits of Rorty's radical pragmatism is precisely that it makes their relevance to political theory clear. Thus the paradox that Rorty's 'pragmatic' rejection of metaphysics has led to so much metaphysical debate is only an apparent one. (The real paradox of radical scepticism such as Rorty's lies rather in its implicit subscription to the idea that only the truths based on metaphysical meta-narratives are indeed 'real' 'Truths'.[60]) But it continues to be difficult to elucidate these issues, for three main reasons. In the first place, they are not articulated by many of the participants in the debate. Second, the realism/anti-realism dichotomy encompasses a diversity of issues. Within the broad categories of ontology and epistemology, we can identify a number of more specific questions on which the views of the writers need to be located: realism versus anti-realism in values, and in the social and natural worlds: realist, interpretivist and constructionist positions in ethics, social and natural sciences. In Rorty the embrace of constructionism is wholehearted and radical: the contingency of the world, as well as of knowledge, identity and politics is celebrated in a thoroughly 'post-modernist' manner. In others, notably MacIntyre and Walzer, the rejection of realism is more ambiguous, and acceptance of the view that we cannot have pre-interpretive access to reality has led rather to a form of conventionalism which roots identity, meaning and value in traditions and practices which themselves become in some sense 'reified'. Like most characterisations, this is not an absolute divide: post-modernists too depend on practices to generate meaning.

Third, the very notion of realism is ambiguous. On one view, realism adverts to the idea of truth – as a matter of *logic*, the claim that something is real is a truth claim about a proposition.

On a second, realism may be understood in terms of causal efficacy – the claim, for example, that class or gender structures are real means that they cause consequences which are felt in our experience. And in a third version, realism may be understood in terms of claims about the independent existence of what is referred to. Here, too, ambiguity re-emerges. Whilst it seems perfectly clear what is meant by the claim that a table or chair or indeed another person exists 'independently of us', can the same be said of such 'material' things as our hearts or livers? And what of human practices? Furthermore, it may be questioned whether the first and third sense of realism are actually distinct from each other. The logic of a truth claim could be argued to entail something about the state of an independently existing world.

We want to set out our own position on these matters and in doing so to make a final clarification of a key methodological question in the communitarian–liberal debate – the relationship between ontology and advocacy.[61] What, if any, is the relationship between metaphysics and political and social theory? And, if there is a relationship, what position do we take on metaphysical issues? On the first point, we do consider that political theory and indeed political practice (we would want to emphasise the close relationship between the two) presuppose a metaphysics, that is, that they imply a position on a range of ontological and epistemological questions which are not necessarily articulated by the political theory itself.[62] On this our view differs markedly from that of Rawls or Rorty. But to think that political and social theory in fact assume positions in metaphysics is not to say that political and social theorists should spend much of their time doing metaphysics, let alone become preoccupied by second-order arguments. Nor is it to suppose that metaphysics *determines* the shape of any particular political theory. It is rather to argue that political and social theorists must be astute to the assumptions they are making and hence to the possibility that specific disputes or misunderstandings in political theory *may* relate to differences at a metaphysical level. It is also to aver that metaphysical assumptions provide a *framework* within which political views are developed. This entails that onotological assumptions have *some* influence in shaping political arguments, albeit not decisive influence.

In the specific context of the liberal–communitarian debate, we would acknowledge that it is logically possible, as Taylor points out, to be an ontological holist and a political individualist.[63] For example, one might envisage a world in which the challenge to identity posed by ontological inter-subjectivity is kept at bay by the institutionalisation of individual rights. It would also be possible, conversely, to be an ontological atomist and a political collectivist. For example, one might believe that only publicly oriented politics can enable 'human' atoms to coexist. This would conduce to the kind of view Sandel refers to as 'instrumental communitarianism'.[64] Much of our argument in Chapter 5 is devoted to showing that ontologically holist communitarians may turn out to be either conservative or socialist in their political orientation. But we do argue that *as a matter of the interpretation of contemporary debates in political theory* an ontologically atomistic view of humanity has fed into an influential form of political individualism in the shape of contemporary American liberalism, with its focus on individual rights, negative freedom and a lack of focus on public goods and collective life.

We now turn to the metaphysical question itself. On this, as far as the terrain of the social sciences is concerned, we take up a modified realist position in the second and, possibly, the third of the senses outlined above. In other words, it is an important assumption of our argument that women's oppression, and particular aspects of it such as the hierarchically-gendered division of labour and sexual harassment, are 'real' in the sense that they cause consequences which are the objects of our experience. We also want to leave room for the idea that certain human needs or interests, flowing from and contingent upon aspects of embodied existence, can sensibly be said to be 'real', albeit that their precise shape and hence the appropriate means of satisfying them are open to human interpretation. Furthermore, there is certainly a sense in which aspects of gender are socially real in that they exist independently of us. We have already noted the ambiguity of the idea of 'independence of us' even in the context of organs of the body. The ambiguity deepens when we think about the subject matter of social science, that is, human practices. Clearly, human practices do not exist independently 'of us' in the sense of 'independently of human beings', yet they do exist independently of any particular person, who may or may not be a participant in those practices. The ideas of dependence and independence seem to present us with an unnecessarily rigid dichotomy here. Similarly, we would argue that systems of moral or political values have a reality in the senses both of having causal effects in the world and as existing *within* and as part of human practices. Thus whilst we do not hold a realist position in terms of making appeals to any 'objective' regime of truth which transcends particular human contexts, we certainly do believe that it makes sense to speak of 'social reality' and of systems of values as aspects of the social world.

Finally, the question of fact and value and the parallel opposition between description and prescription requires attention. We drew on this distinction in our analysis and critique of communitarianism: we argued that communitarians sometimes make an illicit inference from the facts of the matter – how a society or tradition *is* – to an *evaluation* of its worth. We suggested that communitarianism was particularly defective in its ability to speak evaluatively or prescriptively. Yet we also acknowledged that the description/prescription divide is problematic, and that it is blurred by the adoption of interpretivist methodology – a method with which we are sympathetic. To see why interpretivism does not entail that there is no difference at all between description and prescription we need to unravel some distinct sources of dissatisfaction which often get lumped together. An important theme in much critical theoretical work in the social sciences and elsewhere has been the problematic nature of any simple idea of description. We have already rehearsed the reasons for this. In some areas, it is the very idea of the *existence* of a 'fact of the matter' which is in question. In others, it is the question of our *access* to such facts, particularly in the light of the critique of the idea of language as representational. On the interpretive view, any linguistic 'description' is already an interpretation – it *gives* rather than merely *finds* meaning. But to say that such description is selective and interpretive is not the same as saying that it is *prescriptive* in a strong sense. Our descriptive or explanatory utterances do reflect an interpretive framework which helps us to make sense of the world, although they do not advocate particular practical measures.

Critical dissatisfaction with a distinct idea of *prescription* rests on a somewhat different foundation. Here most of the argument has concerned the *basis* for prescription, and in particular the idea that normative utterances can be universally valid or 'objective'; that they can 'speak from nowhere'.[65] On a thoroughly sceptical view, ethical utterances are just reports of emotions or 'subjective' opinions, and hence collapse into either 'descriptive' statements about 'how the speaker sees the world' or expressions of emotion. Certainly, the rejection of the idea of an objective basis for prescription, like the interpretive theory of language, undermines the notion of a reified *dichotomy* between description and prescription. It allows for certain continuities between them, and for the idea of statements which combine descriptive and prescriptive aspects. What these arguments do not undermine, however, is the idea that description and prescription are importantly different as *stances*, that whilst composite statements are common, particularly in political discourse, one can ultimately unpick the aspect of a statement which offers an *analysis* or *explanation* of how aspects of the world work or are from that which offers an *assessment* of that state of affairs. We want to insist upon this difference not least because we think that it is of fundamental *political* importance. This is implicit in our realist position on social structures such as women's subordination, racism and class hierarchy.

Reconstructing political theory

In the last two sections, our analysis of certain underlying issues has revealed the ways in which dichotomised thinking has over-simplified the liberal–communitarian debate and presented us with an unnecessarily circumscribed set of political theoretical options. It has also helped us to see the extent to which the liberal–communitarian debate is itself fragmented and plural. It is, of course, important to look at the liberal–communitarian debate as a cultural phenomenon whose significance is not exhausted by a stage-by-stage analysis of its central elements. But this is not a substitute for a detailed focus on the specific underlying issues we have identified.

We have now located the liberal–communitarian debate both as a cultural phenomenon and within the fundamental questions of social theory which form an important part of its intellectual context. It remains for us to explain how an application of the insights of feminist critique and the techniques of modern social theory can help us to develop a more satisfactory approach to political theory than that offered by those who identify themselves as either liberals or communitarians. We shall sketch what amounts to a post-liberal, post-structuralist conception of political theory. In doing so we do not start with a blank sheet. Our approach draws upon and coheres in important respects with the work of a number of writers, several of them associated with communitarianism.[66] In this section we offer a brief characterisation of our own position and consider a number of possible objections to it.

We start from a basic political commitment to equality and the absence of oppression. By *equality* we mean not merely formal equality or even equality of material resources, but rather a commitment to the idea that substantial differences in levels of power and well-being themselves raise central issues of social justice wherever their correction is within the ambit of collective effort or social policy. The core idea which dictates this broad approach to equality is a commitment to the view that each person's welfare, encompassing their autonomy conceived in a positive way,[67] is of equal concern in the ordering of our political life. It is consistent with the view, which we have argued to be important to dismantling the objectivism/relativism dichotomy, that certain human needs generate claims to our moral and political attention which transcend particular human contexts. Meeting, to an adequate degree, (the criteria of 'adequacy' would include but not be exhausted by standards of fairness in the division of available resources) human needs for food, shelter, nurturance, education, leisure, companionship, self-esteem, interpreted on the basis of current sociological, scientific and psychological understandings of what human beings are like, can plausibly be argued to be central to the substantial ideal of equality.

The ideal of substantial equality entails that politics, broadly conceived as 'the critical activity of raising issues and deciding how institutional and social relations should be organized',[68] is about the positive empowerment of citizens as well as about the negative respect for their freedom and privacy. On this view, women's double burden of labour inherent in current social arrangements, like the disempowering impact of sexual harassment in the workplace, raise genuinely *political* questions about inequality. One aspect, then, of the ideal of equality is a cardinal conception – a commitment to equality entails the adequate meeting of what are conceived as fundamentally important human interests and needs. However, we also need to focus on ordinal equality, the absence of very great differences in distributions of power, resources and levels of well-being which, given the degree to which our identity is constituted in terms of our relations with others and with social structures, are likely to be central to our sense of our own worth.[69] Institutionally, the commitment to equality issues in a concomitant commitment to a form of welfare state which would express a meaningful conception of egalitarian citizenship and help to provide the concrete conditions necessary for such citizenship to be realised.[70] These normative commitments, of course, raise a number of complex economic and social issues: how can a society create the wealth needed to maintain the decent levels of welfare to which it aspires; and how can political processes be designed effectively to nudge an inegalitarian, disintegrated society closer to an egalitarian one? These, too, would have to be central to a reconstructed political theory rooted, as we have argued political theory must be, in the sociologically astute analysis of human practices and discourses.

We conceive *oppression* in terms of structural social and political disadvantage for which some person, persons or (in principle) identifiable practices are responsible. This kind of structural disadvantage is one of the things which modern liberal theory is badly equipped to identify. As we have argued, the decisive impact of oppression on the welfare levels and quality of citizenship attained by members of particular, relatively stable groups in modern societies marks this liberal myopia out as a significant failing. And a focus on the idea of oppression has several further recommendations. It enables us to escape the constraints of the 'distributive paradigm' – not every political evil can be reduced to a matter of unjust distribution or corrected by redistribution, because social injustice inheres in ongoing social *processes* which are themselves in need of critical scrutiny and correction.[71] The redistribution of jobs in, say, manufacturing industries equally to women and men, for example, will not secure political justice, for it addresses a symptom rather than a cause. The processes which constructed a gendered division of labour will reproduce the original distribution if they are not themselves confronted. These influential processes inhere in a variety of powerful discourses and practices which in turn constitute a distinctive and constraining social structure.

This analysis allows us to see the power of social structure without portraying it as monolithic or, even more importantly, as beyond the sphere of human agency and hence of political responsibility. Thus the resolution of the political injustices which social structures generate depends on their being addressed in political action and critique in a range of 'publics' which stretch well beyond the sphere of the state. Policies which focus on the redistribution of resources are similarly inapt in addressing problems of sexual violence or the voicelessness that comes not just from under-representation of women in particular contexts but also the lower value or audibility of women's voices in contexts where we are present. As we shall see, the concept of oppression can accommodate the variety and specificity of different sources and types of social injustice in modern societies, a variety which calls for differentiated modes of analysis and political responses.

A focus on oppression, then, suggests the need for a commitment to a political framework and a political practice which give a central place to dialogue and the ongoing democratic involvement of members of the political community. For only within such a framework is there any hope that the power relations which are an inevitable feature of any society will be adequately negotiated and scrutinised. This kind of approach has sometimes been called '*dialogic communitarianism*'.[72] We shall now move on to look at the features of this approach in more detail, and to consider possible objections to our position.

Power and oppression
We have already argued that the main substantive component of an adequate political theory – one which is equally lacking in liberal and communitarian arguments – is a theory of power. In her recent work, Iris Marion Young has argued for a political theory based not on primarily distributional conceptions of social justice but on a sophisticated notion of oppression and domination, conceived in terms of five aspects: exploitation, marginalisation, powerlessness, cultural imperialism and violence.[73] Young shows how the pervasive assumption in political theory that the fundamental problems of social injustice have to do with unjust distributions of social goods continually misses the boat by ignoring the more fundamental problems about the decision-making and other institutional processes which generate the unjust outcomes on which political theory focuses. She argues that we should rather focus on the idea of oppression, with the five discrete aspects mentioned above. Along each of these dimensions, social practices continually and structurally reproduce the unjust distributions which liberal governments vainly try to correct via welfare, educational or other policies, and which represent the symptom rather than the main cause of social injustice. The commitment to equality entails, of course, that we must attend to the fact that in actual societies unequal outcomes are themselves powerful in reproducing those injustices in many areas.[74]

As we noted in Chapter 1, an adequate theory of power must accommodate the ways in which power inheres in practices and discourses such as law, education, psychiatry, which are socially pervasive. The traditionally exclusive focus on power as 'sovereignty' or as 'property', as something which is 'held' or 'exercised' by those with authority, typically by government, has contributed to the myopia of political theory by blinding it to the pervasiveness of powerful discourses in every area of social life. However, we do not share the view expressed by Young among others that it is inappropriate to speak of power as something which can be the object of (re)distribution.[75] We recognise the importance of conceiving power as inhering in discourses and practices. In Chapter 1 we called this the 'structural' conception, but our subsequent argument would suggest it should be reconceptualised as the 'practice' conception so as to mark up the relevance of agency and hence the possibility of political responsibility in these as well as in 'property' arenas of power. Conceived in this way, power is clearly not susceptible of analysis as a 'thing' to be distributed. But we think that it is possible to incorporate in our analysis both 'property' and 'practice' conceptions of power. Certainly, it is the case that many social policies for which feminists have campaigned have as both an effect and an object *changes in power relations.*

For example, the proscription of marital rape incontrovertibly (albeit only moderately) changes the distribution of power between wife and husband, in that the proscription constitutes a necessary albeit not sufficient condition for her to invoke a particular form of state protection. When combined with other social and legal policies such as the provision of adequate refuges for abused women, powers to remove abusing husbands from a shared home and adequate provisions for financial support, a woman's situation following the abolition of the marital rape exemption is certainly to be described as *more powerful* than it was beforehand. Exactly the same could be said about the extension of suffrage and the opening of formerly exclusively male occupations to women. It is also the case that discursive changes such as those which have marked the transition from the social construction of certain forms of behaviour as 'chivalry' to their construction as 'sexual harassment' have the effect of changing power relations. Whilst the goal of equalising power may generally be an unfeasible political strategy, the ideal of relatively equal power in many areas of life strikes us as a valuable and indeed central feminist, anti-racist and socialist ideal. To recognise this need not, as Young fears, entail a lack of focus on the ways in which the powerful enact and reproduce their power. We recognise that power exists in action but we do not accept that power exists *only* in action. Indeed, we think that in this respect Young's position is internally inconsistent: her focus on powerlessness as a form of oppression implies a concern with the distribution of power, and hence the inadequacy of an exclusively Foucaultian conception of power.

The idea of power as inhering in discourses and practices means that the pervasiveness of power is inevitable: the relevant political ideal would therefore seem to be the just arrangement of all forms of social power. The practice conception, however, presents a deep challenge for the political theorist. For since it identifies the operations of power literally everywhere, it opens up wide-ranging normative questions about the justification of power as well as complex institutional and sociological questions about the legitimation of power.[76] This leaves to the political theorist the task of conceiving of political processes adequate to the recognition and democratisation of power. It also raises questions about the implications of the ubiquity and inevitability of power for a political critique which aspires to be reconstructive. We think that these challenges can be confronted successfully, however, if we read the practice conception of power through a critical theory of oppression and a substantive theory of equality. For by doing so we can generate a manageable conception of the focus of political theoretical critique. Hence we can argue that where power is used to exploit, to marginalise, to do violence, to deprive of a voice, to violate the autonomy of citizens, or to create or perpetuate avoidable inequalities, it is susceptible of political critique.

But we should also note that, contrary to the view which often seems to be assumed, power is not an inevitably negative political phenomenon. 'Sovereignty' or 'property' power such as that held by a government minister, youth worker, employer, mother or anyone who finds themselves in a position of authority can be used in productive, 'empowering', legitimate ways. Similarly, particular practices and discourses such as psychotherapy, mothering, education, the administration of welfare can be positively empowering, legitimate, democratic. Whilst power is always open to abuse and always calls for justification, it is an essential means of social coordination and hence of the realisation of valued political goals such as equality, the dismantling of subordination, the provision of decent levels of welfare.[77]

One useful way of thinking about this is in terms of the idea of 'power with' as opposed to 'power over'. Although the operation or exercise of power inevitably reduces the freedom of some, where it operates within democratically endorsed and accountable practices to achieve ends or realise goods to which the polity or the relevant group has collectively subscribed, power is used in a substantial sense in the interests of all and hence constitutes 'power with' as opposed to merely 'power over'.[78] On this conception, power can be thought of as a vital social resource whose creation, allocation and management in the service of the social good is the primary concern of democratic politics. The development of democratic structures, a variety of 'civic public' consultative and deliberative processes, and genuinely empowering rather than dependency-fostering welfare agencies is, on this view, the means by which the exercise and practice of 'power with' may gradually be realised.

We should note one final implication of the idea of power as inhering in practices and discourses. This is that it renders inappropriate the liberal conception of public and private spheres, and suggests that every area of social life must be opened up to political critique. This fits well with both the feminist critique of public/private dichotomies and the view that in the modern world of corporate power and the interpenetration of public and private spheres the political realm can no longer be seen merely in terms of the state. It also gives us a further critical perspective on the liberal construction of *absence* of power – negative freedom – as both a possibility and an ideal. The construction of the liberal public/private distinction does not entail either the automatic legitimacy of state intervention in the 'private' or the abandonment of the idea of a sphere in which subjects can legitimately claim the right to keep others out. It rather generates a broader conception of the political, which must bring with it reconstructed political institutions. It entails the need for a variety of public but not exclusively or even mainly state-sponsored forums which allow for genuine involvement in self-government without being unrealistically time-consuming and without entailing that we must all live our lives primarily as *citizens*.[79] On this view, not just central and local government but also representative or participatory workplace organisation, pressure groups and a whole range of other institutions and benefits (such as welfare benefits, legal aid, rules about office hours) designed to facilitate directly or indirectly people's access to deliberation and decision-making about the organisation of the social order would become central to our conception of the political and hence to political theory.

Only once political theorists have absorbed the implications of arguments about the pervasiveness of power and hence of questions of legitimacy, about the extension of the political beyond the state, and about the way power inheres in structures and practices rather than merely in individual persons or person-like institutions, will the kinds of problems our feminist critique of liberal and communitarian theories revealed be overcome. Deconstruction of the individual-society dichotomy shows us how power is exercised through social practices – it infuses our lives rather than staying in manageable locations where we can reify, identify and control it. By espousing a partial theory of power or by failing to have one altogether, political theorists have disabled themselves from producing theories which could genuinely cast light on pervasively unequal distributions of social goods, and on the persistence of powerlessness and marginalisation for certain social groups. To include the notion of a social group as a tool of political theoretical analysis is, positively, to recognise that our social positions, our identities, the operations of power on us, are largely determined not just by our actions as 'individuals', but by our social relations and locations, which will, of course, be multiple and shifting. Only by placing the relevance of different kinds of social groups and group membership, including questions of power and access to that membership, at the core of political theory can we properly acknowledge the importance of group membership in the constitution of human identity, and recognise and attend to the question of social justice raised by group-based patterns of disadvantage.

Furthermore, the accommodation of the idea of social groups brings with it a richer set of possibilities for the reconstruction of a realistic ideal of participative, active citizenship, for it is likely to be as members of groups rather than as individuals that our participation in the varied civic public forums mentioned above can give us access to genuinely political power. We would deny that to draw on the idea of a social group in political theory is inevitably to participate in an essentialising or repressive move. Nor would we accept that it assumes a homogeneous and stable social profile. A welter of different kinds of group membership, central to citizens' identity, shifting over time, is what needs to be envisaged. To recognise the relational self and the incoherence of any rigid public/private divide need not, and should not, amount to an uncritical embrace of intersubjectivity or the assumption of a static, homogeneous community which would be repressive of difference. What the expanded conception of the political allows us to do is to embrace as instances of genuinely political participation activities of people in the roles and groups which make up their identity – as workers, students, members of pressure groups, members of living units such as families. This helps us to escape both from an unduly narrow conception of citizenship and from the spectre of an oppressive or unrealistic expansion of citizenship responsibilities tied to direct participation in the processes of central government.

In other words, we need to take the powerful practices of the variety of meaning-generating geographical, functional and cultural groups or 'communities' discussed in Chapter 5 to the heart of political theory. Certainly, this does not imply a political primacy for questions arising for social groupings based on gender. Rather, the kind of political structure which we have argued that this reconstructed political theory could help to develop would facilitate the political expression of views and demands based on other aspects of social situation – class, race, age, ethnicity – associated with oppression and inequality. Indeed, many of the arguments for 'dialogic communitarianism', made in this book from a feminist perspective, could equally have been made from an anti-racist or socialist perspective. These critical perspectives interact in a potentially transformative way in terms of the radical implications they have for the critique of political theory and practice.[80]

Subject, society and practice

We have argued that a post-liberal, post-structuralist political theory must engage in a sociologically informed and critical study of a wide range of human practices and discourses. In order to do so, it must have the conceptual tools to illuminate the relationship of subjects to social structures. In other words, it must draw on both sociological knowledge and social theory. In terms of an adequate theory of the subject, we have already argued for the attractions of what we have called the 'relational theory of the self', which draws upon both the Hegelian tradition in philosophy and psychoanalytic insights into the achievement of subjectivity. By deconstructing the agency/structure dichotomy, we were able to see that the situated subject need not be an engulfed, acritical, non-reflective subject. The moments of self-consciousness which the relational conception of the self describes already express the duality of the subject: in recognising itself through its relation to others, it embraces both connection and separation, and retains the potential for a reflective and critical stance towards itself and the world it encounters. Doubtless the fragmentation of subjectivity can and does cause problems for all of us at particular times, but we can also sense our ability to hold multiple and even conflicting views and interpretations of particular events or aspects of our lives without total disintegration. This should make us suspicious of the strong assumption made in much (both liberal and communitarian) political theory of the essential *unity* of subjectivity. Whilst a baseline of coherence is probably necessary to stay more or less sane, most people's experience of themselves is not of stable coherence but rather of not just interpersonal but also *intrapersonal* dialogue.[81]

In Chapter 5 we considered the argument that the ideal of community participated in the 'logic of identity', the authoritarian assumption that persons or practices can be reduced to a unity, which inevitably represses difference.[82] One aspect of this argument was the suggestion that an emphasis on inter-subjectivity presupposes a naive view not only of how transparent we can be to one another but also, more fundamentally, of how transparent we are to ourselves.[83] Once we recognise the complexity of human subjectivity – the way in which we can hold multiple commitments, relationships, views, desires and roles together without collapsing under the weight of incoherence – the idea of the unitary subject becomes less plausible, just as the ideal of the unitary subject becomes less attractive. Conversely, the spectre of the fragmented subject becomes less frightening.[84] In terms of a revised conception of subjectivity, then, three points emerge as crucial. First, the relational account of the subject allows for the existence of critical reflection, including reflection on one's self and identity. Second, the multiple and fragmented experience, consciousness and, to some extent, identity which comes from the situated conception of the self is revealed as something which we can and do accept without paralysis, insanity or disintegration. Third, even in areas of experience where particular structures are dominant and hence where the possibility of determinism seems to threaten, the relational subject can achieve a degree of critical purchase because of the openness, not only of language but hence of other structures, revealed by deconstruction. Even, that is, where power seems at its most monolithic, the very language in which that power is exercised or justified contains the echoes of what might have been or what could yet be. The possibility of transformative politics is never closed off.

The idea of the self as relational refers, of course, not only to relations with other subjects but also to the subject's relationship to society. As we saw in Chapter 5, communitarian writers often seem either to evoke an extraordinarily homogeneous conception of community or 'culture' as the context in which identity and value are created, or to be exceedingly vague about just what is intended by references to 'community'. In what has been justly dubbed the romantic vein in communitarian thought, notions of 'shared under-standings', 'traditions' and 'overlapping consensus' are referred to as if they reflected an unproblematic view of human society. However, we have moved on from the small, homogeneous, stable communities evoked (selectively) by MacIntyre, and any return to them seems not only unrealistically romantic but also powerfully unattractive given the repressive implications of life in unitary value-generating communities.

As we have seen, not all communitarians share the pre-modern fantasy of *Gemeinschaft*. To different extents and in different ways, many of them envision a more complex and diverse social sphere, one which provides a useful model for post-liberal, post-structuralist theory. Walzer, for example, sees society in terms of a number of coexisting distributive spheres, each generating its own criteria of membership, distribution, excellence and so on. Notwithstanding some signs in his work of a tendency to resurrect the idea of an overarching community which is in some strong sense homogeneous, his principle of non-domination between spheres is premissed on the recognition that people do live their lives across distributive spheres within the wider geo-political communities which characterise the modern world.

Both common sense experience and sociological interpretation tell us that modern societies are made up of multiple 'communities-within-communities' – practices, crafts, roles, traditions, discourses, languages – all of which generate meanings, evaluations, norms, expectations and so on. This cultural heterogeneity has been under-emphasised by communitarians because of its inconsistency with the cosy, pre-modern conception of community from which the *ideal* of community gets much of its rhetorical force, and because of fears about a multiplicity of meaning-generating communities leading to fragmentation and incoherence in the communitarian picture of the world. Of course, this kind of fragmentation is indeed a threat to social order if it is thought to entail that there is simply no way of making sense of ourselves, of reconciling our differences, of living peaceably together. But, at a sociological level, this kind of fragmentation is precisely what we are confronted with in the modern (or perhaps post-modern) world, and the great political challenge we face is to learn how to manage it in ways which do not deny our interdependence, repress difference or seek stability via the institutionalisation of unjust inequality in ways which construct such inequality as 'normal' or 'natural'.

The revised conception of community, then, like that of subjectivity, must embrace rather than suppress diversity and fragmentation. Indeed, what this amounts to is not so much a conception of community but rather a social ontology which emphasises the role of linguistic and other interpretive, meaning-generating communities within broader societies, and their role in the constitution of subjectivity. How does this social ontology help us to theorise gender? It directs our attention to a range of communities – workplaces, families, consciousness-raising groups – organised on a variety of lines – geographical, evaluative, relational, functional. And it reveals the relevance of a multiplicity of practices – paid and unpaid work of many kinds, including child-rearing, the reading of novels and poems, watching television and films, participating in many different political, cultural and aesthetic activities. Life in society generates multi-layered consciousness, but critically reflective subjects are capable of, and do, to different degrees, think about, rationalise, and compare notes among their many experiences. Some of these aspects of consciousness will be relatively stable across many of the communities and practices in which they live their lives. In a society in which gender is a significant category of social differentiation, gender itself will generate powerful discourses and will be a feature of all the practices in which subjects participate. In such a society, a woman will have a relatively continuous experience (albeit one which is affected by other aspects of her position such as her race, class or work situation) of the ways in which her femaleness affects her place in various communities and the reactions of other persons and groups to her, of the cultural meanings with which her body, voice, dress and comportment can be inscribed, her relation to social and geographical space determined. Indeed, she will to a greater or lesser extent have internalised cultural messages about gender and other identity-constituting structures.

But it is unlikely that the social meaning of gender will be fixed or stable in any relatively complex society. This is for two main reasons. In the first place, the openness of human behaviour to competing interpretations means that even within a relatively closed and unitary interpretive community, alternative meanings of gender are constantly implicitly evoked, even if only to be repressed. The boss who recognises and relies on his secretary's talents evokes the possibility of a less hierarchical relation between them, even if he is the same person who makes constant reference to her sexual attractiveness in contexts where this is irrelevant to the work being done. Even within a particular context, then, women are likely to experience gender as multiple and contradictory: being treated as a competent worker and as a 'woman as object' seem to go together, yet how?

Second, we add to this the fact that our lives are lived across many practices and communities. The female teacher, secretary, nurse is also daughter, mother, friend, member of a reading group, watcher of television, reader of short stories, amateur football player and so on. These different experiences themselves bring her up against not only other meanings of gender but other feelings (pleasure, empowerment, entitlement, to name some positive ones) which feed into her experience of herself and grate against feelings of powerlessness and worthlessness which her experience of being a woman may involve in other contexts. Social structure is not so coherent, so univocal that all her experiences, albeit inevitably gendered, are so in identical ways. The tension or straightforward comparison between them is one source of critical reflection on both the adequacy and the inevitability of current gender arrangements. Another is the sense of recognition and empathy to which the experience of gender-related powerlessness may give rise in a woman who works and lives alongside people whose race or class links to structures of oppression analogous to gender, and to which the internal reflection multiple experience of oppression give rise in those whose embodied situation exposes them to different sources of oppression.

Attention to the transformative potential of conflicts between the competing value-creating communities in any society is bound to be an important source of political consciousness, as subjects reflect upon and try to make some sense of their multiple experiences.[85] Both the multiplicity of meaning-generating communities and the openness of social structures lay the groundwork for the development of dissent, struggle and change. Immanent critique arises within particular practices, made possible by the existence of fundamental tensions in dichotomised thought, which can be unsettled by exposing the suppressed reference to the other. In many areas, our grasp of the multiplicity of difference can help us to understand the way in which dichotomised thought constitutes a powerful strategy for controlling the world, stabilising contingent hierarchies by constructing them as rational and inevitable. This combines with critique arising out of competing experience and subjectivity across practices, critique which is still 'immanent' to social situation, but which achieves a degree of 'externality' to particular features of social experience, precisely because of the fragmentation of society (thus resisting yet another dichotomy, that between 'immanence' and 'transcendence'). This suggests that the implication of a post-structuralist reading of the communitarian critique of liberalism is dynamic rather than conservative. But this is far from a complete basis for political theory. It fails, for example, to address the fundamental question of who has the power to engage in critique, and to be heard in doing so. To resolve this issue, we have to develop an adequate conception of the process of political debate.

The dialogic process

In thinking about both the structure of legitimate political institutions and the nature of an adequate political process, we would argue, as we have already suggested, for the attractions of what has been called 'dialogic communitarianism'. This ideal is dialogic in the sense that it assumes democratic institutions providing real access to political processes for all citizens. It is both dialogic and communitarian in the sense of proceeding from the relational theory of the self, recognising the importance of both dialogue and identification with various 'communities' in the constitution of subjectivity and human identity, and it is communitarian in the sense of placing questions of both public goods and the institutions needed to support them, and the ideal of collective life based on mutual acceptance and recognition, at the heart of politics. 'Dialogic communitarianism' starts out, then, from the idea that each of us must be given access to and heard at the bar of informed ethical and political debate.[86] It should go without saying that this needs to be a real debate and not a hypothetical one, in which difference and diversity would tend to be repressed. In Seyla Benhabib's phrase, our politics must confront the 'concrete' and not just the 'generalised' other.[87] Our experiences as women should remind us, however, of the dangerously utopian conclusions about the virtues of participatory democratic structures that sometimes flow from discourse ethics.[88] Formal rights of participation can all too easily serve to disguise inequalities of substantive access to speech and to being heard.

With this caveat, we think that the dialogic conception of the baseline for an adequate political practice is consistent with, if not entailed by, a commitment to deconstruction as one useful theoretical technique. Deconstruction includes an 'ethical moment'. Whilst it is easy to caricature it as an irresponsible embrace of the chaotic indeterminacy attendant on the 'play of difference', the very idea of attending to the repressed-yet-referred-to other in language connects with an ethical impulse to attend to difference.[89] In other words, it leads to the commitment to recognise and be open to 'unassimilated otherness'.[90] This means that we should reject the security and repression of the 'logic of identity' and force ourselves to face up to our differences in a more substantial way than by mere tolerance.

Theorists like Young are concerned about the repression of difference. This is understandable, but we think that they overstate the difficulties inherent in dialogic communitarianism. We agree that much of the civic republican literature envisages an unrealistic and potentially oppressively wide scope for public life and the duties of citizenship, but we think that there is room for a position between liberal pluralism and civic republicanism. If we are right in thinking that realisation of the dialogic ideal need not reconstruct a unified public, and need not privilege face-to-face relations, then Young's position is closer to some of the 'moderate' dialogic communitarians than she allows. The strength of her rejection of republicanism is understandable precisely because of the slippage between different questions and conceptions which has characterised the debate and which we have tried to unravel.[91]

How does this kind of dialogic ideal differ from that of liberal pluralism? In the latter, the facts of heterogeneity are managed by way of a strong public/private divide and by espousing a thin conception of the common life within an area of consensus focused mainly on procedures. This, of course, is Rawls' strategy, and that of many other liberals.[92] It is inadequate from a feminist point of view for several reasons. First, the particular form of public/private divide which it enshrines is destined to continue to privatise questions which feminism has persuasively constructed as questions of social justice. Furthermore, the public/private divide as usually construed issues in an impoverished conception of what counts not just as a political issue but also as political action. As we have seen, the equation of the public with the state and of political action with state regulation assumes a model of political action whose legitimacy and efficacy are questionable in many areas, and marginalises the diversity of practices which feminists have argued to be genuinely political and potentially more effective than state or legal regulation in many contexts: publicity campaigns, debates, boycotts, pickets, consciousness-raising in a variety of forums. The strong dichotomy between critique and action which is assumed by the conception of politics flowing from the public/private dichotomy is contradicted by the feminist conception of political critique *as* a form of political action – a discursive intervention in the production of dominant meanings. The reconstruction of housework as 'domestic labour' and hence as of economic value, like the characterisation of pornography as a form of violence or degradation, although it does not constitute a complete political strategy, forms an important part of feminist political *practice*.

Second, the assumption that an 'overlapping consensus' can be found, whilst it weakens the assumption of social homogeneity, none the less still participates in it. Even the robustly procedural interpretation of Rawls can be shown to rest on substantive premises which are bound to be controversial. This gives further stimulus to the thought that a substantial political life has to be based not on an overlapping consensus in Rawls' sense but rather on a positive framework commitment to living with – even a presumption in favour of respect for[93] – difference, and to drawing on the resources of that diversity in the construction of an inclusive but heterogeneous society. The only kind of 'consensus' (we would prefer to call it 'framework commitment') on the basis of which a heterogeneous society can enjoy peaceable coexistence, in other words, converges around the *ideal* of positive recognition and acknowledgement of diversity, and of the adequate meeting of basic human needs. The former is, of course, an ideal which is inconsistent with the anti-perfectionism to which Rawls continues to subscribe.

Finally, given the relational conception of the self defended above, the interpretation of public life in terms of a minimal overlapping consensus, a limited sphere of justice, and an attitude of tolerance towards 'private' diversity seems inadequate in two respects. First, positively, it seems to give up the hope of the kind of richer public life which human interdependence suggests may be possible, at least in certain areas of life and at certain moments of history. Arguably, this richer conception of the public sphere may be necessary if societies are to resist the disintegrating pull of heterogeneous values and interests. Second, because (like most modern liberal analyses) it under-emphasises the extent to which particular practices and forms of life depend on social structures and on a background culture, it fails to address the need positively to provide for minority interests and needs. The attitude of toleration applies only to forms of life which have managed to survive, and even then supports them negatively rather than positively. Indeed, as Susan Mendus has shown, an adequate moral (as opposed to pragmatic) basis for tolerance inevitably takes liberalism beyond its general espousal of governmental neutrality as between conceptions of the good.[94] And even in perfectionist versions of liberalism such as that of Joseph Raz, the emphasis on autonomy as the central liberal value (indeed, of an autonomous life as the liberal conception of the good, to be endorsed by government) entails that tolerance be limited to those who in effect espouse the government's conception of the good, a conclusion which seems to undercut one of the central tenets of liberalism.[95]

Whilst any political theory, including our own, has to confront the problem of the appropriate stance *vis-à-vis* those who do not themselves respect difference, our explicit perfectionism enables us to do so more satisfactorily than can neutralist liberals like Rawls and Dworkin. Furthermore, our commitment to values beyond that of the autonomy celebrated by Raz's perfectionist liberalism opens the way for a more complex analysis of the issues involved, making relevant questions such as the positive value of respect for diversity in terms of the creation of a supportive social environment in which citizens share a concern about, and even accept a certain responsibility for, each other's well-being. A more expansive commitment not just to autonomy but also to equality, to citizens' well-being and to the just distribution of power, combined with a practical concern for the coordination of society by substantively democratic as opposed to authoritarian means, entails that there are both moral and pragmatic reasons for reflecting on the possibilities for transforming our social world which the recollection of difference repressed in dominant meanings or suppressed in current political practice presents.

Whilst we are certainly not committed to the view that all 'cultures' are automatically entitled to protection or preservation, we do endorse the idea that diversity should be promoted and that certain minority practices or ways of life – not only those characterised by a shared commitment to equality and the absence of oppression conceived as we conceive them, but also those which accept the framework of democratic commitments which inform dialogic communitarianism – should be protected. Indeed, as we have already suggested, the importance of the acceptance and recognition of diversity is both ethical and practical. Since diversity is a fact, learning to live together without defining difference in terms of the 'otherness' which entails political marginalisation and voicelessness is one of the most pressing political problems confronting our societies.[96] If the 'unoppressive city' is not to become an alienating environment, a positive culture of diversity and real dialogue about how to live together, a dialogue in which participants' diverse group affiliations are recognised, will be needed.

We are also wary of the Rawlsian reinterpretation of the original position, which might be taken to suggest both the continuing priority of a pure procedural theory of justice and the idea that a *hypothetical* as opposed to a real debate could be an adequate basis for establishing just political arrangements.[97] To the extent that Rawls' most recent work envisages an actual as opposed to a hypothetical debate, it is incumbent upon him to address the questions raised by the heterogeneity of the participants to a far greater extent than he has so far done. The limits of imagination make the idea of a representative decision-maker problematic, and the failure of Rawls' substantive principles to generate an adequate critical analysis of social structures such as gender oppression should make us wary of too easily assuming that his choosers in the reconstructed original position can necessarily envisage and take account of all relevant forms of unjust disadvantage. Whilst the similarities between Rawls' recent position and Habermas's communicative ethics is striking, we would want to insist on the substantive aspect of deliberations about justice, the links between justice and conceptions of the good, and the need for *actual* debate between real, embodied, socially-situated persons. Only in such debate can the ethical impulse to recognise each other's claims by listening attentively to them, respecting the difference of others whom we identify as in some deep sense having the same moral status as ourselves, be realised.

Certainly, dialogical communitarianism offers no blueprint for the ideal society. What it does is to suggest the ways in which we can begin to see what possibilities for political change exist. Arguably this is the best that can be hoped for from any political theory. The production of blueprints in the past has neither straightforwardly issued in new worlds nor served as a guarantee against catastrophically oppressive political practices. Interpretivism reminds us that in some sense political theory is always an *immanent* critique, a critique from within a particular culture, located in a particular place and time. But the fragmentation of subjectivity and of society, and the openness of language mean that critique is never immanent only to a single structure or context. Our lives and consciousness, and hence our critique, cut across numbers of meaning-generating practices. Most of these are not so radically discontinuous that they operate as the completely separate vocabularies which Rorty rightly reminds us of the difficulties of transcending. The fact that the project of trying to exercise moral persuasion in a dialogue with Hitler seems futile should not lead us to the conclusion that paradigm shifts in ethics never come about or that immanent critique cannot contribute to them. Nor should it be taken to entail that moral critique is 'groundless' and equivalent to socially-determined expressions of preference. The conception of critically reflective subjectivity, abandoned by Rorty, turns out to be central to understanding the meaningfulness of interpretivist conceptions of political and ethical theory. The ideal of dialogic communitarianism, like that of discourse ethics, depends upon that subjectivity being engaged in listening to and recognising the claims and perceptions of others, recognising the need to justify ourselves, and being aware of the importance of existing practices and communities to human identity and life whilst recognising their openness and contingency. Along with the 'primacy of critique' and the willingness to recognise culturally transcendent, polically relevant features of the human condition, discussed above, this is the final idea which we take to be definitional to the enterprise we are advocating, part of the ground rules for the political practice our feminist approach seeks to engender.

How might this conception of the dialogic process realise itself in concrete political practices? The feminist practice of interactive consciousness raising is perhaps the most graphic illustration of the process of forming and developing oppositional political consciousness and of developing transformative politics in a dialogic process. As multiple experiences are exchanged, new interpretations emerge and find strength and validity from the collective practice. These interpretations generate new concepts, new languages, new frameworks through which we interpret the world, and hence in turn change our perceptions and with them, in a significant sense, social reality. But we should be clear that the self-conscious consciousness-raising group of the women's movement is an illustration of this process and not the only or even a privileged medium in which it takes place. As black and working-class feminists have pointed out, access to the institutional practice of consciousness-raising depends on privileges – leisure and articulacy, for example – which are themselves unfairly distributed on class and race lines.

But consciousness-raising is not confined to a self-conscious institutional practice related to a very specific historical moment. It takes place also in casual discussion, and even without the meeting of two persons, via the internal dialogue that we as critically reflective subjects are not only capable of but engaged in when we try to make sense of our lives or formulate our views and claims in the workplace, the family, the union. A chance scene in a film or passage in a novel; reflection on a dream; recollection of one's past feelings and behaviour in certain situations; an argument at work; all these are capable of generating reinterpretations and reconceptualisations of the world. Until these conceptualisations get a foothold in a shared (if minority) language, their power will remain dormant. But the foundations for the kind of reconstruction of the world which comes from reconceptualisation and the spreading of new critical ideas can be laid outside the context of an institutionalised group setting. The reconstructed theory conceives all of these practices as genuinely political.

The critically engaged women of dialogic communitarianism, living their lives across a number of practices and in overlapping communities, could, then, gradually come to a consciousness of certain kinds of behaviour as distinctive, as forming a meaningful pattern, and as oppressive. Their access to a variety of models of the apt treatment of human beings and their reflective capacity prevent them from being engulfed in the cultural dominance of sexist behaviour, because this allows them to glimpse other kinds of practices and worlds. Once this vision is shared, and once the experience of anger, humiliation, shame, guilt, embarrassment, powerlessness is communicated and we recognise we do not have such experiences alone, the groundwork for the feminist consciousness and feminist critique of the political underrepresentation of women, the undervaluation of women's work, sexual violence is laid. What has been constructed by its participants as natural – as paternalism, chivalry, courtesy, flattery, the exercise of rights, joking – is gradually reconstructed in an alternative consciousness which realises itself in the appropriation and reworking of language. Similarly, what has been constructed as women's natural role in the home is slowly being reconstructed as economically valuable labour.

An integral part of this process is the shared understanding of how the implicit social structure of gender is implicated in the experiences shared. Examples include the understanding of how sexuality is implicated in the specific form of power which is exploited by men who harass women, or how gender is implicated in the judgements about the value of work on the basis of which pay is set, and even in the very denomination of a certain activity as 'work'. The openness of language once again helps to explain the process of turning consciousness into power. By making analogies with pre-existing linguistic practices, chivalry or protectionism comes to be called sexism, courtesy insensitivity, flattery hypocrisy, the exercise of rights the abuse of power, 'housework' reproductive labour, the fulfilment of 'natural' duty exploitation. This reconstruction initially develops within small groups who draw on their shared experiences across practices to reconceive the world. It gains power as its use spreads beyond the initial group.

How, though, can the critical usage and the practice it engenders spread in a culture, a relatively stable constellation of discourses and practices, which is predominantly sexist? Once again, the post-structuralist conception helps us to see how this can be the case, because of the fragmented nature of even relatively homogeneous societies. Clearly, there is a sense in which critical arguments have to wait for their time to come. Some radical ideas never gain a toehold beyond minority groups, others (women's suffrage, for example) lurk on the fringes of society for decades or even centuries before getting a purchase in society's most powerful institutions. But participants in consciousness-raising are moving across practices – workplaces, leisure arenas, families, schools – where their reconstructed discourse may find a resonance and prompt further reflection and reconstruction. Culture is not monolithic, and this is what allows for radical critiques to find a voice. In a real sense, to change discursive practice is to change the world. Once unwanted sexual attentions are named as rape or sexual harassment, or a husband's 'chastisement' of a wife recharacterised as 'wife abuse' or 'domestic violence', they are no longer the same.

Of course, such changes in discursive practice are no more monolithic or irreversible than any other cultural practice. For example, those who resist the idea that sexual harassment is an abuse of power will find ways to take the sting out of the political burden of the language of harassment – by trivialising the idea, by marginalising those who have constructed it as humourless or hysterical, by straightforwardly denying its existence. But each of these strategies is a response to the discursive category of harassment, an implicit recognition that the world has changed. The world is now one in which a practice which was formerly taken as a matter of uncontroversial entitlement has been constructed as problematic, as calling for justification, even though the new vision is far from securely established. What ensues is, in effect, a battle for dominant cultural meaning. A similar point can be made about feminist campaigns around pornography. Whilst, as we have argued, both the instrumental and the specifically discursive effects of the legislative strategy against pornography have been of doubtful value to the feminist cause, the construction of pornography as raising questions about the dignity of women, about men's respect for women and women's respect for ourselves, and, hence, about women's citizenship status, has been of enormous importance. For it has now become a sufficiently settled aspect of pornography's cultural meaning that contemporary discussion of pornography almost inevitably has to address the questions raised by the feminist critique. Feminist critique, in other words, has changed the structure of the politics of pornography.

Gaining control of language, then, is a necessary part of the exercise of power but the discursive is not all. To continue the example, the wrongs, harms, abuses, injustices which the idea of harassment renders visible, are felt and have effects beyond the discursive world. And, second, the presence within a culture of a pejorative notion of sexual harassment will not stop the practice any more than the idea of rape, violence, racism or homophobia as wrong or problematic have stopped those social practices. How, then, can our reconstructed political theory help us to envision and realise a world in which sexual harassment and the other examples on which we have focused – political under-representation and a hierarchically gendered division of labour – along with the sexual oppression of which they are both a cause and a symptom, are transcended? The post-structuralist conception can help us to see why the liberal conceptualisation of such problems in terms of sex discrimination is inadequate, for its failure to conceptualise power and social structure disables liberalism from identifying the distinctive cultural meaning and power which derives from a sexually hierarchical social context. Attention to the material effects of discursive change shows us that what may seem to be the most direct way of changing the world – legal proscription of abuses, political reform – is not necessarily the most effective in the longer term. Only once we have recognised the structural aspects of gender – have constructed harassment, the division of labour and so on as social *practices* – can we begin to see not only what is wrong with them but also what a world without them might look like.

The post-structuralist conception suggests that decisions about particular political struggles around issues such as those we have considered are essentially *strategic*. At certain moments, political struggle in terms of getting something like feminist conceptions of sexual harassment recognised as wrongs at union or workplace level, via codes or informal understandings, or at the level of interaction in the family, may be more effective than legal proscription. The same is true of questions such as the appropriate redivision of responsibility for domestic labour and the revaluation of 'women's work'. What the revised conception engenders is a strong sense of realism about the issue. The liberal conception sees harassment as the wrongful actions of deviant individuals which call for punishment or censure, unequal pay as an unfair market practice which can be corrected by legal policy. Communitarianism tends to an uncritical view of the division of labour, harassment and so on as simply features of culture, if indeed they are visible at all. The revised conception sees them as structural, as continuous with other aspects of gendered existence, and hence as outwith the scope of straightforward, deliberate change by government. From this point of view, incrementalism and immanent critique are simply the only alternatives. The actual history of the women's movement shows that they can none the less be genuinely radical. The vision of a world without a gendered division of labour, without sexual subordination, without the silencing of women, is implicit in the very construction of these concepts, although not realised by that discursive change. The realisation of that world will only come from an incremental cultural revolution.

Feminist politics and political theory as critique

Our argument has set out some substantive and procedural ideas, along with conceptions of subject and society and of theoretical method, which could underpin a political theory which escaped many of the problems which feminist critique exposed in both liberal and communitarian approaches. In terms of the impulses discussed at the beginning of this chapter, our position draws on both 'welfare liberal' and 'post-modernist' tendencies; it is sympathetic to aspects of both liberal and communitarian ideas whilst, in keeping with our suspicion

. See Duchen 1986.

. Arguments about feminism and Marxism are rehearsed in Sargent (ed.) 1986 and in Barrett 1980 (2nd edn 1991). Liberal feminism is discussed in Z. Eisenstein 1979, Jaggar 1983, and exemplified by Richards 1980. A. Dworkin 1981, 1983; Jeffreys 1990 emphasise men's direct sexual interest in women's subordination. Whatever respectable biologists and geneticists may say, genetic and biological theories of gender have undoubtedly had a central place in anti-feminist discourses; see Birke 1986, esp. Ch. 3.

. For such arguments and counter-arguments in the British context see Lovenduski and Randall 1993; Phillips 1987a esp. Ch. 5; in the French context, Duchen 1986.

. For a summary and review of the 'domestic labour debate' see Molyneux 1979. For the debates about capitalism and patriarchy, Sargent (ed.) 1986.

. Delphy 1984 theorises men's interest in women's domestic labour; A. Dworkin 1981, 1983, Jeffreys 1990, Cameron and Frazer 1987 men's interest in sexual dominance; Daly 1983, Griffin 1981 emphasise men's fear of women.

. See typically Richards 1980.

. Accounts of women's oppression in relation to psychoanalysis or from a psychoanalytic perspective are Mitchell 1974, Chodorow 1978, Dinnerstein 1976.

. See Bryson 1992, Ch. 9; Z. Eisenstein 1979; Jaggar 1983, Ch. 7.

. See Bryson 1992, Chs 9–12; Lovenduski and Randall 1993, for more detailed accounts.

. Bryson 1992, Chs 1 and 2.

. Bryson 1992, esp. Chs 1, 2, 4–7; Phillips 1987a, esp. Ch. 1; Spelman 1989, esp. pp 88–15.

. Bryson (see n. 12); Phillips 1987a, esp. Ch. 4. Further to this and to n. 12 see also Davis 1982; hooks 1981, 1984, 1989; Phillips (ed.) 1987b.

. The most notable example of a theorist of the universality and continuity of misogyny is Daly 1983. For the continuities between women's friendship and contemporary lesbianism see Jeffreys 1985, Faderman 1985. For criticism see in particular Riley 1988.

. See Spelman 1989, esp. pp 12–13, Chs 4–7; P. Williams 1991.

. Phillips 1987a, Ch. 6, Spelman 1989, Ch. 7. Jordan 1986, Lorde 1984 develop pluralistic concepts of womanhood. cf. Judith Butler's thorough-going constructionist account of gender as performance: Butler 1990.

. Bourdieu 1990, esp. pp 30–52; Connell 1987, Chs 5–6; Giddens 1979.

. Riley 1988.

. As Catharine MacKinnon says: 'I don't use the term *persons*, I guess, because I haven't seen many lately.' (MacKinnon 1987, p. 87).

. For example, women's and girls' sexual discontent can be identified as a foundation for an articulated feminism. See Frazer 1988, 1989; Lees 1986.

of dualistic thinking, resisting classification as either. We have argued that the social theory underlying many liberal and communitarian political philosophies is inadequate, and that only by revising that underlying social theory and by making explicit the methodological assumptions of political theory can the problems of the liberalism–communitarianism debates be understood and transcended. A political theory which started out from a relational and situated conception of the self and a differentiated view of society, which gave a central place to a theory of power and the notion of practice, and which employed a critically interpretivist methodology, would be capable of illuminating the structural aspects of social injustice without sacrificing the values of human freedom and difference. It would, in short, be able to meet the core commitment to equality and the absence of oppression which we found both liberal and communitarian theories incapable of either explicating or sustaining.

Throughout this book, we have identified the deficiencies of liberal and communitarian theories not only in theoretical terms but also with reference to the analysis they could generate of a number of social practices. In this chapter, we have used our recurring examples to show, positively, how the kind of political theory we have advocated would generate something like the feminist analysis and critique of practices like sexual harassment, the hierarchical, gendered division of labour and the exclusion of women from effective political power. We have asked whether our theory could 'see' these issues and characterise them as structured social practices; whether it could explain the senses in which such features of social reality are politically problematic and raise questions of social justice; and whether it could gesture in the direction of, or provide any hope for, transformative political practices in the relevant areas. In each of these respects, we believe that a development of our reconstructed approach to political theory would be more illuminating than the liberal and communitarian approaches analysed earlier in the book.

Underlying our argument is a claim which is central to the critical feminist enterprise. The invisibility of gender in political theory, an influential intellectual discourse in our culture, is symptomatic of a fundamental inadequacy of the social ontology on which that theory is based. We have exposed the structural defects of political theories which leave social institutions such as gender out of account, and have used our examples to show the impossibility of political theory without social theory. In this way, we hope to have contributed to an opening up of the possibility of genuinely critical political theory, to the development of a theory which combines a recognition of the relational nature of subjectivity and the empirical facts of interdependence so as to give questions of both agency and structure their proper place. We also hope that our work will help to undermine the common but indefensible way in which 'feminist theory', like 'anti-racist theory' is constructed as outwith the bounds of political theory, and hence as marginal. A flawed theoretical framework cannot be used, unmodified, to engage in critical political and social thought. For such conceptual frameworks, far from being politically innocent, are in fact of the first importance in determining both what kinds of substantive political visions can be generated by political theory and what kinds of phenomena political theory can 'see' as problematic. Thus no such framework should be allowed to stand. Our argument is a contribution to the reconstruction of the discourse of political theory on feminist and critical terms. It is up to our readers to judge whether the reconstructed conception of political theory which we defend, or the unreconstructed conception which we criticise, should occupy the centre ground of the political theoretical enterprise.

Notes

Introduction

1. We refer to MacIntyre 1981; Sandel 1982, Walzer 198
   as texts which came to be known as 'communit
   problems with this designation in what follows. The m
   which these writers' critique is directed, are Rawls 1
   and Dworkin 1977. Key articles are collected in Av
   (eds) 1992.
2. We are taking as representative texts of 'feminist pc
   1978, 1989a; Jaggar 1983; Phillips 1987a, 1991; Pa
   See also Coole 1988; Evans et al., 1986; Kennedy
   1987; Pateman and Gross (eds) 1986; Shanley and P
   Young 1990a. For discussion see Kymlicka 1990, Ch.
3. Especially structuralist Marxism as exemplified by
   1971b. For discussion see Benton 1984. See Gic
   elucidation of disputes about and between indivic
   turalism.

Chapter 1

1. See Jaggar 1983, H. Eisenstein 1984, Walby 199(
   varieties of feminism and feminist analysis.
2. See Coote and Campbell 1987, Duchen 1986, Kapla
   and Randall 1993, Phillips 1987a, for accounts of rec
   and the fate of 'the' women's movement. For the
   category 'women' is unviable see Riley 1988. Other
   this direction are Spelman 1989 and Butler 1990.

22. For overviews of sociological and related research into labour markets see Crompton and Mann 1986, Walby 1986, McRae 1991.
23. See A. Dworkin 1981; Hanmer and Maynard 1987; MacKinnon 1987, 1989; Smart 1990; Smart and Smart (eds) 1978.
24. See Randall 1987; Phillips 1991; Lister 1990, 1991.
25. We understand Daly 1983 (see n. 15 above), Dworkin 1981, Griffin 1981, and to some extent Jeffreys 1985, 1990, as developing this analysis, while some current feminist ethics also tend to reproduce it; see esp. Noddings 1984, Ruddick 1990.
26. See Sargent (ed.) 1986 for a collection of important contributions to the Marxist feminist debate; see also Nicholson 1987. See Barrett 1980; Walby 1990, Chs 2 and 3, for critical summary and analysis.
27. More, we have to say, by what they don't than by what they do say. See Bryson 1992, Ch. 9; Jaggar 1983, Chs 3 and 7, esp. pp 199–203.
28. Cameron 1985, p. 187.
29. Foucault discusses the significance of the history and development of the social sciences in Foucault 1967, 1973, 1977; see also 1970, Ch. 10. The concept of discourse is developed in Foucault 1970, 1972. See also McNay 1992, pp 24–8.
30. Foucault analyses the power of the medical 'gaze' in Foucault 1973 and the power of 'surveillance' in Foucault 1977.
31. McLellan 1986, Barrett 1991 for clear discussions of the concept of ideology. See Merquior 1979, Ch. 1; Minogue 1985 for contrasting stances.
32. See Barrett 1980, Ch. 3, 1991, Ch. 6; Thompson 1984; MacDonnell 1986.
33. See Barrett 1980, Ch. 3 esp. pp 86–96 where she gives references for key contributions to this position.
34. See Bourdieu 1977, 1990; Connell 1987; Foucault 1972; Giddens 1979; MacIntyre 1985, pp 187–8; MacDonnell 1986, pp 28–32, 90–94, for theoretical and empirical discussions of 'practice'.
35. Giddens 1979 and 1987 emphasises this aspect.
36. See esp. Taylor's papers in 1985a and 1985b for an elaboration of this position.
37. See Hawthorn 1987, Chs 4, 5, and 6 for discussion of the historical link. Taylor 1989b argues that the link is not a logical one.
38. See Craib 1984, Chs 7–9. For debates about structuralist method in literary criticism see Eagleton 1983, Hawkes 1977.
39. For references see Jaggar 1983, Chs 3, 7, and 11.
40. Cameron 1985, 1990; Lakoff 1975; Spender 1980.
41. Benhabib and Cornell (eds) 1987, Fraser 1989b. Current definitions and understandings of the method of 'critique' owe a good deal first to Kant (see Preface to the *Critique of Pure Reason*), and to Marx who uses the

technique in the *Critique of Hegel's Philosophy of Right* and *Critique of the Gotha Programme*, and in his reading of political economy generally.

42. See MacKinnon 1979, 1987, Ch. 9; Oxford University Students' Union 1984; Sedley and Benn 1984.

43. See, for example, definitions of male and female incest in the English *Sexual Offences Act* 1956: *Section 10* It is an offence for a man *to have sexual intercourse with* a woman whom he knows to be his grand-daughter, daughter, sister or mother. *Section 11* It is an offence for a woman of the age of sixteen or over *to permit a man* whom she knows to be her grand-daughter, father, brother or son *to have sexual intercourse with her* by consent. (Our emphasis). Note who is subject and who is object.

44. Lévi-Strauss 1963, Douglas 1966; 'The Kabyle Household', in Bourdieu 1990. For Marxist structuralism see Benton 1984 and Craib 1984. For a general discussion of structuralism see Benoist 1978. For a discussion of structuralist liberary criticism see Hawkes 1977. For discussion of its implications for feminist theory, see Butler 1990, esp. Ch. 1.

45. See for example Lévi Strauss 1969, p. 133 where he suggests that binary oppositions are conceived, not experienced. See also Douglas 1966; Lévi-Strauss 1963; Bourdieu 1990 appendix.

46. Although the tension between determinism and freedom, or structure and agency, keeps recurring in Marxist studies. See Anderson 1980. Also Cohen 1988, esp. Chs 4 and 5.

47. See Benoist 1978, esp. Ch. 1.

48. See Piaget 1965, 1971. For a discussion of Piaget's theory of cognition and morality which is relevant to our concerns see Gilligan 1982.

49. Saussure 1974; but see Rée 1992 for a (brief) argument that Saussure was not a structuralist.

50. See Craib 1984, Chs 7, 8, and 9.

51. Parsons 1949, 1951. For the concept of autopoiesis see Luhmann 1982, 1987; Teubner (ed.) 1987.

52. An important article, marking the turning point from structuralism to deconstruction is Derrida 1978c. See also Derrida 1987b, Ch. 5.

53. See for example Derrida 1978b, p. 281.

54. Benhabib 1986. For feminist suspicion of utopianism see Smart 1989, 1990, 1992.

55. Explicitly philosophical and theoretical discussion in practical application are found in *The Federalist Papers* (Madison, Hamilton and Jay 1987). See White 1987 for discussion.

56. See Skinner 1978; Berki 1977.

57. Featherstone 1988; see also Connolly 1988; Giddens 1991.

58. See Taylor 1989a, Pt. I on the inception of the modern era.

59. See *Communist Manifesto* 'Bourgeois and Proletarians' (Marx and Engels 1968, pp 35–46) and *Capital* Vol. 1, for example Ch. 13 (Marx 1954, p. 316).

60. See Siedentop 1983.
61. Plato 1955, 1970; Aristotle 1962. See Skinner 1978 for discussion of the place of virtue in Renaissance political thought, and for Machiavelli's attack on the importance of virtue (esp. pp 131–5.)
62. Machiavelli *The Prince*, *The Discourses*; see Skinner 1978, Chs 4, 5, and 6.
63. Berki 1977, Ch. 6; Taylor 1989, Pt. I.
64. Pateman 1989, Ch. 3.
65. Compare Burke 1968 with Bentham 1982 and Montesquieu 1989. On conservatism in general see Eccleshall *et al.*, 1984, Ch. 3; O'Sullivan 1976; Scruton 1980. On conservatism and law see esp. Nisbet 1986, p. 53.
66. See for example *German Ideology* 'Private property and communism' (Marx and Engels 1964).
67. Eisenstein 1984, Pt. I; Pateman 1988; 1989, esp. Chs 2, 4, 6, 8, and 9; Walby 1990.
68. See for example Miller 1990b.
69. Mechanical and organic structures of solidarity respectively characterise pre-modern and modern societies for Durkheim (Durkheim 1964). Ferdinand Tönnies (Tönnies 1957) most clearly draws the distinction between 'community' and 'society' (or 'association'). For Weber modern social institutions are based on rationality and rational relations, in contrast to traditional ties (Weber 1968) See Bell and Newby 1971), Ch. 2.
70. Volumes with special relevance for social and political theory are Boyne and Rattansi (eds) 1990; Doherty, Graham and Malek (eds) 1992; Featherstone 1988; Harvey 1989; Jameson 1991; Lyotard 1984; Nicholson 1990; Siedman and Wagner (eds) 1992; White 1991. *Theory Culture and Society*, Vol. 5, 1988 is a special edition entitled 'Postmodernism'.
71. Harvey 1989 emphasises the material aspects of post-modernity. See also Rengger 1992, White 1991.
72. Lyotard 1984. See also Rorty 1989, 1991a and for discussion Guignon and Hailey in Malachowski (ed.) 1990.
73. See Lukes (ed.) 1986 for key readings and bibliography. Also Barnes 1988.
74. The question is most explicitly posed by Thomas Hobbes (Hobbes 1968).
75. Most notably Rawls 1971, although this aspect of the theory is less pronounced in his later papers. See also Hollis 1987, Lessnoff (ed.) 1990.
76. Hollis 1987, McLean 1987, Elster 1991; for a critical discussion of rational choice theory see Hindess 1988, Mansbridge 1990, esp. Ch. 1.
77. Most notably in the sociological tradition of Parsons; Parsons 1951 and 1949. See Craib 1984.

78. Foucault 1980, 1982.
79. See extracts from Russell, Weber, Dahl in Lukes (ed.) 1986.
80. Lukes 1974 elaborates this criticism of exercise or voluntarist conceptions of power.
81. Foucault 1980 (an extract appears in Lukes (ed.) 1986). For other 'decentred' conceptions of power see Parsons, Arendt, in Lukes (ed.) 1986, and see Barnes 1988.
82. Foucault 1980.
83. Walkerdine 1990, Ch. 1.
84. Scott 1990.
85. Young 1990a, pp 30–3 develops this kind of analysis, but in her theoretical exposition tends too nearly to erasing agency. This results in tensions, as later in the book she needs to discuss who 'has' and who is able to exercise power eg. pp 56–8.
86. For example, Cameron *et al.*, 1992; Walkerdine 1990.
87. See Benhabib and Cornell 1987; Coole 1988; Elshtain 1981a; Kennedy and Mendus 1987; Lloyd 1984; Okin 1978; Pateman 1989; Pitkin 1984; Shanley and Pateman (eds) 1991.
88. See Okin 1989a; Pateman 1989.
89. See Rossi (ed.) 1973 for extracts from feminist writings. See Bryson 1992, and Spender (ed.) 1983 for discussion. Mary Wollstonecraft *A Vindication of the Rights of Woman*, Harriet Taylor *The Enfranchisement of Women*, John Stuart Mill *The Subjection of Women* are readily available in current editions (see Mill and Mill 1970).
90. Hence the perceived resonances between feminism and postmodernism. See Nicholson 1990; Morris 1988; Benhabib 1992a.
91. Smart 1989, 1990, 1992; see Lacey 1993a for a critical discussion of this position.
92. For example, Firestone 1971; Utopian thought has especially been developed in the novel – see Charlotte Perkins Gilman *Herland* (1915), Marge Piercey *Woman on the Edge of Time* (1979).
93. Lloyd 1984; Butler 1990, Ch. 1.
94. For historical references to this tension see Bryson 1992; see also Introduction to Frazer, Hornsby and Lovibond (eds) 1992.

Chapter 2

1. However, some critics argue that the early liberal theorists explicitly excluded women from the theory. See esp. Pateman 1988, 1989.
2. For more detailed discussion of the liberal tradition and all its historical and conceptual complexity see Arblaster 1984; Eccleshall *et al.*, 1984,

Ch. 2; Freeden 1978, 1986, 1990b; Jaggar 1983, Ch. 3; Lacey 1988, Ch. 7; MacPherson 1962; Sandel (ed.) 1984.

3. Rawls 1971. For critical discussion of this extraordinarily influential work see in particular Barry 1973; Daniels (ed.) 1975; Kukathas and Pettit 1990.

4. Other central contributions to this version of liberalism are R. Dworkin 1977; Ackerman 1980; and Nozick 1974. Berlin 1989b clearly distinguishes negative from positive liberty and argues in favour of the former. This terminology is used in a number of ways in recent literature, though, which can be confusing, cf. Miller 1990b, Ch. 1. Notable attacks on this strand of the liberal tradition include some from theorists we refer to as communitarians but who are committed to what they understand to be liberal values – as we shall suggest, an increasingly plausible way to understand the communitarian critique is that it has in fact emerged from within liberalism.

5. Locke 1967.

6. Kant 1966. Kant insists that persons are to be treated always as ends, never as means; and that this principle is unconditional – it does not depend on any other circumstance or principle.

7. J-J Rousseau 1968, 1985. The extent to which Rousseau was committed to 'society' as an entity with an independent existence is a vexed question; see Shklar 1969, Ch. 5; Viroli 1988, esp. Ch. 2.

8. Freeden 1978, 1986 analyses the welfare liberal tradition which as he says puts *social* or *societal* needs and a strong conception of social structure at the centre of theory and policy.

9. Bentham 1982; also see Waldron (ed.) 1987 for extracts from *Anarchical Fallacies* fp 1816; Mill 1972. See Kymlicka 1990, Ch. 2.

10. See Freeden 1978, 1990b. Freeden argues vigorously that recent individualist theorists have misunderstood and misrepresented the liberal tradition (especially in his comments on our draft manuscript).

11. See for example Kymlicka 1989, pp 22–3.

12. For discussion of liberalism and embodiment see Jaggar 1983, Ch. 3. See Freeden 1990a for an argument that this is an unacceptably reductionist conception of the person.

13. See Rawls 1971, Ch. 3; also Nagel 1975; R. Dworkin 1975; Sandel 1982, Chs 1 and 3.

14. We should note here that Taylor 1989b, Freeden 1978 (see esp. p. 23) both argue that ontology (eg. individualism) and what Taylor calls 'advocacy' (eg. individuality) are analytically and historically distinct. See also MacPherson 1962.

15. Bentham 1982, Ch. 1 s. 5.

16. Talmon 1952; Popper 1945.

17. Rousseau 1968, Chs 4 and 6.

18. See Freeden 1990b.
19. Arblaster 1984, esp. Chs 15 and 16; Eccleshall *et al.*, 1984, Ch. 2; Freeden 1986. Compare Rawls 1971 and Nozick 1974.
20. Mill 1974. For commentary see Rees 1985; Ryan 1970, 1974; Ten 1980; Honderich 1982; Gray 1983.
21. Wolfenden Committee 1957. But see Freeden 1978 and Arblaster 1984, Ch. 16 on more interventionist liberalism.
22. See R. Dworkin 1975, 1977, 1978; Rawls 1975, 1988.
23. See Phillips (ed.) 1987b, esp. papers by Elshtain (Elshtain 1981b) and Alexander (Alexander 1984). See Bryson 1992 for the history of debates about equality and difference in feminism.
24. Marshall 1950; see Barbalet 1988.
25. Especially Nozick 1974; Friedman 1963.
26. See for example Arblaster 1984, pp 71–5.
27. For further discussion of legitimacy see Beetham 1991.
28. Finnis 1980.
29. Montesquieu 1989; Bentham 1982, 1816.
30. For example, for J. S. Mill there was a link between social science and social progress – see Ryan 1970, Chs 9 and 10. See also Freeden 1978, Chs 2 and 3, and esp. pp 10–12 on the relations between science and ethics in the liberal tradition.
31. Popper 1964, Preface.
32. Hayek 1962.
33. Elster 1983; Elster and Hylland (eds) 1986; Elster 1991.
34. Mill 1859, esp. Ch. 2; 1972, esp. Ch. 8.
35. And we discuss the issue further in Chapter 6.
36. See Lessnoff (ed.) 1990, Intro.
37. Hart 1983b; R. Dworkin 1977, 1985, 1986.
38. Raz 1986; Haksar 1979. But see Mendus 1989, Chs 4 and 5 on the difficulties this causes for liberalism.
39. Rorty 1989; Unger 1987.
40. Arblaster 1984, Chs 13, 14 and 16; Freeden 1986.
41. Fraser 1989b. This is the method used by Pateman (1988) where she retrieves a suppressed contract narrative (the sexual contract) from the classic contract theorists. It is also the method of feminist literary and cultural criticism; see Millett 1977; Modleski 1984.
42. Sandel 1982, pp 54–9; 1984 (ed.) Intro; Jaggar 1983, Ch. 3.
43. See for example Lloyd 1984. For the sociology of 'men's transcendence' see Smith 1987 (also in Harding (ed.) 1987).
44. See Matsuda 1986 for the implications of the disembodied subject for issues of race as well as gender. See also Van Dyke 1975.
45. Sandel 1982, pp 24–8; Nagel 1975; R. Dworkin 1975.
46. Lacey 1988, p. 19, 1992b; Jaggar 1983, p. 47.

47. Rawls 1971, p. 21; 1980, p. 533; 1985, p. 237.
48. Our position here is contrary to Mulhall's understanding in Mulhall 1987, p. 269. See also Kymlicka 1989, Chs 3 and 4; Okin 1989a Chs 3, 5, and 6; Lloyd 1984.
49. Cameron *et al.*, 1992 Intro; Harding 1986, 1987; Harding and Hintikka (eds) 1987; Garry and Pearsall 1989; Smith 1988.
50. Taylor 1989b, and cf. Hampton 1989.
51. Cornell 1987a, p. 693.
52. Cornell 1987a, 1990.
53. Certain forms of psychoanalysis may downplay the importance of the social here. We think this is a weakness and a potential point of incoherence in psychoanalysis. But see Rose 1983, who protests that feminists have 'socialised' psychoanalysis to its detriment.
54. See Benhabib 1987, p. 77; Balbus 1987, p. 110 and pp 124–6; Sandel 1982.
55. Gauthier 1986, and Rawls in his later articles, concede that the liberal individual is a social and historical construction, but argue that this does not threaten the status of liberal theory. We disagree, as we go on to argue.
56. Okin 1989a, pp 101–9. For a critical discussion see Lacey 1992b.
57. Rawls 1975, 1980, 1985, 1987, 1988.
58. Rawls 1980, pp 552, 570.
59. See Rawls 1980, p. 570 for the importance of the social point of view and for the primacy of the social 1980, p. 552. For the importance of public institutions, Rawls 1985, pp 228–9. Also relevant is Rawls' idea of an 'overlapping consensus', see Rawls 1987, 1985 p. 225.
60. See Kymlicka 1989, Chs 3 and 4; Mulhall 1987, p. 269; Okin 1989b, Chs 3, 5 and 6.
61. Rawls 1985, p. 236, n. 19; R. Dworkin 1975, 1977 Ch. 6.
62. Rawls 1985, p. 241.
63. Kymlicka 1989, pp 55–9.
64. Young 1987b, p. 56; Sandel 1982, Ch. 1; Pateman 1988.
65. This ideal is most famously expressed in J. S. Mill's *On Liberty*. See also Kant *Critique of Pure Reason* ss A316/B373.
66. Mill 1974; see Berlin 1989b. For Berlin Mill's concept of freedom is 'negative' (albeit somewhat muddled), although some have seen Mill's concept of freedom as autonomy as 'positive'. See Freeden 1978 and Mendus 1989, Ch. 3.
67. See Miller 1990b, Ch. 1.
68. See for example Cohen 1988, Chs 12, 13 and 14; MacKinnon 1989, Ch. 8.
69. Hindess 1988; Mansbridge (ed.) 1990; Sen 1977.
70. See MacIntyre 1981, 1988; Max Weber is a most notable theorist of the historical specificity of conceptions of rationality, see for example Gerth and Mills (eds) 1948, p. 293. Also see Kant 1966.

71. Nagel 1986.
72. Young 1989, p. 60.
73. For example, Marx 1954, p. 571 n. 2.
74. Young 1990a, pp 98–102.
75. Lloyd 1984.
76. Gilligan 1982; for discussion see *Ethics* vol. 97.
77. Young 1989, p. 63.
78. Lloyd 1984.
79. Young 1989; see also Rorty, 1989, Chs 1–3.
80. Rawls 1988; see Sandel 1982, pp 16–20. Critics include Raz 1986, Chs 5 and 6; Haksar 1979.
81. Dworkin 1978.
82. Sandel 1982, p. 145.
83. Raz 1986, pp 117–24.
84. See Mendus 1989, Chs 3, 4 and 5.
85. Neither did much older liberalism, but for different reasons – for example, it tended to be assumed that harmony between individual goods and wills either existed or could be attained.
86. See for example Raz 1986.
87. Freeden 1978, 1990b, pp 62–3.
88. Cohen 1992.
89. For example R. Dworkin 1986, pp 195–202; Raz 1986, Chs 10, 14 and 15.
90. Rawls 1971 p. 105ff.
91. R. Dworkin 1986, pp 200–201. In R. Dworkin 1989 and 1990 the idea of community is introduced but in ways which court the dangers of both liberalism *and* communitarianism. See Cornell 1986, 1987b.
92. Kymlicka 1989, Ch. 8.
93. Raz 1986.
94. Mendus 1989, Ch. 6 argues that actually perfectionism must pull us in a more socialist direction, towards the non-derivative value of community of a certain sort.
95. Gilligan's (1982) research suggests this to be the case. See also O'Brien 1981; Lloyd 1984; Mansbridge 1992.
96. Spender 1980; Cameron 1985; Cameron (ed.) 1990.
97. Pateman 1989, Ch. 2.
98. Okin 1989a, pp 10–13.
99. Woods 1984; Cockburn 1983, 1985; Connell 1987, Ch. 6; Brod 1987, Ch. 3.
100. R. Dworkin, 1981.
101. Pateman 1988, 1989, Ch. 2.
102. Rawls 1971, pp 128, 146; see Okin 1989a, Ch. 2.
103. See Wolfenden 1957; J. S. Mill 1974; Hart 1963.

104. There is a vast feminist literature on this topic. See for example Elshtain 1981a; Pateman 1989, Ch. 6; MacKinnon 1989, Ch. 10; Jaggar 1983; Olsen 1983; O'Donovan 1985, Okin 1989a.

105. Lacey 1993b, p. 91.

106. Young 1989; MacKinnon 1989; Smart 1989.

107. Young 1989, pp 116–21; Dietz 1991; Lacey 1993b.

108. Of course, feminist theorists are not the only ones to have argued for the inadequacy of traditional conceptions of political institutions. Marxists have always challenged them, so have 'pluralist' political scientists from a broadly liberal perspective such as Dahl (Dahl 1961, 1983). The sociological perspective of political scientists like Dahl represented a challenge to traditional conceptions of 'politics' as the realm of constitutions and state institutions proper.

109. Some theorists have argued that feminists too share in this aversion to power. We think this is a misreading of feminist politics and we discuss it further in Chapter 4. Meanwhile see Phillips 1992 and Braidotti 1991.

Chapter 3

1. For an assessment of the contribution of liberal analysis to women's struggles in a number of political spheres see Walby 1990; Bryson 1992, Ch. 8.

2. For general discussion of equality of opportunity in liberalism see Kymlicka 1990, Ch. 3.

3. See generally *Feminist Review* (ed.) 1986.

4. See Walby 1986; Brown and Pechman 1987; Hernes 1987; McRae 1991; Bradley 1989; Crompton and Mann (eds) 1986. On the role of particular working practices in maintaining male dominance see Cockburn 1985.

5. Feminist doubts are voiced in O'Donovan and Szyszczak 1988; Smart 1989, Ch. 7.

6. O'Donovan and Szyszczak 1988, pp 176–85; Rhode 1989, p. 121.

7. *Turley* v. *Allders Department Stores* (1980) *ICR* 66; *Hayes* v. *Malleable Working Men's Club* (1985) *ICR* 703; *Webb* v. *EMO Air Cargo UK* (1990) *IRLR* 124.

8. *Sex Discrimination Act* 1975 section 1(i)(a). The SDA also covers housing, education, the provision of goods and services, and a number of other specific practices such as advertising.

9. For further discussion see Lacey 1986.

10. *Sex Discrimination Act* 1975 s. 1(i)(b).

11. See Lacey 1986 and Lacey 1992b.

12. Lacey 1986, 1992c; McCrudden 1985.

13. Waldron 1985.

14. O'Donovan and Szyszczak 1988; for more general discussion of equal value and comparable worth policies see Evans and Nelson 1989; Blum 1991.
15. Op. cit.
16. See R. Dworkin 1977, Ch. 9; 1985 Chs 14, 15 and 16; Sandel 1982, pp 135–47.
17. Rubenstein 1983, 1987. For a critical but constructive discussion of legal approaches to sexual harassment see MacKinnon 1987, Ch. 9.
18. Berlin 1989b for a liberal objection to 'positive' conceptions of freedom.
19. Lloyd 1984; Benhabib 1989.
20. This is particularly true of the existentialists and some of their forebears. See Cameron and Frazer 1987, Chs 2 and 5. See also Hegel *Phenomenology* (Hegel 1977) S.463 where 'the union of man and woman' is analysed as peculiarly ethically significant. See Lloyd 1984.
21. For critical discussion see Lacey, Wells and Meure 1990, Ch. 5.
22. Temkin 1987. See also Smart 1989, Ch. 2; MacKinnon 1987, Ch. 6; Rhode 1989, Ch. 10.
23. Williams 1983, p. 238. It is interesting that he uses the term 'masterful'; see Lloyd 1984; Cameron and Frazer 1987. Also, Pateman 1989, Ch. 4 'Women and consent'.
24. MacKinnon 1989, Ch. 11; MacKinnon 1987, Part III; A. Dworkin 1981; Brown 1981, pp 5–18; Kappeler 1986; Smart 1989, Ch. 6.
25. We consider, though, that Kappeler 1986 offers a better analysis of what is really at issue in pornography; it raises difficult questions about what legislation and social policy feminists want.
26. For a critical discussion of this problem see Cameron and Frazer 1992. See also Lacey 1993b.
27. *Hudnut* v. *American Booksellers' Association Inc.* 475 US 1001 (1986). See Lacey 1993b.
28. For more detailed discussion see Lacey 1993b.
29. Brownmiller 1985; *Feminist Review* (ed.) 1987; Temkin 1987; Hanmer and Maynard 1987; Coward 1984.
30. See Randall 1987; Rendel 1987, Stiehm 1987, Jones and Jonasdottir (eds) 1988; Hernes 1987; Watson 1990 discusses women's political participation in Australia.
31. On the relation between poverty and political participation see Lister 1990 and 1991. See also Gordon (ed.) 1990; Dale and Foster 1986; Lacey 1992b; Pateman 1989, Ch. 8.
32. Pateman 1989, esp. pp 182–5.
33. Phillips 1991, Ch. 3.
34. Pateman 1970; Phillips 1991; see also Barber 1984.
35. Benhabib 1989; Cornell 1987b; see also 1992, Ch. 2.

Chapter 4

1. Avineri and de-Shalit (eds) 1992 collect together some key articles in the communitarianism debate. For a clear and accessible introduction to the main communitarian thinkers see Mulhall and Swift 1992. Sandel (ed.) 1984 gives a good idea of the range of issues encompassed in the communitarian critique of liberalism.

2. Those who are identified as communitarians are MacIntyre 1981, 1988, 1990; Taylor 1985a and b; Sandel 1982; Walzer 1983; Selznick 1987, 1988.

3. Like all such intellectual movements, the 'New Public Law' is a relatively broad umbrella covering a range of views. Among the most important contributions to the debate are articles by Brest 1988; Michelman 1988; Sherry 1986; Sunstein 1988; Rubin 1991. Critics include Bell and Bansal 1988; Kahn 1989; Sullivan 1988. Gardbaum makes explicit the links between civic republicanism and communitarianism, as do Taylor 1989a and Tushnet 1991.

4. For discussion of the hermeneutic tradition and its place in social science see Giddens 1979, 1987; also Taylor 1985a and b. For interpretivism in legal theory see Dworkin 1986; Fish 1989; Goodrich 1986.

5. For discussions of the work of the Frankfurt School see Benhabib and Dallmayr (eds) 1990; Craib 1984, Ch. 11; Thompson and Held (eds) 1982.

6. Rorty 1979, 1989, 1991a.

7. Socialist feminism is discussed and developed in Jaggar 1983, Chs 6 and 10, discussed in Segal 1987, Ch. 2. 'Cultural feminism' designates those feminists who reject biological essentialism, economic reductivism, and traditional psychoanalysis. Instead they emphasise how all social reality (including our sexuality) is socially constructed. Although it is likely that socialist and cultural feminists will have a great deal in common, cultural feminism has been sceptical about commitment to any existing political parties or projects. See Lovenduski and Randall 1993. The editorial to the first issue of *Trouble and Strife* (1983) sets out one version of what is distinctive about cultural feminism.

8. Sandel 1982, 1984 Introduction.

9. Walzer 1983; Unger 1987.

10. MacIntyre 1981, 1988, 1990.

11. Unger 1983, p. 602; Rorty 1988.

12. Miller 1989.

13. Taylor 1989b, p. 161.

14. Berlin 1989a; Hayek 1960.

15. Holmes 1989.

16. See n. 3 above.
17. Dewey 1930a, 1930b; Arendt 1958.
18. See n. 4 above.
19. See n. 4 above; see also Gadamer 1976, 1991.
20. For discussion of reflexive methods in social science and the principles of the social interpretive construction of reality see Berger and Luckmann 1966; Filmer *et al.*, 1972; Heritage 1985; Blumer 1986.
21. Dewey 1930a, 1930b. See also Putnam 1990; C. West 1989, 1990; Grey 1990; Radin 1990; Matsuda 1990 – all of which are contributions to a symposium on pragmatism which occupies a whole issue of *Southern California Law Review*. Also see Brint and Weaver (eds) 1991.
22. Rorty 1979, 1989, 1991a.
23. See n. 5 above for references to work of the Frankfurt School.
24. For critical analysis of Habermas's recent theory see Fraser 1989b; Benhabib 1989; Benhabib and Dallmayr 1990. See also McCarthy 1978; Baynes 1992.
25. Baynes 1992.
26. See n. 7 above.
27. See n. 7 above.
28. See contrast between Sandel and Taylor on the one hand, and MacIntyre on the other. See Frazer and Lacey forthcoming; Passerin d'Entreves, 1991.
29. Sandel 1982, pp 147–54.
30. Unger 1987, vol. 1 pp 3–4, 88–9, 194–5 for discussion of 'institutional and imaginative formative contexts'. See also Habermas 1981; MacIntyre 1981.
31. Hegel is the most notable modern proponent. See Lloyd 1984; Taylor 1979, Ch. 1.
32. This movement is evocatively captured in Taylor 1989.
33. Nagel 1986; Rorty 1991a, pt. 1.
34. Rorty 1991b, for example.
35. Taylor 1989, Chs 3–5 and pp 513ff.
36. See Lacey 1993c for further discussion.
37. For discussion of club goods see Sandler and Tschirhart 1980.
38. Walzer 1983, Ch. 3; Sandel 1982, Ch. 4 and conclusion.
39. Unger 1987, Vol. I pp 43–7; Rorty 1989, Ch. 9.
40. Gilligan 1982; Noddings 1984; Ruddick 1984, 1990.
41. Devlin 1968.
42. Rorty 1989, 1991a; for comment see Malachowski (ed.) 1990.
43. Sandel 1982.
44. Taylor 1992; Walzer 1992.
45. Rawls 1988.
46. Rorty 1991a, p. 175 and p. 197.

47. Dworkin 1986, 1989, 1990.
48. Dworkin 1989, 1990.
49. Kymlicka 1989, p. 178.
50. For a particularly clear statement of this position see Walzer 1987.
51. Cf. Hampton 1989.
52. Rawls 1980, 1985; Rorty 1991a.
53. Taylor 1989a, pp 342ff.
54. Benhabib 1989.
55. Walzer 1987.
56. This idea is developed by Cornell 1986, 1991; see further in Ch. 6.
57. Coote and Campbell 1987, Ch. 1; Kaplan 1992; Lovenduski and Randall, 1993 for historical reviews of organisational debates and developments in women's movements. See also, for example, Henry 1984, Kelly 1985, Viennot 1986 – examples of contemporary interventions and comments.
58. Braidotti 1991.
59. Phillips 1992, p. 74.
60. Lovenduski and Randall, 1993.
61. Kaplan 1992; Coote and Campbell 1987; Lovenduski and Randall, 1993. (However, at the time of going to press there is an attempt to launch a 'Women's Party' in the UK.).
62. Sargent (ed.) 1986.
63. Lovenduski and Randall, 1993.
64. See Coote and Campbell 1987 for information about umbrella groups and national networks in the UK. See Kaplan 1992 for comparative data on Europe.
65. Smart 1989.
66. Barrett and MacIntosh 1982, Ch. 1.
67. Taylor 1989a, Ch. 11.
68. Feminists are not the only people concerned about processes in groups – counselling and group therapy practices have long emphasised the importance of such factors. See Ernst and Goodison 1981.
69. For references see n. 39 above.
70. What follows is the result of a thought experiment based on Nozick's *Anarchy State and Utopia* (Nozick 1974) – given his market principles and principles of individual autonomy and rights, how *is* childcare to be done?
71. For critical discussion see Phillips 1991, esp. Ch. 5, and Lovenduski and Randall, 1993.
72. See Gunn 1989, esp. pp 198–9.
73. Harding 1986, Ch. 6; 1987, Ch. 1.
74. Smith 1987, esp. pp 88–91; 1988 esp. Chs 2 and 3.
75. Radin 1990.
76. See Matsuda 1986; Williams 1991; Scott 1990.
77. Smith 1987, esp. p. 92.

Chapter 5

1. See A. Dworkin 1983; B. Campbell 1987.
2. See for example Bryson 1992; Segal 1987; Smart 1989, Ch. 6.
3. Gilligan 1982; Noddings 1984; Ruddick 1984, 1990; Sherry 1986; R. West 1988; for critical comment see Bryson 1992; Flanagan and Jackson 1987; Okin 1990; Tronto 1989.
4. See for example, Taylor 1992.
5. See in particular Harris 1990; P. Williams 1991. As Gisela Kaplan shows (Kaplan 1992, Ch. 1), questions about diversity have preoccupied women's movements at various stages in their history.
6. For a discussion of this dilemma, see Butler 1990, Ch. 1.
7. See Spelman 1989.
8. This relates to the realist position in the social sciences which we defend in Chapter 6. A similar position in respect of race – acknowledging the dual need to recognise its reality and its contingency – is expressed by Patricia Williams (P. Williams 1991): for comment, see Halley 1991, pp 196–7. The position we take up is also similar to that of Mansbridge (Mansbridge 1991, p. 32). For a helpful general discussion of essentialism, see Fuss 1989. Fuss's defence of 'strategic essentialism' is criticised by Cornell (Cornell 1991, pp 181–4): for critical analysis of essentialist traces in Cornell's own position, see Lacey 1993a; S. Williams 1990.
9. See Wilson 1992; Lacey 1993b.
10. Carol Gilligan, whose work is often invoked in support of the latter claim, is herself careful to avoid any such generalisation. But other writers have not always been so restrained in their use of her data, which is itself based on relatively small-scale research. For more detailed discussion of Gilligan, see Chapter 2.
11. Catharine MacKinnon expresses this point eloquently in her well-known critique of Gilligan: MacKinnon 1989, pp 51–2. See also Susan Wolf's comment on Taylor (1992) (Wolf 1992). We do not mean to imply that the cultural recognition argument is by any means straightforward in the case of the other groups we mention: for them, too, significant aspects of 'their' culture may have been imposed or developed in response to oppression. None the less, the claim to cultural recognition seems to us to be a more central and potentially less problematic feature of, for example, native American politics than could be the case for feminist politics.
12. Kaplan 1992, Ch. 1.
13. Daly 1983; A. Dworkin 1981; Firestone 1971; Griffin 1981; MacKinnon 1987, 1989. For critical comment, see Segal 1987, 1990.
14. See A. Dworkin 1983.

15. See MacKinnon 1987, Part III; 1989, Ch. 9; the ordinance was held to be unconstitutional by the US Supreme Court in *Hudnut* v. *American Booksellers Association Inc.* 475 US 1001 (1986). On the political alliances involved, see Segal 1990, p. 225. For a more detailed discussion, see Chapter 3.

16. An interesting example of the political ambiguity of certain communitarian and feminist ideas is to be found in Elshtain 1981a.

17. See Scruton 1980; Scruton (ed.) 1991.

18. HMSO 1988, 1990.

19. See Young 1989; 1990a, Ch. 8; 1990b.

20. Cf. Glendon 1991: whilst much of Glendon's critique of the individualistic rights discourse which dominates American political debate would evoke a sympathetic response from the political left, several of her policy suggestions have undoubtedly conservative implications.

21. Lukes 1973, 1974; Thompson 1978; R. Williams, 1960, 1973; MacPherson 1962, 1966, 1973.

22. R. Dworkin 1989; Freeden 1978, 1986; Okin 1989a; Rawls 1980, 1985; Raz 1986; Rosenblum 1987; Walzer 1990.

23. For a critique of the ahistoricism of much communitarian thought, facilitated by its abstractness, see Holmes 1989.

24. For useful assessments of this and other aspects of communitarianism, see Buchanan 1989, Gutmann 1985, Kymlicka 1988.

25. Bernstein 1983.

26. MacIntyre 1981, 1988.

27. MacIntyre 1981, p. 187.

28. See Frazer and Lacey 1993 for a fuller discussion of this problem.

29. Rorty 1991b: this also seems to be an implication of Taylor's recent argument (Taylor 1992): cf. n. 11 above and accompanying text.

30. See Waldron 1989.

31. See Mansbridge 1991, pp 15–18.

32. See Mansbridge 1991; Pateman, 'The fraternal social contract' in Pateman 1989: Pateman's views are discussed in more detail in Chapter 2.

33. On this point see Holmes 1989 and Rosenblum 1989b.

34. On the distinction between public goods and club goods, see Sandler and Tschirhart (1980). There is, of course, a vast economic literature on clubs which further differentiates among club goods on the basis of criteria such as distribution of access to benefits within the club itself. For our purposes, however, the distinction helps to mark up two essential points. The first is that club goods constitute one empirically and politically significant instance of 'impure' public goods – i.e. public goods from which it is possible to exclude some people; the second is that, in the real world, far more public goods (clean air included) are impure than pure. Our thanks to David Soskice for alerting us to the literature on clubs.

35. We discuss this further in Chapter 6.
36. For further critical discussion of the communitarian (non)-treatment of the issue of membership, see Gardbaum 1992; Hirsch 1986; Okin 1989a, Ch. 3; Waldron 1989 and 1992.
37. Okin 1989a, Ch. 6.
38. In Walzer's more recent work the implicit answer seems to be that the basis for such a judgement is essentially a liberal one: Walzer, 1990, 1992.
39. Pateman 1988, p. 142.
40. MacIntyre 1981 pp 221–4.
41. Rorty 1991b.
42. See Burrows 1990; Fraser 1989c; Hollis 1990; Taylor 1990 and B. Williams 1990: cf. Nussbaum 1991, Ch. 8.
43. Lovibond 1989, 1992: these questions are dealt with more fully in Ch. 6.
44. But for constructively critical discussion of these issues, see Benhabib 1989, 1992b; Young 1990c, Ch. 7; Fraser 1989a, pp 126–7, 166–71; Mansbridge 1991.
45. Taylor 1989a, Chs 1–5 passim: see particularly p. 100.
46. Taylor 1992; in his comment on Taylor's essay, Walzer too identifies himself as a liberal (Walzer 1992). Walzer goes further than Taylor in endorsing the choice by particular countries (including the US) of a neutralist version of liberalism such as that defended by Ronald Dworkin (R. Dworkin 1978) as the best political framework for accommodating cultural diversity. On the question of the possibility and adequacy of a non-atomistic and perfectionist liberalism, see Mendus 1989, Chs 4 and 5.
47. See, for example, R. Dworkin 1989, 1990: for comment, see Selznick 1989; Waldron 1989; B. Williams 1989.
48. See Young 1990a, Chs. 4–6.
49. Mansbridge 1991, pp 15–18.
50. Walzer 1983, pp 28–9, 223.
51. For critical comment, see Young 1987b; 1990a, Ch 4; Benhabib and Dallmayr (eds) 1990; Thompson and Held (eds) 1982.
52. See n. 11 above and accompanying text.
53. Sandel 1982, pp 170ff.
54. Pateman 1988.
55. See Richards 1980.
56. Particularly in his most recent work, Taylor (1992) distances himself from a simple socialisation model in favour of a dialogical account of the acquisition of identity. The same is true of Walzer: see n. 72 below. For further discussion, see Chapter 6.
57. On problems of accommodating critical reflexivity in communitarian thought, see Downing and Thigpen 1986; Passerin d'Entreves 1991.
58. Cf. R. Williams 1960; Kenny 1991.

59. Tönnies 1957.
60. MacIntyre 1981; see Frazer and Lacey 1993; Okin 1989a, Ch. 3.
61. Unger 1983, p. 602.
62. Rorty 1989: cf. Rorty's view of Unger's romanticism: Rorty 1988.
63. See Burrows, 1990; Hollis 1990. On the tension between communitarian and 'existentialist' strands in Rorty's thought, see Guignon and Hiley 1990.
64. Walzer 1983, pp 28–9. Walzer does advert to the fragmentation of subjectivity in his more recent work (Walzer 1990), in which he takes a line more sympathetic to Rawlsian liberalism than that of *Spheres of Justice*; see also Walzer 1992.
65. Sandel 1982, p. 144.
66. Sandel 1982, p. 172.
67. For stylistic reasons, we shall from now on use the term 'reflective' to encompass both 'reflective' and 'reflexive' as here defined, except where the context is one in which we mean specifically to focus on reflexivity.
68. Taylor 1989a.
69. Taylor 1989a, Chs 1–5 and pp 342ff: see Mulhall and Swift 1992, Ch. 3.
70. Cf. Nussbaum 1991, Ch. 15.
71. See Chapter 6 for further discussion of such intermediate accounts of subjectivity.
72. Here we are referring to Walzer 1983; his ideas on subjectivity have developed, however, and have been expounded more fully in Walzer 1987, 1988. In his more recent work (Walzer 1990, 1992) he places himself nearer to the Sandel/Taylor view.
73. See MacIntyre 1981; for critical discussion see Okin 1989a, Ch. 3; Frazer and Lacey 1993.
74. Unger 1987; see Hutchinson 1990. Hutchinson notes in particular Unger's assumption (in Vol. 2, p. 398) that human reproduction will take care of itself.
75. Okin 1989a, Chs 3 and 6.
76. See for example Taylor 1989a, pp 8, 100, 291.
77. Habermas 1981, Vol. 2.
78. Fraser 1989b. See also Taylor 1989a, pp 509ff.
79. Gardbaum (1992) develops this argument.
80. Walzer 1983, Ch. 9.
81. See Okin 1989a, Chs 3 and 6.
82. Rorty 1991b.
83. For a critique of this and other feminist implications of Rorty's position, including his individualism, see Fraser 1989b; Hutchinson 1989; Lovibond 1992. For further discussion of the problems pragmatism presents for the critical foothold of radical politics, see Chapter 6. In a recent lecture on Human Rights in the Amnesty International Series, delivered in Oxford on February 26 1993, Rorty's analysis did give

gender, as a critical and theoretical tool, the central place feminist writers such as ourselves argue it should have. We look forward to seeing whether this development in his thinking prompts Rorty to reassess his position on 'public and private'.

Chapter 6

1. Rawls, 1980, 1985, 1987, 1988: for comment on the continuities between liberalism and communitarianism, see Ryan 1993.
2. R. Dworkin 1986, 1989.
3. Rosenblum 1987, 1989b.
4. Raz 1986.
5. Hobhouse 1922; Hobson, 1901; see Freeden 1990a, 1990b.
6. See Taylor 1992; Walzer 1990, 1992.
7. See his 'Postmodernist Bourgeois Liberalism' in Rorty 1991a, p. 197: the communitarian strand in Rorty's work is discussed in Guignon and Hiley 1990.
8. Rorty 1991a, p. 198.
9. Walzer 1982, p. 19.
10. See in particular Unger 1983.
11. Jaggar 1983, 1989 Chs 3–5; Lloyd 1984, 1989; Butler 1990, Ch. 1.
12. Derrida 1976, 1978a; Lacan 1977; Mitchell and Rose 1982.
13. See Laclau and Mouffe 1985; see Bourdieu 1990 for an account of a development away from binary structuralism (which is not, however, 'deconstructionist').
14. See in particular, Cornell 1986, 1991.
15. Cornell 1991, pp 92–118 and Ch. 4.
16. Radin and Michelman 1991, pp 1053–4.
17. See Young 1990a, pp 169ff.
18. This kind of argument for and use of deconstruction is to be found in Fraser 1989b; Radin and Michelman 1991; Rhode 1990a; Young 1990a.
19. See for example, Giddens 1979, 1987.
20. See Elster 1983, 1989, 1991.
21. Berger and Luckmann 1966.
22. Giddens 1979, 1987: cf. Unger 1987.
23. See Beetham 1991, Chs 3–6.
24. Foucault 1976, 1977, 1980, 1982.
25. Derrida 1976, 1978a, 1978b, 1991; Lacan 1977; Kristeva 1986.
26. Mitchell 1974; Cornell 1991.
27. Cornell 1986, 1990; Hegel 1969: cf. Schwartzenbach 1991.
28. Chodorow 1978; see also Dinnerstein 1976.

29. Cornell 1991, Ch. 1; Segal 1990, Chs 4 and 10.
30. For the application of such a theory, see Walkerdine 1990, Ch. 19.
31. This has been explicated by Derrida in terms of the concept of '*différance*': see Cornell 1991, Chs 2 and 3.
32. Giddens 1984.
33. Unger 1987, Vols 1 and 3.
34. Benhabib 1988, 1992b.
35. Young 1987b; 1990a Chs 4–6, 8.
36. Held 1985; 1990: our account also has much in common with Cornell's notion of the 'reciprocally constituted subject' (Cornell 1992) and Taylor's account of the 'dialogical' creation of human identity (Taylor 1992).
37. See Walzer 1987.
38. Cornell 1986.
39. See Foucault 1967, 1973, 1977, 1980.
40. For a critical appraisal of this tendency, see Fraser 1989a; Taylor 1989a, Chs 35 and 39; Hartsock 1990.
41. See R. West 1987.
42. Taylor 1989b.
43. Empiricism has also, of course, been associated with scepticism about the existence of an external world; indeed, for many philosophers of science, taking an empiricist stance *entails* that one take a constructionist view of knowledge: see Popper, 1959, 1983; Van Fraassen 1980.
44. See Giddens 1979; Cameron *et. al.*, 1992, Introduction.
45. For discussion of this kind of development in the philosophy of the social sciences, see Bohman 1991; Outhwaite 1987.
46. Minow and Spelman 1990.
47. Dworkin 1989; see also Cornell's analysis (Cornell 1986) of Dworkin 1986. She illustrates the basic tension which Dworkin's notion of the community of principle creates between backward-looking, conventional understandings of community obligations and transcendental, normative ideas.
48. Radin and Michelman 1991.
49. Taylor 1989a: cf. Nussbaum 1991, Ch. 6. Writers committed to deconstruction, too, do not necessarily abandon universalist appeals: see Cornell 1992, Introduction and Ch. 1.
50. This is the view held by Richard Rorty 1989 and 1991a.
51. See particularly 'Postmodernist Bourgeois Liberalism' in Rorty 1991a, p. 197.
52. Lovibond 1992.
53. Taylor 1989a.
54. Dworkin 1986, 1989.
55. Habermas 1981.

56. Freeden 1990b; Nussbaum 1991, Ch. 15.
57. See Freeden 1990a, esp. p. 500; cf. Nussbaum 1991, Ch. 15; Taylor 1989a.
58. See Glover 1977, Chapter 1. By 'modernity as a tradition' we mean to draw on both the historical idea of modernity 'proper' and the cultural idea of 'modernism' as distinguished by Featherstone 1988: see Ch. 1 above pp 6–40.
59. Waldron 1989.
60. See Taylor 1990; cf. Nussbaum 1991, p. 229.
61. Taylor 1989b.
62. Cf. Hampton 1989.
63. See Taylor 1989b; see also Gardbaum 1992; Ryan 1993.
64. Sandel 1982 pp 148–51; see Chapter 4 above.
65. See Nagel 1986.
66. The writers we have in mind are Seyla Benhabib, R. W. Connell, Drucilla Cornell, Nancy Fraser, Michael Freeden, Jane Mansbridge, Charles Taylor, Michael Walzer and Iris Marion Young.
67. Cf. Lacey 1988, Chs 5 and 8; Nedelsky 1989.
68. Young 1990a, p. 240.
69. On the distinction between ordinal and cardinal conceptions of equality, see Honderich 1981.
70. On the links between welfare states and conceptions of citizenship, and for assessment of the deficiencies of current welfare states, see Dale and Foster 1986; Gordon (ed.) 1990; Lacey 1992b; Plant *et al.*, 1980.
71. See Young 1990a, Ch. 1.
72. Benhabib 1989, 1992b; Cornell 1987a, 1987b and 1992 (in the last, her ideal is described as 'communicative freedom'). For some similar ideas, expressed in different terms, see Fraser 1989a, pp 166–71, 1989b; Radin and Michelman 1991, pp 1040–3.
73. Young 1990a, particularly Chs 1 and 2.
74. Cf. Beetham's excellent account of how particular regimes of legitimacy tend to reproduce themselves: Beetham 1991, esp. Ch. 4.
75. Young 1990a, pp 30–3.
76. For Foucault's statement of what we have called the 'practice' conception, see Foucault 1976, pp 92ff; for an excellent critical discussion, see Fraser 1989a, Part 1; McNay 1992. On normative and social science questions concerning the legitimation of power, see Beetham 1991.
77. Cf. Beetham 1991, Ch. 2.
78. The distinction between 'power with' and 'power over' derives from the work of Mary Parker Follett 1942; see also Emmett 1953–4; Hartsock 1974; Lukes 1986; Mansbridge 1991, pp 23ff. On the normative primacy of democratic theories of legitimacy, see Beetham 1991, Chs 3 and 8.
79. Young 1990c, pp 169ff.

80. Harris 1990; Rhode 1990a; Spelman 1989: for further discussion of the problem of essentialism, see Chapter 5 above.
81. For striking illustrations of the complexity of subjectivity revealed by empirical research, see Mansbridge 1992; Walkerdine 1990, Ch. 1.
82. Adorno 1973: see Young 1990a, pp 160–73, 229–32. The same basic idea is sometimes expressed in terms of the 'metaphysics of presence'.
83. See Young 1990a, Ch. 4 and pp 230ff.
84. Waldron 1992.
85. Cf. Mansbridge's discussion of resistance: Mansbridge 1991, pp 27–8.
86. We take this kind of thinking to be represented, explicitly or implicitly, in the work of Seyla Benhabib (1986, 1989, 1992b) and Drucilla Cornell (1987a, 1987b, 1992, Ch. 2). As we argue below, we also think that Iris Marion Young's approach is consistent with this conception. See also Barber 1984; Fraser 1989a, p. 166ff., Gould 1988; Green 1985; Pateman 1970; Phillips 1991.
87. Benhabib 1987.
88. See Fraser 1989a, pp 126–7; Mansbridge 1980, 1991; Phillips 1991.
89. Cornell 1991, 1992.
90. This expression is used by Young (1990a, p. 241).
91. See Young 1990a, Chapters 4, 6 and 8, and in particular pp 230ff.
92. Cf. Rosenblum 1987.
93. As advocated by Taylor (Taylor 1992).
94. Mendus 1989, Chs 3–6; cf. Phillips 1992; Okin 1989b.
95. Raz 1986, Ch. 15; see Mendus 1989, pp 106–9.
96. See Wolf 1992.
97. See Lacey 1992b, discussing Okin 1989a.

Bibliography

Ackerman, Bruce (1980) *Social Justice in the Liberal State*, New Haven: Yale University Press.

Adorno, T. (1973) *Negative Dialectics*, New York: Continuum Press.

Alexander, Sally (1984) 'Women, Class and Sexual Differences', *History Workshop Journal* 17: 124–49; extract reproduced in Phillips (ed.) 1987b.

Althusser, Louis (1969) *For Marx*, transl. B. Brewster, London: New Left Books.

Althusser, Louis (1971a) *Lenin and Philosophy and other essays*, London: New Left Books.

Althusser, Louis (1971b) 'Ideology and Ideological State Apparatuses', in Althusser (1971).

Anderson, Perry (1980) *Arguments Within English Marxism*, London: New Left Books.

Andrews, Richard M. (ed.) (1993) *Punishment: Meanings, Purposes, Practices*, New York: Peter Lang Publishing.

Arblaster, Anthony (1984) *The Rise and Decline of Western Liberalism*, Oxford: Basil Blackwell.

Arendt, Hannah (1958) *The Human Condition*, Chicago: University of Chicago Press.

Aristotle (1962) *The Politics*, Harmondsworth: Penguin.

Avineri, Shlomo and Avner de-Shalit (eds) (1992) *Individualism and Communitarianism*, Oxford: Oxford University Press.

Balbus, Isaac D. (1987) 'Disciplining women', in Benhabib and Cornell (eds) 110–27.

Ball, Terence, James Farr and Russell L. Hanson (eds) (1989) *Political Innovation and Conceptual Change*, Cambridge: Cambridge University Press.

Barbalet, J. M. (1988) *Citizenship*, Milton Keynes: Open University Press.

Barber, Benjamin (1984) *Strong Democracy*, Berkeley: University of California Press.

Barnes, Barry (1988) *The Nature of Power*, Oxford: Polity Press.

Barrett, Michele (1980) *Women's Oppression Today*, London: Verso (2nd Edition 1991).

Barrett, Michele (1991) *The Politics of Truth: From Marx to Foucault*, Oxford: Polity Press.

Barrett, Michele and Mary MacIntosh (1982) *The Anti-Social Family*, London: Verso/New Left Books.

Barry, Brian (1973) *The Liberal Theory of Justice*, Oxford: Clarendon Press.

Barry, Brian (1989) *Theories of Justice: A Treatise on Social Justice*, Hemel Hempstead: Harvester Wheatsheaf.

Baynes, Kenneth (1992) *Normative Grounds of Social Criticism: Kant, Rawls and Habermas*, Albany, New Jersey: State of New York University Press.

Beetham, David (1991) *The Legitimation of Power*, London: Macmillan.

Bell, Colin and Howard Newby (1971) *Community Studies: An introduction to the sociology of the local community*, London: George Allen & Unwin.

Bell, Derrick and Preeta Bansal (1988) 'The Republican revival and racial politics', *Yale Law Journal*, 97: 1609.

Bellah, Robert, Richard Madsen, William Sullivan, Ann Swidler and Steven Tipton (1985) *Habits of the Heart: Individualism and Commitment in American Life*, Berkeley: University of California Press.

Benhabib, Seyla (1986) *Critique, Norm and Utopia*, New York: Columbia University Press.

Benhabib, Seyla (1987) 'The Generalised and the Concrete Other', in Benhabib & Cornell (eds) 77; also in Frazer, Hornsby and Lovibond (eds) and Benhabib (1992a).

Benhabib, Seyla (1988) 'Judgement and the moral foundations of politics in Arendt's thought', *Political Theory*, 16, and in Benhabib (1992a).

Benhabib, Seyla (1989) 'Liberal dialogue versus a Critical Theory of Discursive Legitimation', in Rosenblum (ed.) 143.

Benhabib, Seyla (1992a) *Situating the Self; Gender, Community and Postmodernism in Contemporary Ethics*, Oxford: Polity Press.

Benhabib, Seyla (1992b) 'Autonomy, modernity and community', in Benhabib (1992a).

Benhabib, Seyla and Drucilla Cornell (eds) (1987) *Feminism as Critique*, Oxford: Polity Press.

Benhabib, Seyla and Fred Dallmayr (eds) (1990) *The Discourse Ethics Controversy*, Cambridge: MIT Press.

Benoist, Jean-Marie (1978) *The Structural Revolution*, London: Weidenfeld and Nicolson.

Bentham, Jeremy (1982) *An Introduction to the Principles of Morals and Legislation*, 1789, eds J. Burns and H. L. A. Hart, London: Methuen.

Bentham, Jeremy (1816) *Anarchical Fallacies*, in J. Waldron (ed.) 1987.

Benton, Ted (1984) *The Rise and Fall of Structural Marxism*, London: Macmillan.

Berger, Peter L. and Thomas Luckmann (1966) *The Social Construction of Reality*, London: Allen Lane.

Berki, R. N. (1977) *The History of Political Thought: A short introduction*, London: Dent.

Berlin, Isaiah (1989a) *Four Essays on Liberty*, Oxford: Oxford University Press.

Berlin, Isaiah (1989b) 'Two Concepts of Freedom', in Berlin (1989a); also in Quinton (ed.) 1967.

Bernstein, Richard (1983) *Beyond Objectivism and Relativism*, Oxford: Basil Blackwell.

Birke, Linda (1986) *Women, Feminism and Biology: The feminist challenge*, Brighton: Harvester Press.

Blum, Linda M. (1991) *Between Feminism and Labour: The Significance of the Comparable Worth Movement*, Berkeley and Los Angeles: University of California Press.

Blumer, Herbert (1986) *Symbolic Interactionism: Perspective and Method*, Berkeley: University of California Press.

Bohman, James (1991) *New Philosophy of Social Science*, Oxford: Polity Press.

Bourdieu, Pierre (1977) *Outline of a Theory of Practice*, transl. Richard Nice, Cambridge: Cambridge University Press.

Bourdieu, Pierre (1990) *The Logic of Practice*, transl. Richard Nice, Oxford: Polity Press.

Boyne, R. and Ali Rattansi (eds) (1990) *Post Modernism and Society*, London: Macmillan.

Bradley, Harriet (1989) *Men's Work, Women's Work: A Sociological History of the Sexual Division of Labour in Employment*, Oxford: Polity Press.

Braidotti, Rosi (1991) *Patterns of Dissonance: A Study of Women in Contemporary Philosophy*, New York: Routledge.

Brest, Paul (1988) 'Further beyond the Republican ideal', *Yale Law Journal*, 97: 1623.

Brint, Michael and William Weaver (eds) (1991) *Pragmatism in Law and Society*, Boulder, CO: Westview Press.

Brod, Harry (ed.) (1987) *The Making of Masculinities: The New Men's Studies*, Boston: Allen and Unwin.

Brown, Beverley (1981) 'A feminist interest in pornography: some modest proposals', *m/f* 5 & 6 5.

Brown, Clair and Joseph A. Pechman (1987) *Gender in the Workplace*, Washington: Brookings Institute.

Brownmiller, Susan (1985) *Against Our Will: Men, Women and Rape*, London: Secker & Warburg.

Bryson, Valerie (1992) *Feminist Political Theory: An Introduction*, Basingstoke: Macmillan.

Buchanan, Allen E. (1989) 'Assessing the Communitarian Critique of Liberalism', *Ethics*, 99: 852.

Burke, Edmund (1968) *Reflections on the Revolution in France*, (1790) ed. O'Brien, Harmondsworth: Penguin.

Burrows, Jo (1990) 'Conversational politics: Rorty's pragmatist apology for Liberalism', in Malachowski (ed.) 322.

Butler, Judith (1990) *Gender Trouble: Feminism and the Subversion of Identity*, New York: Routledge.

Cameron, Deborah (1985) *Feminism and Linguistic Theory*, London: Macmillan.

Cameron, Deborah (ed.) (1990) *The Feminist Critique of Language: A reader*, London: Routledge.

Cameron, Deborah and Elizabeth Frazer (1987) *The Lust to Kill: A feminist investigation of sexual murder*, Oxford: Polity Press.

Cameron, Deborah and Elizabeth Frazer (1992) 'On the question of pornography and sexual violence: moving beyond cause and effect', in Catherine Itzin (ed.), *Pornography: women, violence and civil liberties*, Oxford: Oxford University Press.

Cameron, Deborah, Elizabeth Frazer, Penelope Harvey, M. B. H. Rampton, Kay Richardson (1992) *Researching Language: Issues of Power and Method*, London and New York: Routledge.

Campbell, Beatrix (1987) *The Iron Ladies: Why Do Women Vote Tory?*, London: Virago.

Chodorow, Nancy (1978) *The Reproduction of Mothering*, Berkeley: University of California Press.

Cockburn, Cynthia (1983) *Brothers: Male dominance and technical change*, London: Pluto Press.

Cockburn, Cynthia (1985) *Machinery of Dominance: Women, Men and Technical Know-How*, London: Pluto Press.

Cohen, G. A. (1988) *History, Labour and Freedom: Themes from Marx*, Oxford: Clarendon Press.

Cohen, G. A. (1992) *The Tanner Lectures on Human Values*, ed. Grethe B. Peterson, Salt Lake City: University of Utah Press.

Collins, Hugh (1982) *Marxism and Law*, Oxford: Oxford University Press.

Connell, R. W. (1987) *Gender and Power*, Oxford: Polity Press.

Connolly, William E (1988) *Political Theory and Modernity*, Oxford: Basil Blackwell.

Coole, Diana H. (1988) *Women in Political Theory: from ancient misogyny to contemporary feminism*, Hemel Hempstead: Harvester Wheatsheaf.

Coote, Anna and Beatrix Campbell (1987) *Sweet Freedom*, 2nd edition, Oxford: Basil Blackwell.

Cornell, Drucilla (1986) 'Institutionalisation of meaning, recollective imagination and the potential for transformative legal interpretation', *University of Pennsylvania Law Review* 136: 1135.

Cornell, Drucilla (1987a) 'Beyond Tragedy and Complacency', *Northwestern University Law Review* 81: 693.

Cornell, Drucilla (1987b) 'Two lecturers on the normative dimensions of community in the law', *Tennessee Law Review*, 54: 327.

Cornell, Drucilla (1990) 'The doubly prized world: Myth, allegory and the feminine', *Cornell Law Review*, 75, 644.

Cornell, Drucilla (1991) *Beyond Accommodation*, London and New York: Routledge.

Cornell, Drucilla (1992) *The Philosophy of the Limit*, London and New York: Routledge.

Coward, Rosalind (1984) *Female Desire*, London: Paladin.

Craib, Ian (1984) *Modern Social Theory: From Parsons to Habermas*, Brighton: Harvester.

Crompton, Rosemary and Michael Mann (eds) (1986) *Gender and Stratification*, Oxford: Polity Press.

Dahl, Robert A. (1961) *Who Governs: Democracy and Power in an American City*, New Haven: Yale University Press.

Dahl, Robert. A. (1983) *Dilemmas of Pluralist Democracy: Autonomy vs. Control*, New Haven: Yale University Press.

Dale, J. and P. Foster (1986) *Feminists and the Welfare State*, London: Routledge.

Daly, Mary (1983) *Gyn-Ecology: The meta-ethics of radical feminism* London. Women's Press.

Daniels, N. (ed.) (1975) *Reading Rawls*, Oxford: Basil Blackwell.

Davis, Angela (1982) *Women, Race and Class*, London: Women's Press.

Delphy, Christine (1984) *Close to Home: A Materialist Analysis of Women's Oppression*, Transl. and ed. Diana Leonard, London: Hutchinson.

Derrida, Jacques (1976) *Of Grammatology*, Baltimore: Johns Hopkins University Press.

Derrida, Jacques (1978a) *Spurs: Nietzche's Styles*, Transl. B. Harlow, Chicago: University of Chicago Press.

Derrida, Jacques (1978b) *Writing and Difference*, Chicago: University of Chicago Press.

Derrida, Jacques (1978c) 'Structure, sign and play in the discourse of the human sciences', in Derrida 1978b, and reprinted in David Lodge (ed.) 1988.

Derrida, Jacques (1991) *A Derrida Reader*, New York: Columbia University Press.

Devlin, Patrick (1968) *The Enforcement of Morals*, Oxford: Oxford University Press.

Dewey, John (1930a) *Individualism*, New York: Minton, Balch & Co.

Dewey, John (1930b) *Human Nature and Conduct*, New York: The Modern Library.

Dietz Mary G. (1991) 'Hannah Arendt and feminist politics', in Shanley and Patemen (eds).

Dinnerstein, Dorothy (1976) *The Mermaid and the Minotaur: Sexual Arrangements and Human Malaise*, New York: Harper Colophon.

Doherty, Joe, Elspeth Graham and Mo Malek (eds) (1992) *Postmodernism and the Social Sciences*, London: Macmillan.

Douglas, Mary (1966) *Purity and Danger*, London: Routledge and Kegan Paul.

Downing, Lyle A. and Robert B. Thigpen (1986) 'Beyond Shared Understandings', *Political Theory* 14: 451.

Dreyfus, H. and P. Rabinow (eds) (1982) *Beyond Structuralist Hermeneutics*, Chicago: University of Chicago Press.

Duchen, Claire (1986) *Feminism in France: From May '68 to Mitterand*, London: Routledge and Kegan Paul.

Durkheim, Emil (1964) *The Division of Labour in Society*, (1893), New York: Free Press.

Dworkin, Andrea (1981) *Pornography: Men Possessing Women*, London: Women's Press.

Dworkin, Andrea (1983) *Right Wing Women*, London: Women's Press.

Dworkin, Ronald (1975) 'The original position', in Daniels (ed.) 16.

Dworkin, Ronald (1977) *Taking Rights Seriously*, London: Duckworth.

Dworkin, Ronald (1978) 'Liberalism', in S. Hampshire (ed.), and in Dworkin (1985).

Dworkin, Ronald (1981) 'What is Equality?', Parts 1 & 2 *Philosophy and Public Affairs*, 10: 185 & 283.

Dworkin, Ronald (1985) *A Matter of Principle*, Cambridge, Mass: Harvard University Press.

Dworkin, Ronald (1986) *Law's Empire*, London: Fontana.

Dworkin, Ronald (1989) 'Liberal Community', *California Law Review*, 77: 479.

Dworkin, Ronald (1990) 'Equality, democracy and the constitution: We the people in court', *Alberta Law Review*, XXVIII: 324.

Eagleton, Terry (1983) *Literary Theory: An Introduction*, Minneapolis: University of Minnesota Press.

Eagleton, Terry (1991) *Ideology: An Introduction*, London and New York: Verso/Routledge.

Eccleshall, Robert, Vincent Geoghegan, Richard Jay and Rick Wilford (1984) *Political Ideologies: An introduction*, London: Unwin Hyman.

Ehrenreich, Barbara (1983) *The Hearts of Men: American dreams and the flight from commitment*, London: Pluto Press.

Eisenstein, Hester (1984) *Contemporary Feminist Thought*, London: Unwin Hyman.

Eisenstein, Zillah (1979) *The Radical Future of Liberal Feminism*, London and New York: Longman.

Elshtain, Jean Bethke (1981a) *Public Man, Private Woman; woman in social and political thought*, Princeton, NJ: Princeton University Press.

Elshtain, Jean Bethke (1981b) 'Against Androgyny', *Telos*, 47: 5–21; reprinted in Phillips (ed.) 1987b.

Elster, Jon (1983) *Sour Grapes* Cambridge: Cambridge University Press.

Elster, Jon (1989) *Solomonic Judgments*, Cambridge: Cambridge University Press.

Elster, Jon (1991) 'The possibility of rational politics', in Held (ed.) 115.

Elster, Jon and Aalund Hylland (eds) (1986) *Foundations of Social Choice Theory*, Cambridge: Cambridge University Press

Emmett, Dorothy (1953–4) 'The Concept of Power, *Proceedings of the Aristotelian Society*, 54: 1–26.

Engels, F. and K. Marx (1964) *The German Ideology*, (c.1844), London: Lawrence and Wishart.

Engels, F. and K. Marx (1968) *Marx/Engels Selected Works in One Volume*, London: Lawrence and Wishart.

Ernst, Sheila and Lucy Goodison (1981) *In our Own Hands: A Book of Self-Help Therapy*, London: Women's Press.

Evans, Judith *et al*., (1986) *Feminism and Political Theory*, London: Sage.

Evans, Sara M. and Barbara J. Nelson (1989) *Wage Justice: Comparable Worth and the Paradox of Technical Reform*, Chicago: University of Chicago Press.

Faderman, Lilian (1985) *Surpassing the Love of Men: Romantic friendship and love between women from the Renaissance to the present*, Women's Press: London.

Featherstone, Mike (1988) 'In Pursuit of the Post-Modern', *Theory Culture and Society*, vol. 5.

Feminist Review (ed.) (1986) *Waged Work: A Reader*, London: Virago Press.

Feminist Review (1987) *Sexuality: A Reader*, London: Virago Press.

Filmer, Paul, M. Phillipson, D. Silverman and D. Walsh (1972) *New Directions in Sociological Theory*, London: Collier Macmillan.

Finnis, J. M. (1980) *Natural Law and Natural Rights*, Oxford: Clarendon Press.

Firestone, Shulamith (1971) *The Dialectic of Sex*, London: Paladin.

Fish, Stanley (1989) *Doing What Comes Naturally*, Durham, NC: Duke University Press.

Flanagan, Owen and Kathryn Jackson (1987) 'Justice, care and gender: The Kohlberg–Gilligan Debate Revisited', *Ethics* 97: 622–37.

Foucault, Michel (1967) *Madness and Civilisation*, London: Tavistock.

Foucault, Michel (1970) *The Order of Things*, London: Tavistock.

Foucault, Michel (1972) *The Archaeology of Knowledge*, London: Tavistock.

Foucault, Michel (1973) *The Birth of the Clinic*, London: Tavistock.

Foucault, Michel (1976) *The History of Sexuality* Vol. 1, Harmondsworth: Penguin (1981).

Foucault, Michel (1977) *Discipline and Punish*, Harmondsworth: Penguin.

Foucault, Michel (1980) *Power/Knowledge: Selected writings and interviews*, Brighton: Harvester.

Foucault, Michel (1982) 'The subject and power', in Dreyfus and Rabinow (eds) 1982.

Fraser, Nancy (1989a) *Unruly Practices: Power, Discourse and Gender in Contemporary Social Theory*, Oxford: Polity Press.

Fraser, Nancy (1989b) 'What's critical about critical theory?', in Fraser (1989a), and in Benhabib and Cornell (1987).

Fraser, Nancy (1989c) 'Solidarity or singularity? Richard Rorty between Romanticism and technocracy', in Fraser (1989a) and Malachowski (ed) 303.

Frazer, Elizabeth (1988) 'Teenage girls talking about class', *Sociology*, 22.

Frazer, Elizabeth (1989) 'Feminist talk and talking about feminism: Teenage girls' discourses of gender', *Oxford Review of Education*, 15.

Frazer, Elizabeth and Nicola Lacey (1989) 'Communitarianism and feminist lives', *Warwick University Working Papers*.

Frazer, Elizabeth and Nicola Lacey (forthcoming) 'Feminism, MacIntyre and the concept of practice' in Horton and Mendus (eds).

Frazer, Elizabeth and Jennifer Hornsby and Sabina Lovibond (eds) (1992) *Ethics: A feminist reader*, Oxford: Basil Blackwell.

Freeden, Michael (1978) *The New Liberalism: An Ideology of Social Reform*, Oxford: Clarendon Press.

Freeden, Michael (1986) *Liberalism Divided: A Study in British Political Thought 1914–1939*, Oxford: Clarendon Press.

Freeden, Michael (1990a) 'Human Rights and Welfare: A communitarian view', *Ethics*, 100: 489–502.

Freeden, Michael (1990b) 'Rights, needs and community: The emergence of British welfare thought', in Alan Ware and Robert Goodin (eds) *Needs and Welfare*, Sage: London.

Friedman, M. (1963) *Capitalism and Freedom*, Chicago: University of Chicago Press.

Fuss, Diana (1989) *Essentially Speaking: Feminism, Nature and Difference*, London: Routledge.

Gadamer, Hans-Georg (1976) *Philosophical Hermeneutics*, Berkeley: University of California Press.

Gadamer, Hans-Georg (1991) *Gadamer and Hermeneutics: science, culture, literature*, ed. Hugh J. Silverman, London: Routledge.

Gardbaum, Stephen A. (1992) 'Law, politics and the claims of community', *Michigan Law Review*, 90: 685.

Garry, Ann and Marilyn Pearsall (eds) (1989) *Women, Knowledge and Reality: explorations in feminist epistemology*, London: Unwin Hyman.

Gauthier, David (1986) *Morals by Agreement*, Oxford: Oxford University Press.

Gerth, H. H. and C. Wright Mills (eds) (1948) *From Max Weber: Essays in Sociology*, London: Routledge and Kegan Paul.

Giddens, Anthony (1979) *Central Problems in Social Theory*, London: Macmillan.

Giddens, Anthony (1984) *The Constitution of Society*, Oxford: Polity Press.

Giddens, Anthony (1987) *Social Theory and Modern Sociology*, Oxford: Polity Press.

Giddens, Anthony (1991) *Modernity and Self-Identity*, Stanford: Stanford University Press.

Gilligan, Carol (1982) *In a Different Voice: Psychological theory and women's development*, Cambridge, Mass.: Harvard University Press.

Gilman, Charlotte Perkins (1915) *Herland*: published as *Herland: A Lost Feminist Utopian Novel*, 1979, New York: Pantheon.

Glendon, Mary Ann (1991) *Rights Talk: The Impoverishment of Political Discourse*, New York: Free Press.

Glover, Jonathan (1977) *Causing Death and Saving Lives*, London: Penguin.

Goodrich, Peter (1986) *Reading the Law*, Oxford: Basil Blackwell.

Gordon, Linda (ed.) (1990) *Women, the State and Welfare*, Madison: University of Wisconsin Press.

Gould, Carol (1984) *Beyond Domination: New Perspectives on Women and Philosophy*, Totowa, New Jersey: Rowman and Littlefield.

Gould, Carol (1988) *Rethinking Democracy*, Cambridge: Cambridge University Press.

Gray, John (1983) *Mill on Liberty: a defence*, London: Routledge and Kegan Paul.

Gray, John (1989) *Mill's and Other Liberalisms*, London: Routledge.

Grey, Thomas C. (1990) 'Hear the other side: Wallace Stevens and Pragmatist Legal Theory', *Southern California Law Review*, 63: 1567.

Green, Philip (1985) *Retrieving Democracy*, Totowa, N.J.: Rowman & Allanheld.

Griffin, Susan (1981) *Pornography and Silence*, London: Women's Press.

Guest, S. and A. Milne (eds) (1985) *Equality and Discrimination: Essays in Freedom and Justice*, Stuttgart: A.R.S.P., Franz Steiner Verlag Wiesbaden.

Guignon, Charles B. and David R. Hiley (1990) 'Biting the bullet: Rorty on private and public morality', in Malachowski (ed.) p. 339.

Gunn, Jaco (1989) 'Public Interest' in Ball, Farr and Hanson (eds).

Gutmann, Amy (1985) 'Communitarian Critics of Liberalism', *Philosophy and Public Affairs*, 14: 311.

Gutmann, Amy (1992) *Multiculturalism and 'The Politics of Recognition'*, edited with Introduction (see Taylor 1992).

Habermas, Jurgen (1981) *The Theory of Communicative Action*, transl. T. McCarthy, vol. 1 *Reason and the Rationalization of Society*, (1984): vol. 2 *Lifeworld and System: a Critique of Functionalist Reason*, (1987), Boston: Beacon Press.

Habermas, Jurgen (1985) *The Philosophical Discourse of Modernity*, transl. F. G. Lawrence, 1987, Cambridge: MIT Press.

Haksar, Vinit (1979) *Liberty, Equality and Perfectionism*, Oxford: Oxford University Press.

Halley, Janet E. (1991) 'Truth/Value', *Yale Journal of Law and Feminism*, 4: 191.

Hampshire, Stuart (ed.) (1978) *Public and Private Morality*, Oxford: Oxford University Press.

Hampton, Jean (1989) 'Should political philosophy be done without metaphysics?', *Ethics* 99: 91.

Hanmer, Jalna and M. Maynard (1987) *Women, Violence and Social Control*, London: Macmillan.

Harding, Sandra (1986) *The Science Question in Feminism*, Milton Keynes: Open University Press.

Harding, Sandra (ed.) (1987) *Feminism and Methodology*, Milton Keynes: Open University Press.

Harding, Sandra and Merrill B. Hintikka (1987) *Discovering Reality: Feminist Perspectives on Epistemology, Metaphysics, Methodology and the Philosophy of Science*, Reidel: Kluwer.

Harris, Angela P. (1990) 'Race and Essentialism in Feminist Legal Theory', *Stanford Law Review*, 42: 581.

Hart, H. L. A. (1963) *Law, Liberty and Morality*, Oxford: Oxford University Press

Hart, H. L. A. (1983a) *Essays in Jurisprudence and Philosophy*, Oxford: Clarendon Press.

Hart, H. L. A. (1983b) 'Between utility and rights', in Hart (1983a).

Hartsock, Nancy (1974) 'Political change: Two perspectives on power', *Quest* 1: 10–25.

Hartsock, Nancy (1990) 'Foucault on power: a theory for women?', in L. Nicholson (ed.).

Harvey, David (1989) *The Condition of Postmodernity*, Oxford: Basil Blackwell.

Hawkes, Terence (1977) *Structuralism and Semiotics*, Los Angeles and Berkeley: University of California Press.

Hawthorn, Geoffrey (1987) *Enlightenment and Despair: a history of social theory*, Cambridge: Cambridge University Press.

Hayek, F. A. (1960) *The Constitution of Liberty*, London: Routledge and Kegan Paul.

Hayek, F. A. (1962) *The Counter-Revolution of Science*, London: Routledge and Kegan Paul.

Hayek, F. A. (1976) *Law, Legislation and Liberty: ii: The Mirage of Social Justice*, London: Routledge and Kegan Paul.

Hegel, G. W. (1969) *Hegel's Science of Logic*, (1812), Transl. A. V. Miller, New York: Humanities Press International.

Hegel, G. W. (1977) *Phenomenology of Spirit*, (1807), transl. A. V. Miller, New York: Oxford University Press.

Held, David (ed.) (1991) *Political Theory Today*, Oxford: Polity Press.

Held, Virginia (1984) *Rights and Goods*, Chicago: University of Chicago Press.

Held, Virginia (1985) 'Feminism and Epistemology: recent work on the connection between gender and knowledge', *Philosophy and Public Affairs*, 14: 296–307.

Held, Virgina (1990) 'Feminist transformations of moral theory',: *Philosophy and Phenomenological Research*, 1: 321.

Henry, Alice (1984) 'Whose right to decide?', *Trouble and Strife*, no. 2.

Heritage, John (1985) *Garfinkel and Ethnomethodology*, Oxford: Polity Press.

Hernes, Helga Maria (1987) *Welfare State and Woman Power*, Oslo: Norwegian University Press.

Hindess, Barry (1988) *Choice, Rationality and Social Theory*, London: Unwin Hyman.

Hirsch, H. N. (1986) 'The threnody of liberalism: Constitutional liberty and the renewal of community, *Political Theory*, 14: 423.

HMSO (1988) *Green Paper: Punishment, Custody and the Community*.

HMSO (1990) *White Paper: Crime, Justice and Protecting the Public.*

Hobbes, Thomas (1968) *Leviathan*, (1651), ed. C. B. MacPherson, London: Penguin.

Hobhouse, L. T. (1922) *The Elements of Social Justice*, London: Allen and Unwin.

Hobson, J. A. (1901) *The Social Problem*, London: J. Nisbet.

Hollis, Martin (1987) *The Cunning of Reason*, Cambridge: Cambridge University Press.

Hollis, Martin (1990) 'The poetics of personhood', in Malachowski (ed.) 244.

Holmes, Stephen (1989) 'The permanent structure of anti-liberal thought' in Rosenblum (ed.) 227.

Honderich, Ted (1982) '*On Liberty* and morality-dependent harms', *Political Studies*, 30: 504.

Honderich, Ted (1981) 'The question of well-being and the principle of equality', *Mind* XC: 481–504.

hooks, bell (1981) *Ain't I a Woman? Black Women and Feminism*, Boston: South End Press.

hooks, bell (1984) *Feminist Theory: From Margin to Centre*, Boston: South End Press.

hooks, bell (1989) *Talking Back: Thinking Feminist, Thinking Black*, Boston: South End Press.

Horton, J. and S. Mendus (eds) (forthcoming) *After MacIntyre*, Oxford: Polity Press.

Hutchinson, Allan (1989) 'The Three R's: Reading/Rorty/Radically', *Harvard Law Review*, 103: 555.

Hutchinson, Allan (1990) 'A poetic champion composes: Unger (not) on ecology and women', *University of Toronto Law Journal*, 40: 271.

Jaggar, Alison M. (1983) *Feminist Politics and Human Nature*, Brighton: Harvester.

Jaggar, Alison M (1989) 'Love and knowledge: Emotion in feminist epistemology', in Garry and Pearsall (eds).

Jaggar, Alison and Susan R. Bordo (1989) *Gender/Body/Knowledge*, New Brunswick: Rutgers University Press.

Jameson, Frederic (1991) *Post-Modernism, or the Cultural Logic of Late Capitalism*, London: Verso.

Jeffreys, Sheila (1985) *The Spinster and Her Enemies: feminism and sexuality 1800–1930*, London: Pandora.

Jeffreys, Sheila (1990) *Anti-Climax: A feminist perspective on the Sexual Revolution*, London: Women's Press.

Jones, Kathleen B. and Anna G. Jonasdottir (eds) (1988) *The Political Interests of Gender*, London: Sage.

Jordan, June (1986a) *On Call: Political Essays*, London: Pluto Press.

Jordan, June (1986b) 'Report from the Bahamas', in Jordan (1986); and in Frazer, Hornsby and Lovibond (eds).

Kahn, Paul W. (1989) 'Community in Contemporary Constitutional Theory' *Yale Law Journal*, 99: 1.

Kant, Immanuel (1966) *Groundwork for a Metaphysic of Morals*, (1785), transl. and ed. H. J. Paton, as *The Moral Law*, London: Hutchinson.

Kant, Immanuel (1968) *Critique of Pure Reason*, (1787), transl. and ed. J. Kemp Smith, London: Macmillan.

Kaplan, Gisela (1992) *Contemporary Western European Feminism*, London: UCL Press/Allen & Unwin.

Kappeler, Suzanne (1986) *The Pornography of Representation*, Oxford: Polity Press.

Kelly, Liz (1985) 'Feminist v. Feminist', *Trouble and Strife* no. 7.

Kennedy, Ellen and Susan Mendus (eds) (1987) *Women in Western Political Philosophy*, Brighton: Harvester.

Kenny, Michael (1991) 'Facing up to the future: Community in the work of Raymond Williams in the fifties and sixties', *Politics*, 11: 14.

Kristeva, Julia (1986) *The Kristeva Reader*, ed. Toril Moi, New York: Columbia University Press.

Kukathas, Chandran and Philip Pettit (1990) *A Theory of Justice and its Critics*, Oxford: Polity Press.

Kymlicka, Will (1988) 'Liberalism and Communitarianism', *Canadian Journal of Philosophy*, 18: 181.

Kymlicka, Will (1989) *Liberalism, Community and Culture*, Oxford: Clarendon Press.

Kymlicka, Will (1990) *Contemporary Political Philosophy: An introduction*, Oxford: Clarendon Press.

Lacan, Jacques (1977) *Ecrits*, transl. Alan Sheridan, New York: W. W. Norton and Co.

Lacey, Nicola (1988) *State Punishment*, London: Routledge.

Lacey, Nicola (1986) 'Legislation against sex discrimination: Questions from a feminist perspective', *Journal of Law and Society*, 14.

Lacey, Nicola, Celia Wells and Dirk Meure (1990) *Reconstructing Criminal Law*, London: Weidenfeld and Nicolson.

Lacey, Nicola (1992a) 'From individual to group?', in B. Hepple and E. Szyszczak, *Discrimination and the Limits of Law*, London: Mansell.

Lacey, Nicola (1992b) 'Theories of Justice and the Welfare State', in *Social and Legal Studies*, 1 and in W. Maihofer and G. Sprenger (eds) *Praktische Vernunft und Theorien der Gerechtigkeit*, 1992, Stuttgart: Franz Steiner Verlag (ARSP Beiheft 50).

Lacey, Nicola (1993a) 'Closure and critique in feminist jurisprudence: transcending the dichotomy or a foot in both camps?', in A. Norrie (ed.) *Closure and Critique: Current Directions in Legal Theory*, Edinburgh: Edinburgh University Press.

Lacey, Nicola (1993b) 'Theory into practice? Pornography and the public/private dichotomy', *Journal of Law and Society*, 20.

Lacey, Nicola (1993c) 'Punishment; A Communitarian Approach', in Andrews (ed.)

Laclau, Ernesto and Chantal Mouffe (1985) *Hegemony and Socialist Strategy: Towards a Radical Democratic Politics*, London: Verso.

Lakoff, Robin (1975) *Language and Woman's Place*, New York: Harper and Row.

Lees, Sue (1986) *Losing Out: Sexuality and adolescent girls*, London: Hutchinson.

Lessnoff, Michael (ed.) (1990) *Social Contract Theory*, Oxford: Basil Blackwell.

Lévi-Strauss, Claude (1963) *Structural Anthropology*, New York: Basic Books.

Lévi-Strauss, Claude (1969) *Totemism*, Harmondsworth: Penguin.

Lister, Ruth (1990) 'Women, economic dependency and citizenship', *Journal of Social Policy*, 19: 445–67.

Lister, Ruth (1991) 'Citizenship engendered', *Critical Social Policy*, 32: 65–71.

Lloyd, Genevieve (1984) *The Man of Reason: 'Male' and 'Female' in Western Philosophy*, London: Methuen.

Lloyd, Genevieve (1986) 'Selfhood, War and Masculinity', in Pateman and Gross (eds).

Lloyd, Genevieve (1989) 'The man of reason' in Garry and Pearsall (eds).

Locke, John (1967) *Two Treatises of Government*, (1689) ed. P. Laslett, Cambridge: Cambridge University Press.

Lodge, David (ed.) (1988) *Modern Criticism and Theory: A Reader*, London: Longman.

Lorde, Audre (1984a) *Sister Outsider*, New York: Crossing Press.

Lorde, Audre (1984b) 'Age, race, class and sex: Women redefining difference', in Lorde (1984), and in Frazer, Hornsby and Lovibond (eds).

Lovenduski, Joni and Vicky Randall (1993) *Contemporary Feminist Politics: Women and power in Britain*, Oxford: Oxford University Press.

Lovibond, Sabina (1983) *Realism and Imagination in Ethics*, Oxford: Blackwell.

Lovibond, Sabina (1989) 'Feminism and Postmodernism', *New Left Review*, 12.

Lovibond, Sabina (1992) 'A Reply to Richard Rorty', *New Left Review*, 193.

Luhmann, Niklas (1982) *The Differentiation of Society*, transl. Stephen Holmes and Charles Larmore, New York: Columbia University Press.

Luhmann, Niklas (1987) 'Closure and openness: On reality in the world of law', in Teubner (ed.) (1987).

Lukes, Steven (1973) *Individualism*, Oxford: Basil Blackwell.

Lukes, Steven (1974) *Power: A radical view*, B.S.A.; London: Macmillan.

Lukes, Steven (ed.) (1986) *Power*, Oxford: Basil Blackwell.

Lyotard, Jean-Francois (1984) *The Post-Modern Condition: A Report on Knowledge*, Minneapolis: University of Minnesota Press.

McCarthy, Thomas (1978) *The Critical Theory of Jurgen Habermas*, Cambridge: MIT Press.

McCrudden, Christopher (1985) 'Changing notions of discrimination', in Guest and Milne (eds), p. 83.

Macdonell, Diane (1986) *Theories of Discourse*, Oxford: Basil Blackwell.

Machiavelli, Niccolo (1961) *The Prince*, transl. George Bull, Harmondsworth: Penguin.

Machiavelli, Niccolo (1970) *The Discourses*, ed. Bernard Crick, Harmondsworth: Penguin.

MacIntyre, Alasdair (1981) *After Virtue*, London: Duckworth: 2nd edn., 1985.

MacIntyre, Alasdair (1988) *Whose Justice, Which Rationality?*, London: Duckworth.

MacIntyre, Aladair (1990) *Three Rival Versions of Moral Theory*, London: Duckworth.

MacKinnon, Catharine A. (1979) *The Sexual Harassment of Working Women*, New Haven: Yale University Press.

MacKinnon, Catharine A. (1987) *Feminism Unmodified*, Cambridge, Mass: Harvard University Press.

MacKinnon, Catharine A. (1989) *Toward a Feminist Theory of the State*, Cambridge, Mass: Harvard University Press.

McLean, Iain (1987) *Public Choice*, Oxford: Basil Blackwell.

McLellan, David (1986) *Ideology*, Milton Keynes: Open University Press.

McNay, Lois (1992) *Foucault and Feminism*, Oxford: Polity Press.

MacPherson, C. B. (1962) *The Political Theory of Possessive Individualism*, Oxford: Clarendon Press.

MacPherson, C. B. (1966) *The Real World of Democracy*, Oxford: Oxford University Press.

MacPherson, C. B. (1973) *Democratic Theory: Essays in Retrieval*, Oxford: Clarendon Press.

McRae, Susan (1991) *Maternity Rights in Britain*, London: Policy Studies Institute.

MacRobbie, Angela and Mica Nava (eds) (1984) *Gender and Generation*, London: Macmillan.

Madison, James, Alexander Hamilton and John Jay (1987) *The Federalist Papers*, (1788) ed. I. Kramnick, Harmondsworth: Penguin.

Malachowski, Alan (ed.) (1990) *Reading Rorty*, Oxford: Basil Blackwell.

Mansbridge, Jane (1980) *Beyond Adversary Democracy*, New York: Basic Books.

Mansbridge, Jane (ed.) (1990) *Beyond Self-Interest*, Chicago: University of Chicago Press.

Mansbridge, Jane (1991) 'Feminism and democratic community', in John W. Chapman and Ian Shapiro (eds), *Democratic Community: NOMOS XXXXV*, New York: New York University Press.

Mansbridge, Jane (1992) 'Feminist identity: The voices of African-American and White Working-Class Women', unpublished paper delivered at the Graduate Faculty of the New School for Social Research, New York, March 1992.

Marshall, T. E. (1950) *Citizenship and Social Class and Other Essays*, Cambridge: Cambridge University Press.

Marx, Karl (1954) *Capital*, Volume I, (1867 German, 1887 English) London: Lawrence and Wishart.

Marx, Karl and F. Engels (1964) *The German Ideology*, (c.1844), London: Lawrence and Wishart.

Marx, Karl and F. Engels (1968) *Marx/Engels Selected Works in One Volume*, London: Lawrence and Wishart.

Matsuda, Mari (1986) 'Liberal jurisprudence and abstracted visions of human nature', *New Mexico Law Review*, 16: 613.

Matsuda, Mari (1990) 'Pragmatism modified', *Southern California Law Review*, 63: 1763.

Maynard, Mary (1990) 'The re-shaping of sociology: Trends in the study of gender', *Sociology*, 24.

Mendus, Susan (1989) *Toleration and the Limits of Liberalism*, London: Macmillan.

Merquior, J. G. (1979) *The Veil and the Mask*, London: Routledge and Kegan Paul.

Michelman, Frank (1988) 'Law's Republic', *Yale Law Journal*, 97: 1493.

Mill, Harriet Taylor and John Stuart Mill (1970) *Essays on Sex Equality*, ed. Alice Rossi, Chicago: University of Chicago Press.

Mill, John Stuart (1972) *Utilitarianism, Liberty and Representative Government*, (1859, 1861, 1863), ed. H. Acton, London: J.M. Dent and Sons.

Mill, John Stuart (1974) *On Liberty*, (1859), Harmondsworth: Penguin.

Miller, David (1989) 'In what sense must socialism be communitarian?', *Social Philosophy and Policy*, 6, pp 51–73.

Miller, David (1990a) 'The resurgence of political theory', *Political Studies*, XXXVIII: 421.

Miller, David (1990b) *Market, State and Community*, Oxford: Clarendon Press.

Miller, David and Larry Siedentop (eds) (1983) *The Nature of Political Theory*, Oxford: Oxford University Press.

Millett, Kate (1977) *Sexual Politics*, London: Virago.

Minogue, Kenneth (1985) *Alien Powers: The pure theory of ideology*, London: Weidenfeld and Nicolson.

Minow, Martha and Elizabeth Spelman (1990) 'In Context', *Southern California Law Review*, 63: 1597.

Mitchell, Juliet (1974) *Psychoanalysis and Feminism*, London: Allen Lane.

Mitchell, Juliet and Jacqueline Rose (eds) (1982) *Feminine Sexuality: Jacques Lacan and the Ecole Freudienne*, New York: W. W. Norton & Co.

Modleski, Tania (1984) *Loving with a Vengeance: Mass produced fantasies for women*, London: Methuen.

Molyneux, Maxine (1979) 'Beyond the domestic labour debate', *New Left Review*, 116.

Montesquieu (1989) *The Spirit of the Laws* (1748), Cambridge: Cambridge University Press.

Morris, Meghan (1988) *The Pirate's Fiancée: Feminism Reading Postmodernism*, London: Verso.

Mulhall, Stephen (1987) 'The theoretical foundations of liberalism', *Archive of European Sociology*, XXVIII: 269.

Mulhall, Stephen and Adam Swift (1992) *Liberals and Communitarians*, Oxford: Basil Blackwell.

Nagel, T. (1975) 'Rawls on Justice', in Daniels (ed.) 1.

Nagel, T. (1986) *The View From Nowhere*, Oxford: Oxford University Press.

Nedelsky, Jennifer (1989) 'Reconceiving Autonomy', *Yale Journal of Law and Feminism*, 1: 7–36.

Nicholson, Linda J. (1987) 'Feminism and Marx: Integrating kinship with the economic', in Benhabib and Cornell (eds).

Nicholson, Linda J. (ed.) (1990) *Feminism/Postmodernism*, London, Routledge.

Nisbet, Robert (1986) *Conservatism*, Milton Keynes: Open University Press.

Noddings, Nel (1984) *Caring: A feminine approach to ethics and moral education*, Berkeley: University of California Press.

Nozick, Robert (1974) *Anarchy, State and Utopia*, New York: Basic Books.

Nussbaum, Martha (1991) *Love's Knowledge*, Oxford: Oxford University Press.

O'Brien, Mary (1981) *The Politics of Reproduction*, London and New York: Routledge and Kegan Paul.

O'Donovan, Katherine (1985) *Sexual Divisions in Law*, London: Weidenfeld & Nicolson.

O'Donovan, Katherine and Erika Szyszczak (1988) *Equality and Sex Discrimination Law*, Oxford: Basil Blackwell.

Okin, Susan Moller (1978) *Women in Western Political Thought*, Princeton NJ: Princeton University Press.

Okin, Susan Moller (1989a) *Justice, Gender and the Family*, New York: Basic Books.

Okin, Susan Moller (1989b) 'Humanist liberalism', in Rosenblum (ed.) 39.

Okin, Susan Moller (1990) 'Thinking like a woman', in Rhode (ed.) (1990b).

Olsen, Frances (1983) 'The family and the market, *Harvard Law Review*, 96: 1497.

O'Sullivan, Noel K. (1976) *Conservatism*, London: J. M. Dent.

Outhwaite, William (1987) *New Philosophies of Social Science: Realism, Hermeneutics and Critical Theory*, London: Macmillan.

Oxford University Students' Union (1984) *The Ones Who Just Patronise Seem Genial by Comparison: An Enquiry into Sexual Harassment of Women in Oxford University*, Oxford: OUSU.

Parker Follett, Mary (1942) 'Power', in Henry C. Metcalf (ed.) *Dynamic Administration: The Collected Papers of Mary Parker Follett*, New York: Harper.

Parsons, Talcott (1949) *The Structure of Social Action*, New York: Free Press.

Parsons, Talcott (1951) *The Social System*, New York: Free Press.

Passerin d'Entrèves, M. (1991) 'Communitarianism and the question of tolerance', *Journal of Social Philosophy*, 77.

Pateman, Carole (1970) *Participation and Democratic Theory*, Cambridge: Cambridge University Press.

Pateman, Carole (1988) *The Sexual Contract*, Oxford: Polity Press.

Pateman, Carole (1989) *The Disorder of Women*, Oxford: Polity Press.

Pateman, Carole and Elizabeth Gross (eds) (1986) *Feminist Challenges: Social and Political Theory*, Boston: Northeastern University Press.

Pateman, Carole and Mary Lyndon Shanley (eds) (1991) *Feminist Interpretations and Political Theory*, Oxford: Polity Press.

Phillips, Anne (1987a) *Divided Loyalties: dilemmas of sex and class*, London: Virago.

Phillips, Anne (ed.) (1987b) *Feminism and Equality*, Oxford: Basil Blackwell.

Phillips, Anne (1991) *Engendering Democracy*, Oxford: Polity Press.

Phillips, Anne (1992) 'Must Feminists give up on liberal democracy?' in David Held (ed.), *Prospects for Democracy*, *Political Studies* Vol. XL.

Piaget, Jean (1965) *The Moral Judgement of the Child* (f.p. 1932) New York: Free Press.

Piaget, Jean (1971) *Structuralism*, London: Routledge and Kegan Paul.

Piercey, Marge (1979) *Woman On the Edge of Time*, London: Women's Press.

Pitkin, Hannah (1984) *Fortune is a Woman: gender and politics in the thought of Niccolo Machiavelli*, Berkeley and Los Angeles: University of California Press.

Plant, R., H. Lesser and P. Taylor-Gooby (1980) *Political Philosophy and Social Welfare*, London: Routledge and Kegan Paul.

Plato (1955) *Republic*, Harmondsworth: Viking Penguin.

Plato (1970) *Laws*, Harmondsworth: Viking Penguin.

Popper, K. R. (1945) *The Open Society and Its Enemies*, I: *Plato*; II: *Hegel and Marx*, London: Routledge and Kegan Paul.

Popper, K. R. (1959) *The Logic of Scientific Discovery*, London: Unwin Hyman.

Popper, K. R. (1964) *The Poverty of Historicism*, London: Routledge and Kegan Paul.

Popper, K. R. (1983) *Realism and the Aim of Science*, London: Hutchinson.

Putman, Hilary (1990) 'A reconsideration of Deweyan Democracy', *Southern California Law Review*, 63: 1671.

Quinton, Anthony (ed.) (1967) *Political Philosophy*, Oxford: Oxford University Press.

Radin, Margaret Jane (1990) 'The feminist and the pragmatist', *Southern California Law Review*, 63: 1699.

Radin, Margaret Jane and Frank Michelman (1991) 'Pragmatist and poststructuralist critical legal practice', *University of Pennsylvania Law Review*, 139: 1019.

Randall, Vicky (1987) *Women and Politics: An international perspective*, 2nd edition, London: Macmillan.

Rawls, John (1971) *A Theory of Justice*, Cambridge, Mass: Harvard University Press.

Rawls, John (1975) 'Fairness to goodness', *Philosophical Review*, LXXXIV: 536.

Rawls, John (1980) 'Kantian constructivism in moral theory', *Journal of Philosophy*, 77: 515.

Rawls, John (1985) 'Justice as fairness: Political not metaphysical', *Philosophy and Public Affairs*, 14: 223 and in Strong (ed.) (1992).

Rawls, John (1987) 'The idea of an overlapping consensus', *Oxford Journal of Legal Studies*, 7: 1.

Rawls, John (1988) 'The priority of the right and ideas of the good', *Philosophy and Public Affairs*, 17: 251.

Raz, Joseph (1986) *The Morality of Freedom*, Oxford: Clarendon Press.

Rée, Jonathan (1992) 'Language? What language?', Review of David Holdcroft, *Saussure: Signs, Systems and Arbitrariness*, Cambridge: Cambridge University Press., 1991, and David Crystal, *The Cambridge Encyclopaedia of Language*, Cambridge: Cambridge University Press, 1991, *Radical Philosophy* 61.

Rees, John C. (1985) *John Stuart Mill's 'On Liberty'*, Oxford: Oxford University Press.

Rendel, Margherita (ed.) (1987) *Women, Power and Political Systems*, London: Croom Helm.

Rengger, N. J. (1992) 'No time like the present? Post-modernism and political theory', *Political Studies*, XL.

Rhode, Deborah L. (1989) *Justice and Gender*, Cambridge, Mass: Harvard University Press.

Rhode, Deborah L. (1990a) 'Feminist critical theories', *Stanford Law Review*, 42: 617.

Rhode, Deborah L. (ed.) (1990b) *Feminist Perspectives on Sexual Difference*, New Haven: Yale University Press.

Richards, Janet Radcliffe (1980) *The Sceptical Feminist: A philosophical enquiry* London: Routledge and Kegan Paul and Harmondsworth: Penguin.

Riley, Denise (1988) *'Am I That Name?' Feminism and the Category of 'Woman' in History*, Minnesota: University of Minneapolis Press.

Rorty, Richard (1979) *Philosophy and the Mirror of Nature*, Princeton: Princeton University Press.

Rorty, Richard (1988) 'Unger, Castoriadis and the romance of a national future', *Northwestern University Law Review*, 82: 355.

Rorty, Richard (1989) *Contingency, Irony and Solidarity*, Cambridge: Cambridge University Press.

Rorty, Richard (1991a) *Objectivity, Relativism and Truth*, Cambridge, Cambridge University Press.

Rorty, Richard (1991b) 'Feminism and Pragmatism', *Radical Philosophy* 59: 3.

Rose, Jacqueline (1983) 'Femininity and its discontents', *Feminist Review* 14, reprinted in Frazer, Hornsby and Lovibond (eds) 1992.

Rosenblum, Nancy (1987) *Another Liberalism: Romanticism and Reconstruction in Liberal Thought*, Cambridge, Mass: Harvard University Press.

Rosenblum, Nancy (ed.) (1989a) *Liberalism and the Moral Life*, Cambridge, Mass: Harvard University Press.

Rosenblum, Nancy (1989b) 'Pluralism and self-defence', in Rosenblum (ed.) 207.

Rossi, Alice (ed.) (1973) *The Feminist Papers: From Adams to de Beauvoir*, New York: Columbia University Press.

Rousseau, Jean-Jacques (1968) *The Social Contract*, (1762), transl. M. Cranston, Harmondsworth: Penguin.

Rousseau, Jean-Jacques (1985) *A Discourse on Inequality*, (1750), Harmondsworth: Viking Penguin.

Rubenstein, Michael (1983) 'The law of sexual harassment at work', *Industrial Law Journal*, 12: 1.

Rubenstein, Michael (1987) *The Dignity of Women at Work: A Report of the Problem of Sexual Harassment in the Member States of the European Communities* V/412/1/87 Report to the European Commission.

Rubin, Edward L. (1991) 'The concept of law and the new public law scholarship', *Michigan Law Review*, 792.

Ruddick, Sara (1984) 'Maternal thinking', in Joyce Trebilcot (ed.) *Mothering: Essays in Feminist Theory*, New York: Rowman and Allanheld.

Ruddick, Sara (1990) *Maternal Thinking: Towards a politics of peace*, London: Women's Press.

Ryan, Alan (1970) *The Philosophy of John Stuart Mill*, London: Macmillan.

Ryan, Alan (1974) *J.S Mill*, London: Routledge and Kegan Paul.

Ryan, Alan (1993) 'The Liberal Community', *Nomos*, 35, New York: New York University Press.

Sandel, Michael (1982) *Liberalism and the Limits of Justice*, Cambridge: Cambridge University Press.

Sandel, Michael (1984a) 'The procedural republic and the unencumbered self', *Political Theory*, 12: 81, and in Strong (ed.) (1992).

Sandel, Michael (ed.) (1984b) *Liberalism and Its Critics*, Oxford: Basil Blackwell.

Sandler, Todd and John T. Tschirhart (1980) 'The economic theory of clubs: An evaluative survey', *Journal of Economic Literature*, XVIII: 1481–1521.

Sargent, Lydia (ed.) (1986) *The Unhappy Marriage of Marxism and Feminism*, London: Pluto Press.

Saussure, Ferdinand de (1974) *Course in General Linguistics*, 1916, transl. Wade Baskin, London: Fontana.

Schwartzenbach, Sibyl A. (1991) 'Rawls, Hegel and communitarianism', *Political Theory*, 19: 539.

Scott, James C. (1990) *Domination and the Arts of Resistance: Hidden Transcripts*, New Haven: Yale University Press.

Scruton, Roger (1980) *The Meaning of Conservatism*, London: Macmillan.

Scruton, Roger (1991) *Conservative Texts: An anthology*, London: Macmillan.

Sedley, A. and M. Benn (1984) *Sexual Harassment at Work*, London: National Council for Civil Liberties.

Segal, Lynn (1987) *Is the Future Female? Troubled Thoughts on Contemporary Feminism*, London: Virago.

Segal, Lynn (1990) *Slow Motion: Changing Masculinities, Changing Men*, London: Virago.

Selznick, Philip (1987) 'The idea of a communitarian morality', *California Law Review*, 75: 445.

Selznick, Philip (1988) 'Communitarianism and the socially implicated self', *California Law Review*.

Selznick, Philip (1989) 'Dworkin's unfinished task', *California Law Review* 77: 505.

Sen, Amartya K. (1977) 'Rational fools: A critique of the behavioural foundations of economic theory', *Philosophy and Public Affairs*, 6:.

Shanley, Mary Lyndon and Carole Pateman (eds) (1991) *Feminist Interpretations and Political Theory*, Oxford: Polity Press.

Sherry, Suzanna (1986) 'Civic virtue and the feminine voice in constitutional adjudication', *Virginia Law Review*, 72: 543.

Shklar, Judith (1969) *Men and Citizens: A Study of Rousseau's Social Theory*, Cambridge: Cambridge University Press.

Siedentop, Larry (1983) 'Political theory and ideology: The case of the state', in Miller and Siedentop (eds).

Siedman, Steven and David G. Wagner (eds) (1992) *Post-modernism and Social Theory*, Oxford: Basil Blackwell.

Skinner, Quentin (1978) *Foundations of Modern Political Thought Volume I: The*

Renaissance, Cambridge: Cambridge University Press.

Smart, Carol (1989) *Feminism and the power of law*, London: Routledge.

Smart, Carol (1990) 'Law, the sexed body and feminist discourse', *Journal of Law and Society*, vol. 17: 194.

Smart, Carol (1992) 'The woman of legal discourse', *Social and Legal Studies*, vol. 1.

Smart, Carol and Barry Smart (eds) (1978) *Women, Sexuality and Social Control*, London: Routledge and Kegan Paul.

Smith, Dorothy (1987) 'A sociology for women', in Harding (ed.).

Smith, Dorothy (1988) *The Everyday World as Problematic*, Milton Keynes: Open University Press.

Spelman, Elizabeth (1989) *Inessential Woman: Problems of Exclusion in Feminist Thought*, Boston: Beacon Press.

Spender, Dale (1980) *Man Made Language*, London: Routledge and Kegan Paul.

Spender, Dale (ed.) (1983) *Feminist Theorists: Three Centuries of Women's Intellectual Traditions*, London: Women's Press.

Stiehm, Judith (1987) 'Women and citizenship: Mobilisation, participation, representation', in M. Rendel (ed.).

Strong, Tracy B. (ed.) (1992) *The Self and the Political Order*, Oxford: Basil Blackwell.

Sullivan, Kathleen (1988) 'Rainbow Republicanism', *Yale Law Journal*, 97: 1713.

Sunstein, Cass (1988) 'Beyond the republican revival', *Yale Law Journal*, 97: 1539.

Talmon, J.L. (1952) *The Origins of Totalitarian Democracy*, London: Secker and Warburg.

Taylor, Charles (1979) *Hegel and Modern Society*, Cambridge: Cambridge University Press.

Taylor, Charles (1985a) *Human Agency and Language*, Cambridge: Cambridge University Press.

Taylor, Charles (1985b) *Philosophy and the Human Sciences*, Cambridge: Cambridge University Press.

Taylor, Charles (1989a) *Sources of the Self*, Cambridge: Cambridge University Press.

Taylor, Charles (1989b) 'Cross-Purposes: the Liberal-communitarian Debate' in N. Rosenblum (ed.).

Taylor, Charles (1990) 'Rorty in the epistemological tradition', in Malachowski (ed.) 257.

Taylor, Charles (1992) *Multiculturalism and 'The Politics of Recognition'*, ed. A. Gutmann, Princeton, NJ: Princeton University Press.

Temkin, Jennifer (1987) *Rape and the Legal Process*, London: Sweet and Maxwell.

Ten, C. L. (1980) *Mill on Liberty*, Oxford: Oxford University Press.

Teubner, Gunther (ed.) (1987) *Autopoietic Law: A New Approach to Law and Society*, transl. Ian Fraser, Berlin: De Gruyter.

Theory, Culture and Society (1988) 'Postmodernism', Special Issue, Volume 5.

Thompson, Edward P. (1978) *The Poverty of Theory and Other Essays*, London: Merlin Press.

Thompson, John (1984) *Studies in the Theory of Ideology*, Oxford: Polity Press.

Thompson, John and D. Held (eds) (1982) *Habermas: Critical Debates*, London: Macmillan Press.

Tönnies, Ferdinand (1957) *Community and Society*, (*Gemeinschaft und Gesellschaft*, 1887), transl. and ed. Charles P. Loomis, E. Lansing, Michigan State University Press.

Tronto, Joan C. (1989) 'Women and caring: What can feminists learn about morality from caring?' in Jaggar and Bordo (eds).

Tushnet, Mark (1991) 'The possibilities of interpretive liberalism', *Alberta Law Review*, XXIX: 276.

Unger, Roberto M. (1987) *Politics: a Work in Constructive Social Theory* (3 volumes: *Social Theory: Its Situation and Its Task*; *False Necessity*; *Plasticity into Power*), Cambridge: Cambridge University Press.

Unger, Roberto M. (1983) 'The critical legal studies movement in America', *Harvard Law Review*, 99: 561

Van Dyke, Vernon (1975) 'Justice as fairness: For groups?', *American Political Science Review*, 69: 607.

Van Fraassen, Bas C. (1980) *The Scientific Image*, Oxford: Clarendon Press.

Viennot, Eliane (1986) 'Au Revoir to all that', *Trouble and Strife*, No. 8.

Viroli, Maurizio (1988) *Jean-Jacques Rousseau and the 'Well-Ordered Society'*, Cambridge: Cambridge University Press.

Walby, Sylvia (1986) *Patriarchy at Work*, Oxford: Polity Press.

Walby, Sylvia (1990) *Theorising Patriarchy*, Oxford: Basil Blackwell.

Waldron, Jeremy (1985) 'Indirect discrimination', in Guest and Milne (eds) p. 93.

Waldron, Jeremy (ed.) (1987) *Nonsense Upon Stilts: Bentham, Burke and Marx on the Rights of Man*, London and New York: Methuen.

Waldron, Jeremy (1989) 'Particular values and critical morality', *California Law Review*, 77: 561.

Waldron, Jeremy (1992) 'Minority cultures and the cosmopolitan alternative', *Michigan Journal of Law Reform*.

Walkerdine, Valerie (1990) *Schoolgirl Fictions*, London: Verso.

Walzer, Michael (1983) *Spheres of Justice*, New York: Basic Books.

Walzer, Michael (1987) *Interpretation and Social Criticism*, Cambridge, Mass: Harvard University Press.

Walzer, Michael (1988) *The Company of Critics*, New York: Basic Books.

Walzer, Michael (1990) 'The Communitarian Critique of Liberalism', *Political Theory*, 18: 3.

Walzer, Michael (1992) Comment, in Taylor (1992), p. 99.

Watson, Sophie (ed.) (1990) *Playing the State*, London: Verso.

Weber, Max (1968) *Economy and Society*, (1925), Berkeley: University of California Press.

Weedon, Chris (1987) *Feminist Practice and Post-structuralist Theory*, Oxford: Basil Blackwell.

West, Cornel (1989) *The American Evasion of Philosophy: A Genealogy of Pragmatism*, Madison: University of Wisconsin Press.

West, Cornel (1990) 'Pragmatism, oppression and the flight to substance', *Southern California Law Review* 63: 1753.

West Robin (1987) 'Adjudication is not interpretation', *Tennessee Law Review*, 54: 203.

West, Robin (1988) 'Jurisprudence and gender', *University of Chicago Law Review*, 55: 1–72.

White, Morton (1987) *Philosophy, the Federalist and the Constitution*, Oxford: Oxford University Press.

White, Stephen K. (1991) *Political Theory and Post-Modernism*, Cambridge: Cambridge University Press.

Williams, Bernard (1989) 'Dworkin and cultural interests', *California Law Review*, 77: 515.

Williams, Bernard (1990) 'Auto-da-Fé: Consequences of pragmatism', in Malachowski (ed.) 26.

Williams, Glanville (1983) *A Textbook of Criminal Law*, 2nd edition, London: Stevens.

Williams, Patricia (1991) *The Alchemy of Race and Rights*, Cambridge, Mass: Harvard University Press.

Williams, Raymond (1960) *Culture and Society*, London: Chatto and Windus.

Williams, Raymond (1973) *The Country and the City*, Oxford: Oxford University Press.

Williams, Susan (1990) 'Feminism's search for the feminine: essentialism, utopianism and community', *Cornell Law Review*, 700.

Willis, Paul (1977) *Learning to Labour: How working class kids get working class jobs*, Farnborough: Saxon House.

Wilson, Elizabeth (1988) *Hallucinations: Life in the Post-Modern City*, London: Hutchinson-Radius.

Wilson, Elizabeth (1992) 'The invisible flaneur', *New Left Review* 191: 90–110.

Wolf, Susan (1992) 'Comment', in Taylor (1992) p. 75.

Wolfenden Committee (1957) *Report of the Committee on Homosexual Offences and Prostitution*, Cmnd. 247, London, HMSO.

Wollstonecraft, Mary (1975) *A Vindication of the Rights of Women*, (1792), Harmondsworth: Penguin.

Woods, Julian (1984) 'Groping towards sexism', in MacRobbie and Nava (eds).

Young, Iris Marion (1987a) 'Towards a critical theory of justice', *Social Theory and Practice*, 7: 279.

Young, Iris Marion (1987b) 'Impartiality and the civic public', in Benhabib and Cornell (eds) 56 (and in revised form in Young (1990a)).

Young, Iris Marion (1989) 'Politics and group difference: A critique of the ideal of universal citizenship', *Ethics*, 99.

Young, Iris Marion (1990a) *Justice and the Politics of Difference*, Princeton, NJ: Princeton University Press.

Young, Iris Marion (1990b) 'The ideal of community and the politics of difference', in L. Nichoson (ed.).

Young, Iris Marion (1990c) *Throwing Like a Girl*, Bloomington: Indiana University Press.

Index